A Guide to

European Union Funding

for the voluntary sector

PETER SLUITER
LAURENCE WATTIER

DIRECTORY OF SOCIAL CHANGE

Published by
The Directory of Social Change
24 Stephenson Way
London NW1 2DP
Tel: 0171 209 5151, fax: 0171 209 5049
e-mail: info@dsc.org.uk
from whom further copies and a full publications list are available.

The Directory of Social Change is a Registered Charity no. 800517

ISBN 1 900360 50 0

British Library Cataloguing in Publication Data
A catalogue record for this book is available from the British Library

Cover design by Linda Parker
Typeset by Linda Parker
Printed and bound by Antony Rowe, Chippenham

Directory of Social Change London office:
Courses and Conferences tel: 0171 209 4949
Charity Centre tel: 0171 209 1015
Research tel: 0171 209 4422
Finance and Administration tel: 0171 209 0902

Directory of Social Change Liverpool Office:
Federation House, Hope Street, Liverpool L1 9BW
Research tel: 0151 708 0136
Courses and Conferences tel: 0151 708 0117

Acknowledgements

The authors have benefited from the expertise of John Griffiths on the Structural Funds and would like to thank the following for their invaluable help and support: Monica Blum, Shereen Karmali, Pauline Crick, Odyle Delcoigne, Emmanuel Klimis, Elie Klimis, Marc Mathieu and the Associatif financier, Angela Scillia and Karin Ulmer.

About the authors

The authors are independent consultants in Brussels and have a long and varied track record in working for the voluntary sector. They specialise in relations between the non-profit sector and EU institutions: lobbying, policy analysis, fundraising, international partnerships and network building, project design and implementation. They can be contacted through the publishers or e-mail: peter.sluiter@wxs.nl and id.s@skynet.be (Laurence Wattier)

Contents

INTRODUCTION

European Union (EU) funds have increasingly become available in the last decade for activities involving many various sectors of civil society, outside governmental or commercial circles. The 150-plus budget lines and programmes which are described in detail in this book are only a small part of the multi-million euro annual budget of the EU. Still, financial support ranging from several thousand to over a million euros is attractive enough for many non-profit organisations to enter the uncertain terrain of requesting EU financial support for their activities.

If you want to use the EU as a milch cow, you have to know the animal fairly well if you are to get at least a few drops in your bucket. You may even develop a genuine interest in (though not necessarily a great sympathy for) the cows most relevant to you. A short introduction to the history, current developments and future prospects of the EU provides the general context into which your activities and application will have to fit; it will teach you some of the correct Euro-jargon and give you clues about what to stress in the content and description of your project.

You will then need some practical and tactical guidance for choosing one or more promising budget lines, for obtaining full information on the detailed and complicated criteria, procedures and time schedules, and for drafting and submitting your application. If you are lucky enough to receive some funding, you will have to report on the results of your projects and to justify your expenses. If your application is not successful, you may want to try your luck with the same budget line the following year, or submit a different proposal elsewhere in the EU labyrinth even earlier than that.

You do not have to be or become a Europhile to find it an informative and rewarding experience applying for financial support from the EU, often with partners from other EU countries. We hope that this book will give you the basic background information and practical guidance you need to make a successful application for EU funding.

Note At the time of writing (autumn 1999), a number of key programmes, including the 1994–1999 Structural Funds and several in the area of Education, Youth, Training and Culture, were coming to an end, and were due to be replaced by new programmes starting in 2000. We have given what information was available to us on the new programmes, with details of where to go for up-to-date advice. We have also included information about the old programmes, in the belief that this background will help you assess where your activities may fit in the future.

DEALING WITH THE EUROPEAN UNION

How to use this book

Employment, environment, education, research, health, overseas development ... whatever your area of work, European Union policy has an impact on it to a greater or lesser degree. This growing involvement in policy is matched by increased availability of EU funding for a great variety of activities – not just for national, regional and local authorities, or commercial enterprises, but also for the many and varied organisations and initiatives that make up the non-profit sector.

If you consider the EU as nothing but a milch cow (and you would not buy this book if you did not want some of the milk), you will soon find out that it is more than just that. Your work may offer a useful contribution to EU efforts to find constructive solutions to the issues that concern you both. You will discover that EU financial support is a window of opportunity, adding an international aspect to your work through cooperation and exchange of experiences with colleagues in other European countries. Therefore, you may want to follow and understand general EU policy and developments, how the EU works and how it decides. This is the context for your efforts to get EU funding.

This book will give you some initial background information about the European Union and then provide you with guidance about how to find your way through the promising but sometimes bewildering labyrinth of the hundreds of budget lines and dozens of special programmes. It will help you to find and digest the relevant information efficiently, to avoid tactical pitfalls and unproductive side alleys, and to identify unexpected possibilities that official titles of budget lines do not reveal. It will answer such questions as:

- How do you find out whether your activities have a chance of getting financial support?
- What are realistic targets and the proper tone and phrasing to adopt when you draw up your application?
- Will you need partners in other countries?
- What part of your expenses will the EU grant cover?

Do not be discouraged by the effort it takes to draft a proper application and the uncertainty of the outcome. You will be surprised how systematic strategy and method, informal advice and a bit of gut feeling can produce positive results.

A note about the Structural Funds

The central aim of this guide is to help you identify and access funding from the complete list of EU budget lines; in many instances this means that you are likely to have direct contact with the Directorates General in Brussels as well as with sources of advice in the UK. The Structural Funds, including the European Social Fund (ESF) and the Community Initiatives, are administered differently from other EU programmes and we have therefore allocated them a special place in this guide, at the beginning of the section *Inside the European Union*. Information and assistance in applying to these programmes is available from a variety of sources in the UK and does not require the same degree of familiarity with the workings of the European Commission or contact with its services in Brussels.

Identify the right budget line(s)

The EU spends millions of euros each year on a broad range of subjects. In each policy area, a varying part of that money is available to finance the activities of organisations other than EU agencies themselves, both commercial and non-commercial. This chapter will help you to make an initial selection from the more than 150 EU budget lines that are relevant to the non-profit sector.

First try to identify under which main heading your application will be eligible and make your choice from our selection of relevant budget lines, which we have listed in the same order as they appear in the official 1999 EU budget and with their official titles, numbers and available funds (see pages 37–43). Only the Structural Funds have a different place, as noted above. If you find one or more promising titles, look at the detailed description, which you will find by following the numerical order of the budget lines through the book.

Do not despair if your initial search by title does not point convincingly at any budget line that seems worth further investigation. And even if the detailed description does appear to confirm that your organisation's activity may be eligible, do not be too sure that you have found your pot of gold and need only access this one. In either case it may prove fruitful to do a second round of searching and find budget lines where your favourite subject is hidden behind the official title but will become apparent if you read the detailed descriptions in this book and in the official documentation from the European Commission. How do you go about finding these budget lines if the title does not give clear indications and has at first glance little or nothing to do with your activities?

If you want to set up a *network* for *volunteers* to *train disabled women* living in *rural areas*, who suffer from *social* or *cultural exclusion*, who need *information* on *farm modernisation* in *under-developed regions*, while taking *environmental* concerns into account, you will certainly find budget lines containing the words we have highlighted here, but there may well be other EU budget lines and programmes where, for instance, *women*, *exclusion* or *environment* are not easily recognisable aspects.

On pages 44–48 you will find 'search tools' which categorise budget lines according to:

- fields of activity (such as environment, training, human rights)
- target groups (such as disabled people, migrants, the unemployed)
- the area (geographical) where your project takes place, inside or outside the EU

If you are working in the field of education, training or youth, the official titles will already have guided you to the 7 budget lines starting with B3-10. But you will need our references under *field of activity* to find the many more budget lines that may be relevant to you. Similarly, if your field is consumer interests, how would you have found that not only budget lines B5-100 and B5-102 are relevant for you, but also B6-6111 and 6121 in the research section and B7-500 on central and eastern Europe? And those dealing with research will be happy not only to find the 9 budget lines in chapter B6, but also quite a selection from the A, B2, B3, B5 and B7 chapters.

How to read a budget line description in this book and what to do next

Finally in this chapter, we explain how to interpret the descriptions given of each budget. Have a more careful look at the one or two budget lines that you find the most promising to start with – or the least complicated, if you are discouraged by the complexity of some others. The format of nearly every description uses the same categories: number and official title, available budget in 1999, eligibility, beneficial areas, partners needed, types of grant, information and applications. We have given an example on pages 10–11.

Notes

1 **DGs and Units** At the time of writing changes in the structure of Directorates General (number, names, division of responsibilities) were announced, to become effective by the end of 1999. Some of our references to DGs and possibly also some titles of units may therefore be out-of-date. But in practice these changes are likely to be less drastic than they seem, as the same units and people may very well continue to deal with the subject in the changed setting and remain contactable as before.

2 **Addresses** For reasons of space, we have not included *Belgium* at the end of Brussels addresses or *UK* at the end of UK addresses, but where a contact is given in another country e.g. Luxembourg, this is always specified.

   Telephone numbers are consistently given in international format, so if you are calling within the UK, you will of course need to replace the international code *+44* with the national code *0*. From 22 April 2000 six geographic areas across the UK will be given new area codes beginning with 02. Each of these areas will have a new three digit area code followed by an eight digit local telephone number, as below:

Cardiff	(01222)xxxxxx becomes (029) 20xx xxxx
Coventry	(01203)xxxxxx becomes (024) 76xx xxxx
London	(0171)xxx xxxx becomes (020) 7xxx xxxx
	(0181)xxx xxxx becomes (020) 8xxx xxxx
Portsmouth	(01705)xxxxxx becomes (023) 92xx xxxx
Southampton	(01703)xxxxxx becomes (023) 80xx xxxx

Finding out more

At the end of the book the section *The EU from A to Z* provides short explanations of the main aspects of the European Union and the most common abbreviations and acronyms. This is followed by a list of contact addresses, both at EU level (in Brussels and elsewhere) and in the United Kingdom.

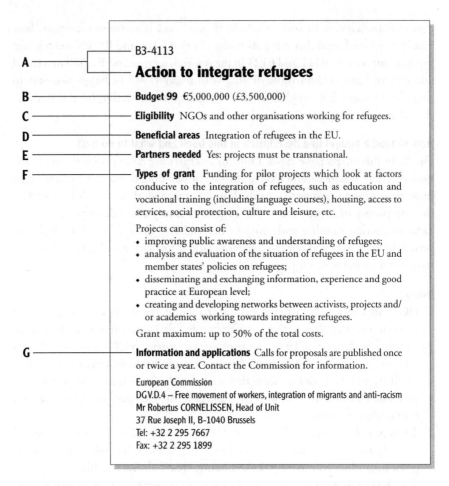

A. Number and title Each individual description of a budget line starts with its official title (which you may find unduly complicated, vaguely phrased or even plain bad English!). Under this heading we have stuck to the official terminology to avoid confusion when you investigate official documentation, but otherwise we have tried to avoid jargon while at the same time remaining close to the original text in order not to lose precision and completeness.

B. Budget 99 Gives the total amount available for this budget line in 1999 in euros € and £ sterling. This is usually not entirely available for subsidies. We have consistently used the rate as at 1 January 1999 when the euro was officially introduced, which was €1 = £0.70, but as the rate fluctuates within certain limits, it may well be different when you read this, when you submit your application, and most importantly, when you actually receive your money.

In some cases the official budget does not give an amount but 'p.m.' for *pro memoria*. This indicates that no money is made available for the year in question, for instance because there is no legal basis for such expenditure, but that the subject is considered important enough to mention and money may well become available in a later year. It may also indicate that there is still money to spend from the previous year.

Using this Guide – following departmental reorganisation (July 2001)

Grant programmes: The departmental changes and the new ministerial appointments may well lead to reviews of the funding programmes noted in the guide. Funding programmes and their criteria are usually announced between early summer and early autumn. There are likely to be delays with announcements for many programmes. Readers need to check the position with each of the individual programmes and be alert to the development of new ones.

Websites: Many of the new websites were not operational at the time of printing this leaflet (early July 2001).

Addresses: There may well be some changes in the future but at the time of compiling this leaflet the programmes could be located via the addresses as shown in the guide. However, it is always essential to check first.

Contact personnel: Movements of staff inevitably occur, throughout the course of any year.

THE NEW DEPARTMENTS

Office of the Deputy Prime Minister
In the Cabinet Office the Deputy Prime Minister will chair a number of key Cabinet Committees as well as dealing with important cross-departmental issues and structures including:

the Regional Co-ordination Unit;

the Government Offices for the Regions;

the Social Exclusion Unit.

Website: www.cabinet-office.gov.uk

Department for Education and Skills
Responsibilities include:
pre-school education, schools, further and higher education, work-based training, and lifelong learning.

(Employment Service and New Deal programme transferred to the Department for Work and Pensions.)

Website: www.dfes.gov.uk

Department for the Environment, Food and Rural Affairs
Responsibilities include:
agriculture, the food industry and fisheries – the functions of the former Ministry of Agriculture, Fisheries and Food (MAFF);

environment, rural development, countryside, wildlife and sustainable development, i.e. Environment Protection Group and Wildlife and Countryside Directorate from the former Department of the Environment, Transport and the Regions (DETR);

animal welfare and hunting (transferred from the Home Office);

funding the Countryside Agency, English Nature and the Environment Agency.

Website: www.defra.gov.uk.

Throughout the transitional period users are advised to continue to consult:

www.maff.gov.uk – for information on responsibilities previously exercised by the Ministry of Agriculture, Fisheries and Food;

www.detr.gov.uk – for information on environmental protection and wildlife and countryside issues;

www.homeoffice.gov.uk – for information on certain animal welfare issues

The Home Office
Responsibilities include:
tackling crime, promoting good race relations, immigration and asylum, war on drugs.

The UK Anti-Drugs Co-ordination Unit has transferred from the Cabinet Office.

The Active Community Unit stays based within the Home Office.

Website: www.homeoffice.gov.uk

The Department of Trade and Industry
Responsibilities include:
industry; energy; innovative science; competition and consumer affairs.

Regional Development Agencies are now alongside the department's regional economic responsibilities.

Sponsorship of the construction industry has transferred from the DETR.

Website: www.dti.gov.uk

Department for Transport, Local Government and the Regions
Responsibilities include:
transport; local government; housing and homelessness; planning; regeneration and neighbourhood renewal; urban and regional policy (from the former Department of Environment, Transport and the Regions, DETR);

fire service and electoral law (transferred from the Home Office).

(The Regional Co-ordination Unit, the Government Offices in the Regions, and the Social Exclusion Unit, which have cross-departmental responsibilities, report to the Deputy Prime Minister in the Cabinet Office.)

Website: www.dtlr.gov.uk

Lord Chancellor's Department
Responsibilities now include:
freedom of information; data protection; human rights (taken over from the Home Office).

New website: www.lcd.gov.uk

Department for Work and Pensions
Responsibilities include:
the employment and disability responsibilities of the former DfEE, i.e. the Employment Service, with the welfare and pensions responsibilities of the DSS;

New Deal programme to get the jobless into work;

Working Age Agency (now Jobcentre Plus) to be established.

Website: www.dwp.gov.uk

PAGE BY PAGE CHANGES
49–55 now within the Department for the Environment, Food and Rural Affairs

81–104 now within the Department for Education and Skills

104 Work-Life Balance Challenge Fund – destination unknown in late June 2001 – probably Department for Work and Pensions, maybe Department of Trade and Industry

105 Learning and Skills Council funded by the Department for Education and Skills

107–12 Employment Service to become part of the Department of Work and Pensions

117–20 now within the Department for the Environment, Food and Rural Affairs

121–31 now within the Department for Transport, Local Government and the Regions

132–34 Housing Corporation agency now funded by the Department for Transport, Local Government and the Regions

138–41 English Nature now funded by the Department for the Environment, Food and Rural Affairs

141–43 Forestry Commission funded by the Treasury (and EEC money)

143–45 National Forest Company funded by the Department for the Environment, Food and Rural Affairs

145-51 Countryside Agency (plus contributions to the Local Heritage Initiative and Walking the Way to Health) now funded by the Department for the Environment, Food and Rural Affairs

211–15 Disability and Carer Benefits grant-in-aid now within the Department for Work and Pensions

231–34 Regional Development Agencies now with the Department of Trade and Industry

236–38 Regional Coordination Unit and Government Offices for the Regions now with the Office of the Deputy Prime Minister

241–46 Single Regeneration Budget now with the Regional Development Agencies

246–47 New Deal for Communities now with the Department for Transport, Local Government and the Regions

247–48 Local Strategic Partnerships now with the Department for Transport, Local Government and the Regions

248–49 Neighbourhood Renewal Unit now with the Department for Transport, Local Government and the Regions

250 Early Years Development and Childcare Partnerships with the Department for Education and Skills

250–54 Sure Start Unit – cross-departmental, no change of address

260–62 Education Action Zones with the Department for Education and Skills

262–65 Connexions Service National Unit and Neighbourhood Support Fund – cross-departmental, no change of address

265–67 Community Champions Fund coordinated within the Department for Education and Skills, no change of address

282–83 London Borough Grants has merged with the Association of London Government. For information on grants contact: Association of London Government, Social Policy and Grants, 59$^{1/2}$ Southwark Street, London SE1 OAL, Tel: 020 7934 9999; Fax: 020 7934 9991; Website: www.alg.gov.uk

C. Eligibility Explains who is eligible for a grant. Is it enough to be non-commercial to qualify for EU support? Usually not, as not all non-profit organisations or NGOs (non-governmental organisations) may apply for a grant under any particular budget line. The sector is broad and differentiated: associations and foundations, charities, self-help groups, grass-roots organisations, civil society groups, non-profit lobbyists (some find 'single-issue or advocacy groups' more civilised), trade unions or employers' and professional organisations, educational and research institutes, hospitals, even local or regional authorities and some small and medium enterprises (SMEs). As applicants for EU support, all that they have in common is that they must not (directly or indirectly) work for commercial aims, must have status as a legal entity and should be able to prove that they can do the job properly. For many of the budget lines listed (especially the larger ones), applicants from the commercial sector may also be eligible, but we have limited ourselves to indicating which categories of non-profit organisation qualify for funding.

D. Beneficial areas Summarises the main subject or objective of a budget line and gives its particular geographical area of concern, if there is one.

E. Partners needed Specifies the minimum number and type of partner organisations that you are advised to involve or that you need to team up with in order to be eligible for a grant.

F. Types of grant Describes the type of projects and activities that can receive EU support under this budget line and provides where possible examples of previously approved projects. It also gives an idea of the size of grants given and the percentage of co-financing (sometimes known as 'match funding') which is necessary.

G. Information and applications How, where and when to apply for what, usually in the European Commission. Though desk officers are in charge of the actual work on applications, we prefer to give the name and contact numbers of the Head of Unit as they change jobs less frequently. If the Head of Unit has also been replaced, the title of the unit helps you to find the relevant people. Individual officials take their phone numbers with them to their new jobs, but they will tell you who has succeeded them and the fax numbers and web-sites mentioned remain with their old units. If you write to the Commission, the official postal address of any DG or unit in Brussels is 200 Rue de la Loi, B-1049 Brussels, Belgium but delivery may be a little faster if you add the address of the actual building in which the unit has its offices – which you need for a personal visit, to collect documentation or to deposit your mail by hand.

The European Union: a short introduction

After World War II, 6 of the currently 15 member states of the European Union (EU) started cooperating in coal and steel production and trade. Nowadays the EU jointly deals with a broad range of policy issues and some member states may choose to go further than others. Most member states have replaced their national currencies with the euro and others may follow, which leads to the question of whether joint monetary policy is possible without closer cooperation in general economic policy. Agricultural expenditure and support to less developed EU regions and industries are about to be thoroughly revised. EU membership will be further expanded to over 20 member states. This reinforces the debate about current methods of common EU policy and decision making: What should the balance of EU, national, regional and local decision making be? How will EU policies be decided and implemented with 20 or more member states?

Since the original 6 European countries started cooperating with each other, the European Union has grown to 15 member states and has gradually become involved in such an increasingly broad range of policy issues that it is becoming more and more relevant to the non-profit sector.

This economic and political cooperation was initially set in the context of cold war East–West confrontation: US-led Marshall aid and NATO in Western Europe and North America, COMECON and the Warsaw Pact under the domination of the former Soviet Union in the East. Western European politicians and business circles soon realised that more comprehensive cooperation amongst themselves was needed to achieve reconstruction of their war-shaken economies and the preservation of peace between West Germany and its former enemies (at least those in Western Europe).

Prompted by a mixture of idealism ('no more war on European soil') and down-to-earth economic and foreign policy considerations, the European Coal and Steel Community (ECSC) was set up in 1952, to which were soon added agricultural and nuclear policies in the European Economic Community (EEC) and Euratom in 1956. It was a modest beginning in limited fields and few key players of the time will have foreseen (or indeed wished for) the extent to which common European policies and structures would develop over the next 40 years.

In the 1950s and 1960s France, Germany (the Federal Republic), Italy and the smaller Benelux countries (the Netherlands, Belgium and Luxembourg) were the initiators of formal and deepening economic cooperation in Western Europe. Though the UK was fully involved in Western cooperation in general terms, it chose to prioritise military and political cooperation within NATO and to keep its economic independence.

Europe and European are not always the same

In this book, as in much official and colloquial EU practice, 'Europe' and 'European' refer almost exclusively to the EU or its components and predecessors, such as the ECSC and the EEC. That is practical but not really fair: 'European' should not be used as a brand name which excludes other countries, that are not (yet) EU members: Poland or Moldova are as European as the current 15 EU member states such as the United Kingdom or Luxembourg.

Moreover, several international organisations have 'European' in their names and they should not be confused with the EU. Best known past and present examples are the Western European Union (WEU), the Council of Europe (CoE), the European Economic Area (EEA) and its better known predecessor, the European Free Trade Area (EFTA), and the Organisation for Security and Cooperation in Europe (OSCE). They are briefly described in the glossary at the end of this book.

Until the UK joined in 1973, the major economic obstacle preventing the Irish Republic from joining the ECSC and EEC was its open border with the UK. Like Sweden, Finland and Austria, it had remained neutral and outside the major economic and political blocks, though all these countries had Western-style capitalist economies. NATO members Denmark and Norway felt that joining the EEC would jeopardise their close relationship with the neutral Nordic countries. Economic backwardness and the absence of democracy until the mid-1970s kept Spain, Portugal and Greece out for many years.

15 current EU member states with year of accession

1956	*1973*	*1981*	*1986*	*1995*
Belgium	Denmark	Greece	Portugal	Austria
France	Irish Republic		Spain	Finland
Germany	United Kingdom			Sweden
Italy				
Luxembourg				
The Netherlands				

After this initial cooperation over coal, steel, agriculture and nuclear energy had stabilised, a start was made with gradual expansion, both geographically and in policy fields. The primary target became the creation of a fully open internal market for goods and services. After Greece, Spain and Portugal had joined, the strengthening of structurally weak economic sectors and entire regions became another focal point. More and more it became clear that a common external economic policy was also needed for the proper functioning of the open internal market. From 1993 onwards, this internal market included the service sector and the free flow of capital and, with certain limitations, people.

This process was rounded off by a common monetary policy and, as of 1999, the introduction of the euro as a common currency, which will fully replace national currencies in 2002 in 11 out of 15 EU countries (but not, as yet, in the UK, Sweden, Denmark and Greece). The exchange rates between these 11 currencies and the euro have been fixed from 1 January 1999, whereas the rates of the other 4, against the euro and amongst each other, will fluctuate, but within set limits. At that date, €1 was worth £0.70, which is the rate we have used throughout. Please note that it may have changed by the time you read this book.

EU involvement beyond politicians, officials and commercial interests

In parallel with deepening European cooperation on strictly economic issues, the EU has gradually become involved, in one form or another, in almost the full range of government policies. These were originally treated as 'appendices' of purely economic policy, but are today increasingly dealt with by the EU because they are important in their own right; they include social affairs and public health, education, training and youth policy, culture, development cooperation and human rights. The list of subjects where non-profit organisations may seek financial support from the EU, which appears on page 31, says it all.

This expansion does not mean that the EU is equally involved in all aspects of what used to be national policy concerns and that national governments no longer have specific national policies in all these fields. Some areas, such as agricultural policy, are totally or nearly totally 'communitarised', whereas environment policy includes EU-wide minimum standards as well as freedom for national governments to implement their own policy according to their local circumstances or political preferences.

As a general principle (which creates new debates every time a concrete decision has to be taken) the EU has accepted that if a problem in any field should be dealt with at EU-level, common policies could range from loose forms of coordination and consultation to comprehensive EU-wide legislation.

In recent years, some issues on which member states have traditionally felt most reluctant to give up their sovereignty have cautiously been added to the common EU agenda: foreign affairs and security policy, justice and home affairs (migration, asylum, drugs, crime). It remains difficult to strike a balance between perceived national interests or traditional policy preferences and the advantages of more coordinated and effective joint policies.

As a result, the structure of the EU can be summarised as follows:

European Union				
European Community				
ECSC European Coal and Steel Community	Euratom European Community for Atomic Energy	EEC European Economic Community	CFSP Common Foreign and Security Policy	CJHA Cooperation on Judicial and Home Affairs
first pillar			*second pillar*	*third pillar*

Alongside this broadening of scope to cover new fields of policy, the EU is increasingly recognising the work of the non-profit sector, with whom cooperation is sought and whose activities have become eligible for financial support. Therefore, the EU has become increasingly relevant beyond the traditional key players in politics and economics. The non-profit sector as a whole is affected, from the smallest charity or solidarity group to large and established institutions dealing with health, education and research or local development.

But these organisations are not just passive objects of EU policy. In addition to the traditional means of political involvement through elections and membership of political parties or interest groups, civil society in all its manifestations can, if it wishes, get involved beyond traditional regional or national boundaries. As nothing comes for free, the areas where the EU budget is spent have expanded beyond the official expenditure of the EU and the governments of its member states, and considerable sums have become accessible for non-profit organisations dealing with the greatly increased variety of issues of concern to the EU.

The EU goes East

In parallel with this expansion into new policy fields, nearly all countries in western, northern and southern Europe have now chosen to be full member states of the EU, with Norway, Iceland and Switzerland the only exceptions. Since the end of Soviet domination of central and eastern Europe, all former Soviet satellites and the newly independent Baltic states have applied for EU membership. Intensive negotiations started in 1998 with the Czech Republic, Estonia, Hungary, Poland, Slovenia and long-time applicant Cyprus; these are expected to come to fruition in the first decade after the year 2000. For a mixture of economic and political reasons, it will take more time before Bulgaria, Latvia, Lithuania, Malta, Romania, the Slovak Republic and Turkey will be able to join. Meanwhile, new forms of economic cooperation were set up with Russia and the New Independent States (NIS) in Europe and central Asia.

The EU beyond the year 2000

The Treaty of Amsterdam, which was signed on 2 October 1997 and came into force in May 1999 after ratification by each of the 15 member states, has updated the existing treaties which are the political and legal framework of the European Union in the following ways:

- more powers for the European Parliament by applying the *codecision procedure* (shared decision making by the parliament and the Council of Ministers);
- the voting system of *qualified majority* inside the Council of Ministers will be applied more extensively, replacing the principle of unanimity by which each member state had a veto on EU decision making;
- extension of EU competencies into various subject areas such as: employment, social policy, health, environment, consumer protection, European citizenship, culture, sport, voluntary work, human rights, non-discrimination, free circulation of persons, immigration and asylum policy, cooperation of the police and judicial system.

Meanwhile, a great number of major issues are still on the political agenda beyond 2000:

- enlargement with countries in central, eastern and southern Europe;
- reform of the common agricultural policy;
- reform of support to economically weak regions and industries (Structural Funds);
- strengthening monetary and socio-economic cooperation, also in the *first pillar* (euro, economic, social and fiscal policy, employment, consumer affairs);
- effective cooperation in the *second pillar* (common foreign and security policy) and the *third pillar* (judicial and home affairs);
- reform of EU decision making and adaptation to an enlarged EU of 20+ member states;
- *transparency*: parliamentary control, openness to the public, access to documents;
- *enhanced cooperation* or *flexibility:* joint policies by less than all 15 member states;
- *subsidiarity and proportionality*: policy formulation and implementation at EU, national, regional or local level.

Who decides and implements what?

EU policy is a mixture of national and European politics. Civil servants and politicians in Brussels play a key role but do not make national governments and parliaments redundant. On the basis of proposals put forward by the European Commission, EU policies are jointly debated and decided by the European Parliament and the Council of Ministers, though each national government also remains responsible to its national parliament. On important issues like agriculture and foreign affairs, the European Parliament has advisory powers only.

EU procedures ensure that decisions on important issues are taken by larger majorities than the bare democratic minimum of 50.01%. This prevents a few larger countries or 2–3 major political groups in the European Parliament dominating the others. The European Commission is the main implementing agency of EU policy, with varying degrees of involvement of the national, regional and local authorities in the member states.

Proposing legislation, deciding on proposals, implementing policy and political control are distinct political and administrative functions which on a national level are shared by the government, the elected parliament and the appointed civil service. In the EU, these roles are played by the European Parliament, the Council of Ministers and the European Commission, but in a slightly different way. Moreover, national governments, parliaments and officials still have a distinctive role to play in political decision making and policy implementation.

The central role in EU decision making is played by the **Council of Ministers**, in which each member state has one member. The presidency of the EU rotates every 6 months amongst the governments of the member states, whose prime ministers (and one head of state, the French president) discuss major policy issues once or twice during every presidency. The main task of the incumbent presidency is to coordinate the process of joint debates and decision making. This does not prevent it from ensuring that issues and positions close to its own political heart feature prominently on the agenda.

Between these European summits, the ministers of foreign affairs discuss more than EU foreign politics. They also deal with EU policies in general and are therefore called the General Affairs Council. The meetings of the other ministers are named after their specific subject, e.g. the Transport Council, the Environment Council, etc. The differences in size and economic power between countries are reflected in a system where the vote of larger countries is accorded more weight than that of the smaller ones. The preparatory work for council meetings is co-ordinated by the permanent representatives of the member states (COREPER in the French abbreviation) with the support of the Secretariat of the Council, all based in Brussels.

The most direct representation of the citizens of the EU is the **European Parliament**, which is elected every 5 years. The differences in size between EU member states are clearly illustrated by their varying number of MEPs (Members of the European Parliament). Under the Treaty of Amsterdam it is stipulated that in each country a system of proportional representation is applied.

Once elected, MEPs work mainly within their political groups (Socialists, Christian-Democrats and Conservatives, Liberals, Greens, etc.) and not in national delegations. But party discipline in political groups in the European Parliament is much looser than in most national parliaments. This allows MEPs to take national and regional interests or private preferences into account and no MEP ever forgets that they are nominated by their national parties and elected by the citizens of their own country.

In comparison with national political systems, the EU has one unique institution: the **European Commission** of 20 members, 2 from each of the 5 larger member states (UK, Germany, France, Italy and Spain) and one from each of the other 10. They are appointed by their governments and confirmed in office as a team by the European Parliament. Once countries from central and eastern Europe have joined the EU, the larger countries will lose their second Commissioner, but this relative weakening will be compensated for by changes in the system of weighted voting in the Council of Ministers.

The *right of initiative* is the main political prerogative of the Commission, as all EU policy proposals are drafted and submitted by the Commission, sometimes after prompting by the Council or the Parliament. The Commission lacks one key prerogative of a national government: a formal share in the final phase of the decision-making process. But it acts like any national government and civil service in implementing common EU policies once they are determined by the Council of Ministers and the European Parliament. Therefore, 'European Commission' sometimes means the 20 commissioners but can also refer to the whole apparatus of officials, as in any national civil service.

EU or national politics: from Brussels to Westminster (and your own constituency)

The national aspect is never far away in European policy making. The Council of Ministers consists of politicians who are politically responsible to their national parliaments, not the European Parliament. All national parliaments are briefed by their governments on the agendas of forthcoming meetings of the Council of Ministers and the positions it intends to take. But it would be very difficult to reverse any decisions after the event.

The alertness of national politicians and the general political culture of government–parliamentary relations therefore determine the impact national parliaments have on the making of EU policy. The strongest example of such control by national politicians is the Danish practice where the parliament defines very strict margins within which the government may manoeuvre in negotiations with its EU partners.

The powers of the European Parliament are limited to EU policy and the EU budget, but MEPs are no less aware than national governments that their political legitimacy is entirely dependant on the electorate back home, as they are selected by national parties and elected by their respective national electorates.

To a lesser extent this applies even to European Commissioners. National politics are decisive in determining who gets the one or two posts available for a country, but once elected European Commissioners are not always able or willing to function without regard to their national and party-political backgrounds.

Big and small countries, majorities and minorities

The differences in size between EU member states have been taken into account in different ways, in order to ensure that the larger countries do not easily overrule smaller ones. Both in the Council of Ministers and in the European Parliament the representation from larger countries is stronger than from the smaller ones, but if one takes numbers of inhabitants as a basis for comparison, smaller countries are slightly over represented. Moreover, decisions on most issues of any importance must be taken with larger majorities than a simple 50.01% of the votes cast.

The European Parliament is the simplest example with its scale of 6 members for Luxembourg and 15 for the Irish Republic, to 81 for the United Kingdom and 99 for Germany. Moreover, a majority of two-thirds of the votes cast is needed for most substantial issues. In other cases, a majority of all 627 elected members (not just voting members) is needed. As attendance at the European Parliaments is rarely much over 500 members, the 314 votes needed amount to a *de facto* majority of 60% or more, if 475 or 525 votes are cast. As no single political group ever has more than one-third of the votes and all groups have members from all or most member states, broad support is needed for major decisions, both from a political and a national perspective.

In the complicated system of weighted voting in the Council of Ministers, the UK and German votes each 'weigh' 10 out of a total of 82 votes, Ireland has 5 and Luxembourg only 2. As in the Parliament, this does not mean that smaller countries can easily be outnumbered by cooperation between larger ones. This is prevented by the provision that many decisions can only be taken with a qualified majority of 62 out of 82 votes (more than 70%) or even by unanimity.

Moreover, voting behaviour is usually not determined by the size of a country but by the political colour of each government or its specific interests. When it comes to agricultural policy or support for underdeveloped regions in the EU, any government in Italy and Spain has more in common with smaller Portugal and Greece than with Germany or the United Kingdom. If the regional aspect is absent, a coalition government with Green and Socialist parties (Belgium, Finland, France and Germany at the time of writing) may take different positions on environmental issues from a solid centre-right government (such as Spain).

Brussels, Strasbourg, Luxembourg

Brussels is equated with 'Europe' in popular perception and the majority of citizens and organisations, whether public, private or non-profit, will do most of their EU business there. Nevertheless, 3 cities are official seats of the European Union. Strasbourg hosts the monthly plenary meetings of the European Parliament and the office of the European Ombudsman. The seats of the European Commission and the secretariat of the Council of Ministers are in Brussels, where the European Parliament hosts the permanent offices of its members and holds most meetings of parliamentary committees, political groups and even a limited number of plenary sessions. The Council of Ministers also has its secretariat in Brussels. The EU Court of Justice and the Court of Auditors are in Luxembourg, as well as a limited number of services of the Commission and the Parliament.

How do they decide?

In spite of simplifications introduced by the Treaty of Amsterdam, EU decision making is still a complicated process where the balance of power amongst governments and between the Council of Ministers and the European Parliament varies according to the subject. As a rough distinction, the system of *codecision* is applied to policies which are determined at EU level and have legally binding force in the member states. Agreement has to be reached between the Council and the Parliament, and the Commission plays a mediating role where the 2 disagree. Within both the Council and the Parliament simple majorities are not enough; qualified majorities are needed for important decisions.

Under the *intergovernmental* procedure the Council of Ministers can only take a decision if no single country opposes it (*unanimity*). It is applied to subjects such as foreign and defence policy, in which national governments have basically kept their independent powers of decision making and the European Parliament is at best informed or consulted. So national parliaments have the last say here, even when sometimes they are under pressure from their governments, who love to point out the great problems that renewed negotiations would cause. In such cases, parliamentary codecision or control does not exist at either a national or a European level.

The EU budget is a special case with aspects of both procedures, as the European Parliament approves the budget as a whole but has no say in the total amount of income and expenditure nor in the details of expenditure on agriculture (there is further explanation about the budget at the beginning of the next chapter).

EU democracy and transparency

What is the democratic deficit of the EU? In fact, it is a catch-all phrase for a number of perceived shortcomings in the democratic quality of the EU. Parliamentary control, which is shared by the European Parliament and national parliaments shows gaps that need to be bridged, not just by politics but also by civil society: the press, individual citizens and their representative organisations are increasingly trying to monitor and influence decision making by the Council of Ministers and implementation by the European Commission.

As explained above, parliamentary control over EU decision making and policy implementation is at risk in cases where the European Parliament does not have full powers of codecision and control and national parliaments are *de facto* not exercising the powers they formally do have. Striking examples are the Common Agricultural Policy (budget and general policy), the Common Foreign and Security Policy and Cooperation on Judicial and Home Affairs. This problem would be solved by extending the powers of the European Parliament or by a more active role for national parliaments in all stages of decision making (including preparation and implementation).

It is too early to judge the effectiveness of new arrangements where national parliaments have 6 weeks to study draft legislative documents, before debates and decisions in the Council of Ministers. They may discuss EU Green and White Papers in which policy alternatives are announced and discussed in general terms and meet their EU colleagues from other national parliaments and the European Parliament in a common Conference of Select Committees on European Affairs.

A related issue is the secretiveness of decision making in the Council of Ministers, which meets behind closed doors and has only recently started publishing its minutes and information on how each country has voted. This limited improvement has been greatly stimulated by the successful case of the British newspaper *The Guardian* and the International Federation of Journalists before the European Court of Justice, which ruled that the Council had unduly refused access to these documents.

In addition to these weak spots in transparent and democratic relations between authorities at national and EU levels, the democratic quality of the EU as a political system is also measured by its accessibility to its citizens either through the press or through citizen-based organisations. Key words are information, documentation, consultation and transparency in decision making.

The right of access to documents of the European Commission and Parliament has been codified in the Treaty of Amsterdam, with exceptions in the case of '… violation of … general and particular interests or if the necessary confidentiality in decision making will be endangered …': a flexible and therefore potentially risky wording, but an improvement on the previous absence of such a legally binding right.

Representation of interest groups at EU level is formalised in the advisory role of the Economic and Social Committee (ESC), where established institutions such as trade unions and employers' organisations are represented, with a third group consisting of 'various interests' (mostly small and medium sized enterprises, farmers' unions, cooperatives, consumers, chambers of commerce).

A very young branch on the EU institutional tree is the Committee of the Regions (CoR), which also has an advisory role. It consists mostly of the representatives of politicians and officials from counties, provinces, Länder etc., some of which are larger than the smaller EU member states. Many regional and even local authorities have their own representative offices in Brussels, not because they are members of the CoR but so that they can operate in the same way as official national representations in advocating their policy interests and promoting financial support to their area.

Citizens and organisations with complaints about the legality of the actions of EU institutions or the application of EU rules and policies by national authorities have several formal means of redress: a court case in the European Court of Justice in Luxembourg, lodging a complaint with the European Ombudsman in Strasbourg or sending a petition to the European Parliament.

From the perspective of the non-profit sector, there are other, more direct and (sometimes) effective forms of involvement and interest representation. Within the principles of parliamentary democracy, charities, advocacy groups and other citizen-based organisations can be seen as a vehicle for information, involvement and representation of the concerns of millions of citizens. Many of them are active and even have representative networks and offices at EU level, and not just for getting financial support for their own work.

They follow and try to influence EU policies in their fields of concern (environment, overseas development, refugees and migrants' issues, social affairs, public health and many more). Their relevance and expertise are increasingly recognised and used by the European Commission and Parliament (less so by the secretariat of the Council of Ministers), as independent, specialised counterparts, rather than as lobbyists for a particular cause. Some play an active role in the European Parliament by liaising closely with or even servicing parliamentary intergroups, which are not the same as official parliamentary select committees but informal gatherings of individual MEPs of various parties and nationalities with shared interests and commitments.

All EU-wide networks have their own style and method of maintaining their independence, whether or not they receive financial support from the EU budget. In all cases they are well informed on policy developments in their fields and are a useful contact for those organisations that are less familiar with daily EU life in Brussels and elsewhere.

The EU is realising that there is an important role to play for civil society in defining and implementing EU policies. One expression of this is the financial support that non-profit organisations can increasingly obtain for their activities. That is what the rest of this book is about.

How to get EU funding for your activities

The making of the EU budget

When you start getting involved in EU policy and project funding, you will need information on general developments and prospects, which are all reflected in or derived from the annual EU budget. It includes dozens of chapters, subdivided into hundreds of separate budget lines, with figures and general descriptions of that year's expenditure, from which detailed EU programmes and annual work plans are elaborated. The budget is adopted in December of the preceding calendar year after a complicated negotiating process in the previous 12 months within and between the European Parliament, the European Commission and the Council of Ministers. The Commission publishes the first official draft in May, but if you want to anticipate or influence the final outcome of the process, you should start earlier than that. Though the Parliament does not have the final say on all details (especially expenditure on agriculture), it does adopt the budget as a whole and has the last word on details in those sections which happen to be the most relevant for the non-profit sector.

The European Union spends around €100 billion annually. That is a lot of money, though relatively modest in the perspective of the economy of the EU as a whole: the EU budget amounts to only a few percent of the combined national budgets of all EU member states and it is even smaller than that of The Netherlands, 'the largest of the smallest EU countries'. On the income side, revenues are stabilised at no more than 1.27% of the Gross National Product of the EU as a whole and must match expenditures. Another essential difference from national budgets is the very different distribution of EU expenses: a disproportionally large share, nearly half of all EU expenses, goes to agriculture. In spite of lively discussions on the EU's agricultural policy and the related costs, it is uncertain whether this will really change in the near future. Moreover, more than one third of the EU budget goes to the Structural Funds and the Cohesion Fund, which are meant to strengthen economically backward regions and sectors, with some budget lines and programmes that are highly relevant to the non-profit sector.

Agriculture and the Structural Funds together tie up more than 80% of the EU budget, so less than €20 billion remain for expenditure in other fields, which tend to be of interest to most institutions and organisations in the non-profit sector hoping for a subsidy from Brussels.

Within the upper limit of 1.27% of EU GNP, the Parliament has the power to adopt or reject the budget as a whole, but its right to determine expenditure in detail does not include the 40% of the budget spent on the Common Agricultural Policy. As far as some expenditure is concerned, such as research programmes, the total amounts and their division over separate subject fields are negotiated between the Council and the Parliament. Over the details of other expenditures, many of which are of great interest to the non-profit sector, the Parliament does have the last word, even against the opinion of the Council.

The making of the EU budget from month to month

European Commission starts discussing the
    budget for the next calendar year .... January

European Commission proposes 'Preliminary
    Draft Budget' (PDB) for the next
    calendar year .... early May
    Published .... no later than 15 June

European Parliament (committees, plenary)
    adopts initial positions and has informal
    discussions with the Council of Ministers .... mid-June to mid-July

Council of Ministers amends PDB and
    publishes its 'Draft Budget' (DB) .... late July

European Parliament discusses, amends
    and adopts DB in first reading:
    Deadline for amendments in
    parliamentary committees .... early September

    Debate and vote in committees .... late September to mid-October

    Debate and vote in plenary session .... 3rd or 4th week of October

Council of Ministers discusses requests
    and amendments with Parliament and
    publishes a new version of the draft
    budget in 'second reading' .... November

European Parliament discusses Council's
    proposal, adopts amendments
    and votes on the budget as a whole, first
    in committees then in plenary session .... early to mid-December
    Adopted amendments available .... late December to early January

Commission publishes the final budget in
    the Official Journal .... mid-February

How much for the non-profit sector?

The 150-plus budget lines summarised in this book, taken together, amount to more than one third of all EU expenditure. From a fund-raising point of view, one should be aware that it is very unusual that all or most available money under one budget line is spent on grants and subsidies. The amounts available per budget line vary between a few million to a few hundreds of millions of euros, and grants from the larger budget lines are mostly spent outside the non-profit sector.

So do not think that there must be a pot of gold within easy reach for any applicant. As long as you are aware that you cannot expect a grant of one or two million euros from a budget line that has only €20 million, the €30,000 or €300,000 that you may get will still make your working life much easier and more effective.

> How much are €100 billion or €30,000 anyway in the UK? Since the euro was introduced in January 1999, the exchange rates between the currencies of most EU member states are fixed, but there will be limited fluctuations in the rate between the euro and sterling, as long as the UK has not joined the euro zone. We have applied the rate on 1 January 1999 of €1 = £0.70 but it may be slightly different when you read this, when you draft your budget, when you hear the good news that your application is successful and when you finally get the first and second instalments of the grant.
>
> As the budget in your application has to be made in euros, you may in the end be slightly better or worse off, depending on the movement of the pound against the euro and price fluctuations inside the UK. These variations in real value may be much bigger if your EU grant is spent outside the European Union: who can predict whether the fluctuations of the Zambian kwanza or the Bulgarian leva against the euro will be to your advantage or not?

Documents and contacts

Once you have identified one or more relevant budget lines, you will first need some documentation in writing and then some friendly advice on how to proceed further. The last section in each budget line description indicates where you can get the full documentation you need to prepare your application, what is known about timing and application procedures and whom you might contact to get further clarification and advice.

European Commission

In most cases, this will be a particular unit in one of the DGs (Directorate General, the EU equivalent of a ministry in a national government). Commission officials are usually more 'client-friendly' than their reputation, but they or their secretaries may try not to be overwhelmed by personal phone calls and visits, especially at busy times (for instance immediately after the deadline for submission of applications which they have to process). Correspondence by fax or e-mail may be a useful preparatory stage and you may limit your oral contacts to loose ends and follow-up questions. Though you may not primarily use such contacts as lobbying tools to get your application approved, it will never harm you if your organisation or project is already positively known with the Commission services.

Technical Assistance Office

For the larger grant programmes, you will be referred to a 'Technical Assistance Office' (TAO) which is created or contracted by the Commission to give information and advice to potential applicants, though they too may suggest that you initially digest their paperwork and talk to them about any follow-up questions only. The same TAO may also do the technical and administrative handling of the applications, but they never take the final decision.

National and regional contacts

For some programmes, there are local contacts to get information and advice and to submit your application, especially for the Structural Funds and other EU programmes which are implemented on a national basis by the Member States.

The Commission has one or more representative offices in all member states, and if they are not experts in your field they may give you useful points of reference in your own country or in Brussels.

National ministries all have sections which are either in charge of implementing EU programmes or have sufficient knowledge of the EU aspects of your work to give you useful information and references.

Many regional and local authorities have appointed staff who specialise in EU programmes and funding. They will primarily try to secure funding for their own projects, but they may well be helpful to others and you may even find opportunities to link in with other initiatives.

For small businesses, including non-commercial organisations in the social or cultural fields, the Euro Info Centres located in all member states will be helpful. They will all have the official documentation you need or will be able to help you find it.

If you know what to look for, you will also get documentation from European Documentation Centres and Depository Libraries, which are usually attached to universities and open to the general public, but for practical advice you will have to go elsewhere unless you want to involve academic circles in your project for education or research.

Permanent Representation of your country, region or city

In Brussels, the Permanent Representation of your country to the EU (with the role of an ordinary embassy) may be able to help you and the number of representations of regional and local authorities in Brussels has grown rapidly since the late 1990s, many of them from the United Kingdom.

Members of the European Parliament

Members of the European Parliament may be useful sources as well, depending on their regional background, specialisation, membership of selected parliamentary committees, personal interests and commitment to maintain their grassroots contacts. Trying to use MEPs for lobbying in your favour after you have submitted your application is a risky business, as the Commission may be allergic to such interference in what they consider the domain of the executive branch. But there are cases of successful 'political interference' from outside or from 'upstairs' inside the Commission structure.

BRUNGOs

All over the EU district of Brussels, you will find offices of BRUNGOs, which are not the EU variations of a QUANGO but EU-wide umbrella organisations of NGOs to which national networks of organisations in your field are affiliated. They will have the necessary experience in translating your plans and needs into an official EU format and will help you finding partners inside or outside the EU if you need or want them. They will have inside information of imminent funding possibilities before a call for proposal is actually published and will know the most relevant people inside the Commission.

How to find the right budget lines

- Be systematic: scan the full list of budget lines and select promising titles.
- Think creatively: find unexpected budget lines from the references by target group, subject, area.
- Make a further selection by reading descriptions in this book.
- Get basic documentation from Commission services, the Technical Advice Office or other contacts (web-site, e-mail, fax, phone).
- Compare your activity with EU grants given earlier.
- Contact EU services in Brussels or national contact points for initial advice.
- Shortlist several options for initial orientation, then narrow down to one or a few for in-depth investigation.
- Ask EU-knowledgeable advisors and colleagues where your best chances are.
- Be patient and persistent, take your time to assess your chances and develop your best approach.
- Learn to read and write EU speak (but don't lose your mother tongue).

From paper chase to paper work

Once the Commission is ready to invite organisations to send in applications for funding, it usually does so in the form of a 'call for proposals' which is published in the Official Journal (OJ) of the EU. Unless you know the day or week of publication, browsing the OJ on paper or via its homepage:

http://europa.eu.int/eur-lex/en/oj/index.html

is like looking for a needle in a haystack. It is easier to use one of the contacts listed above to get the documents. Moreover, you should try to start your investigations and preparations well before the call for proposals is officially published as the deadline for sending in applications may be rather short, two months or only a little longer after publication. Therefore, it is useful to find out beforehand what calls for proposals are in the pipeline. They are usually based on annual work plans and general programme descriptions which you can study in advance to be well prepared once you start drafting your application. If you have access to the Internet, have a look at the general server of the EU:

http://europa.eu.int/

and find your way to one or more relevant DGs in the European Commission. Through:

http://europa.eu.int/comm/dgs_en.htm

many web-sites can be accessed and the more informative ones will have a lot of background documentation on their general policies and grant giving programmes that you can print or download. They will have links to their official calls for proposals and supporting documents. Many calls for proposals also appear on:

http://europa.eu.int/geninfo/whatsnew.htm

where you will also find selected information on the latest policy developments in your field. Our descriptions of individual budget lines will have more specific references to e-mail and other addresses.

Note At the time of writing changes in the structure of Directorates General (number, names, division of responsibilities) were announced, to become effective by the end of 1999. Some of our references to DGs and possibly also some titles of units may be therefore outdated. In practice these changes may be less drastic than they seem, as the same units and people may very well continue to deal with the subject in the changed setting and remain contactable as before.

Learning from the past

Most DGs publish lists of grants given in the current or previous years on their web-sites or supply them on request. You will certainly find such a list useful to get an impression of what activities you may get EU money for, as these are real-life examples of the specified subjects and activities mentioned in the regulations that govern each grant scheme. In the descriptions of each budget line in this book we have quoted from those lists and regulations, with a focus on the most appropriate aspects for the non-profit sector in the larger budget lines, which often deal with a very broad range of activities. If you do not recognise anything similar to what you want to request EU support for, it may be wise to look for better opportunities elsewhere. If you do feel that your subject is actually absent but would be very relevant for the grant scheme in question, contact the Commission: you may be lucky enough to propose a project which the Commission has long been waiting for.

An organisation dealing with traumatised refugees realised that this subject did fall within the mandate of an EU emergency aid programme in one area in crisis, but that only material aid (food, tents, etc.) featured on lists of EU funded activities. So they used that as an extra argument in submitting an application for co-funding their 'immaterial' project (outcome not decided at the time of writing).

Late for this year = early for next year

You may find that you have just missed a deadline or will not manage to meet it, but it may still be useful to look at this 'recent but outdated' documentation, as many programmes do not change very much from one year to the next. So check in good time whether dates, procedures and priorities remain the same as the previous year.

Some budget lines have several deadlines for applications within one year, but there may be less money available for the last one, unless there are fixed amounts and variations in the purposes and criteria for each deadline. If little or no change is expected from one year to the next, you may want to get tactical advice on whether to apply for some of the leftovers of this year or use the documentation available for this year to prepare a better application next year and to have a go at a larger amount.

Larger, multi-annual programmes usually have shifting priorities from year to year, which are often known in advance for the whole period. It will give you time to think and develop your project carefully, seek partners and additional financial sources.

In exceptional cases, there are no fixed deadlines or detailed criteria on fundable activities so you may have more flexibility in setting up your project and draft your application. The later in the calendar year you do so, the smaller your chance of success, as more than half of the available money may well be spent before summer. If you apply in November you may be lucky if there is money left that the Commission finds difficult to allocate before the end of the year, but this is exceptional and unpredictable, so don't count on it.

New starts in 2000

New versions of several larger, multi-annual funding programmes will enter into force as from 2000 (education, training, youth, culture, Structural Funds) and this book combines information on both the outgoing and the revised programmes as available at the time of writing. Aims and criteria of previous years will help you target your search for funding possibilities in the years to come.

Reading the documentation

The first thing to try is to make sense of the often extensive and bureaucratically phrased official documents. Don't be discouraged by official EU phrasing, which is not exactly put in welcoming terms. In addition to bureaucratic and professional jargon, an English text may well be a translation from a French original or have been written by officials who have another native language. They will speak to you in their version of everyday English, but try to imagine how easy your version of English will be for them to understand. Even the authors have to admit that a first round of casual reading often leaves them in the dark. Try to read such texts as if they are written in a remotely familiar foreign language: slowly, carefully and more than once. After some time you will get used to it but don't forget to return to your own language!

Follow the rules

The times are long gone when a mere description of your plans in your own terms, accompanied by a friendly letter requesting financial support, would do the job. Nowadays all subsidies must be applied for through fixed procedures that differ greatly in detail according to the department or budget line, and which can be quite complicated even to insiders. In order to bring some similarity in the procedures and criteria applied by different DGs, the Commission in January 1999 introduced common guidelines. They are published in the *Vademecum on*

Grant Management which serves as a reference guide both for grant seekers and for the EU officials who handle them. At the time of introduction it was expected that it would take more than a few months before the new guidelines were reflected in all procedures and documentation.

Deciding how to proceed (if at all)

- Select one or two of the most promising budget lines or programmes for your actual application.
- Check your choice with EU services (and ask for alternative sources).
- Check the eligibility of your organisation, activity and financial situation.
- Make sure your activity has 'EU added value'.
- Compare your budget with available amounts of EU grants.
- Check your co-funding situation (own or other sources, cash, kind, own paid staff, volunteer work).
- 'Will I apply this year or next?'
- Find partners in other countries if necessary or advisable.

EU policy priorities, buzz words and defending your case

Once you have made your (initial) selection of one or more promising budget lines and have found the relevant documents, you will need to formulate an answer to the question that even the most helpful EU official will put to you:

'You certainly have good reasons of your own why you want some of our money for your project, but can you give me a good reason for my boss to give it to you?'

Many methods, procedures and problems in contacts between fund-raisers and officials are very similar to lobbying or applying for a job: you want something for your own good reasons, but you will only get it if the other party has good reason to agree. The two may be close to each other, but they do not necessarily coincide entirely. Your answer should fit into what is going on in EU policy in your field, demonstrate the importance and quality of your activities and convince those who prepare and make a decision on your application that a financial contribution to your activities is helpful to achieve their policy targets. Therefore, phrase the arguments for your project (motivation, your exact activities, realistic targets) in terms that first of all are relevant to the European Commission, without violating your own aims and considerations.

Some typical concerns that appear in a great variety of EU policies and programmes are: training, job creation, social integration, innovation, information society, multimedia.

Results of a project should always be measurable, evaluated against the stated aims, made publicly available and have a proven impact beyond those immediately involved.

'EU added value' ('additionality') usually features high in the list of selection criteria. Even if no partners in other (applicant) EU countries are needed, the project must fit in with the EU's aims and policies and it is often required that its results are relevant for your sector as a whole and beyond your own country. Other commonly used EU phraseology includes: 'pilot projects', 'exchanges of experiences', 'best practices', 'preparatory' or 'support measures'. You will find them most often in fields where the EU competence is very recent or where national governments have kept most of the policy competencies for themselves. Other popular terminology is 'multiplier effects', 'exchange of experience and best practice', 'visibility', 'benchmarking'. In many cases these phrases are legal niceties to be able to spend any money at all on a subject, but also genuinely indicate the aim of internationalising the activities that the EU gives its money to.

Don't bite the hand that feeds you (or softly only)

Making your project 'EU compatible' means that it will have to fit in with existing policy competencies and political priorities. This does not necessarily mean that you have to be exactly in step with the European Commission. EU officials obviously may not be over-keen to subsidise activities that explicitly oppose EU policy or even the EU as such. On the other hand, there is the democratic principle, applying to the EU as to any governmental institution, of not only supporting its own fan clubs but also other organisations that distribute relevant information and involve their members or public opinion in EU policy. If your own favourite aims and style are 'mobilising forces against ...' it might be wise, without violating your principles, to substitute this with the slightly softer 'informing and actively involving relevant sections of the population in public debate on ...' (The authors apologise for making you speak and write EU jargon ...)

Policy fields in which you may apply for EU funding

There is a great variety of subject areas in which non-profit organisations may apply for EU financial support, which are listed below in the same order as they appear in the official EU budget and in this guide:

Inside the European Union

Structural Funds: European
    Social Fund, Community
    Initiatives, European Regional
    Development Fund
General grants
Education, Youth, Vocational training
Culture
Audio-visual media
Sport
Information and communication
    on the EU
Social dialogue and employment
Social protection

Health
Energy
Environment
Consumer policy
Free movement, social economy,
    tourism
Information society
Labour market initiatives; SMEs
Transports and telecommunication
Justice and home affairs
Research and technological
    development

The European Union in the world

European Development Fund (African, Caribbean, Pacific countries)

Food aid

Humanitarian aid

Asian and Latin American developing countries; South Africa

Mediterranean countries and Middle East

Central and eastern Europe, New Independent States, Mongolia

Support to development NGOs, training, information

Environment, health, drugs, demography in developing countries

Specific aid in the field of development

Other cooperation: transatlantic relations, anti-personnel mines, sex tourism

Democracy and human rights

Environment

Education and vocational training

Be aware that the competence of the EU varies from one policy field to another, which has consequences for the kind of activities it may support. On development cooperation the EU may give aid like any national government. On health the main business of 'treatment and care' remains strictly within national competence. So you may equally try to get money for a hospital project in Burkina Faso from the EU or from your government. The hospital in your home town will never get EU money for its regular activities but the EU may be willing to support an international comparison of diagnostic methods of a certain disease from which not only the project partners benefit but others as well.

In policy fields with restricted EU competence the activities of the Commission may be limited to 'preparatory measures' for further cooperation or 'support measures'. This is reflected in the conditions and eligibility criteria for financial support to what are often called 'pilot projects' or 'support actions'.

Partners needed

One common aspect of most EU funding schemes is that they are conditional on the project having an EU dimension or 'EU added value'. In many cases you will therefore have to design and implement your project jointly with partners in other EU countries so you can complement and learn from each other and transfer your conclusions or experiences even further to other colleagues in your field. Usually a minimum of three partners is required and one of them may or should be from an applicant EU country. In any partnership there must be one 'lead partner' that the European Commission will primarily deal with, but the others must fulfil the same criteria of quality and relevance, have clearly defined assignments, and sign the contract with the EU.

If your project deals specifically with central and eastern Europe or a non-European, developing country, the EU may require that the lead partner is located in the beneficiary country. These partnerships must be real and you will soon be caught out if you try to use or set up fake or 'sleeping' partners. You may have to make an effort to help a non-EU partner in acquiring the necessary experience, which is exactly what the EU increasingly aims at: beneficiary countries and organisations should 'own the project' and determine its main aim and course.

Prepare your application

- Read carefully the application forms, criteria, instructions and the *Vademecum on Grant Management.*
- Find the deadline (if any) for applications.
- 'Why should we spend EU money on your project?'
- Stress reasons, activities and expected results that the EU may like most … but don't overstate your case: you will have to prove results at the end.
- Draft a realistic budget that takes EU funding criteria into account.
- Make sure you have other sources for expenses for which there is no EU (co)funding.
- Find someone who has done it before for help in drafting or for comment.
- Sign the application.
- Observe the deadline scrupulously.
- If 'date sent' is the deadline: send by registered mail and keep your receipt.
- Be patient.

Inside or outside

The tender forms may specify that applicants should be from within or outside the EU; and if there is no regional reference at all, the whole of the EU is eligible. In this guide reference is only made to countries in central and eastern Europe, when they are specifically targeted as eligible. Usually no such reference is made, but their participation may well be possible or even encouraged as applicant EU members. At the time of writing, new policy fields were opening to those 'wannabe' EU countries at high speed, so check the details if you want to give an eastern extension to your project.

A similar situation exists with regard to Norway, Iceland and Liechtenstein, the three remaining members of the former European Free Trade Association (EFTA), after Sweden, Finland and Austria joined the EU. Without being second rank or applicant EU members, they co-operate with the EU in many fields within the European Economic Area (EEA) and may be involved in your EU funded project as equal partners.

Co-financing

In principle, the EU never pays all or even 90% of the project costs, unless the applicant really has no alternative sponsors or resources of its own and the project is considered important enough to make an exception. The 'co-financing' rate usually amounts to 60–80%, but may also be well under 50%. This percentage may be fixed but it is more common that the EU finances 'up to xx%' of eligible costs, which means negotiations are possible on a case-by-case basis with variable results. You will usually have to spend some of your own resources in cash on a project but contributions in kind are sometimes allowed, like involvement of your permanent staff and even volunteer work, if that is an important aspect of your work. An external sponsor may be nearly anyone and will usually be national or local authorities or private sponsors (charities, foundations etc.) You may even get other EU support, though this may usually not serve as a co-financing source, and you must convincingly explain that you are not trying to play the trick of getting the same activity or expense financed twice.

Amounts

There is a great variation in the amounts you can expect, from €10,000 under a budget line of a few millions to several million € under one of the larger, multi-annual programmes. In the documentation of a grant scheme you will find indications on the average range such as *'between €50,000 and €250,000'*, *'mostly over €300,000'* or *'the available €5 million will be spent on 125–150 projects'*. An effective way of estimating how much you may expect (and for what) is consulting the lists of grants given in previous years which most DGs will publish on their web-sites or supply on request.

The Commission tends to alleviate its administrative burden in the selection and administration of projects by sometimes giving preference to larger applications involving several partners and member states, from which it expects a greater visibility of EU grant schemes.

For applicants for smaller projects outside the European Union the solution may be to submit a mini-project (usually from €3,000 to a maximum ranging from €15,000 to €50,000) through a local project partner to the local EU representation.

Some of the smaller budget lines get only minimal publicity if the relevant service wishes to avoid processing hundreds of applications when it can support only a few of them.

Drawing up your project and its budget

You may not use EU money for just any expenses you have. The EU will be very precise in stating, within the agreed budget, which costs are eligible and to what amounts or percentages. Typically, staff costs will usually be funded to a maximum of 50% and your administrative expenses may not be more than 5–7% of total costs. If the project is implemented from your regular offices, you may negotiate to include part of your rent, heating and electricity on the project budget, but in general the running and overhead costs of your organisation as such will be totally excluded. Those will only be (co-)financed if the EU gives 'core funding' to an organisation as such.

If you ask EU support for an activity that lasts longer than one year, you should be aware that an EU grant given in one year may only in certain cases be used over a longer period and you will normally get support on an annual basis only, even if it comes out of an adopted multi-annual EU programme. The Commission can usually not guarantee follow-up grants. This does not exclude a successful follow-up application, but you will normally have to finish the previous project first and send in its financial and substantive report before a new request is even considered.

In all cases, you should try to convince the EU that the activities subsidised by the EU remain viable even if EU support stops after the first year. You may also consider rearranging your project into several viable 'sub-projects' for which you seek EU support in subsequent years.

The Commission's decision

You may be convinced of the quality and eligibility of your project and so may the Commission, but that is no guarantee of a successful application. In many cases the Commission does not have sufficient funds to honour more than one quarter of all eligible applications, or often far less. This should not discourage you from applying again on the next possible occasion, when you may even have improved your application after investigating which proposals were successful and what criteria were decisive in the final selection.

It may also prompt you to look for other potential EU sources of funding for the same or a modestly revised version of your project.

In most cases, you will find EU decision making highly bureaucratic, difficult to follow and time-consuming. EU processing time is measured in months rather than weeks, though efforts are made to avoid the extremely long, complicated and ineffective procedures of the late 1990s. It is difficult and usually a risky business to try and investigate the state of affairs, to speed up the process or to influence the outcome. Most EU financing schemes are politically uncontroversial and your application will normally be processed according to pre-set objectives, rules and criteria, involving little internal EU politicking. There are known cases of effective intervention 'from above', though more in the commercial sector or in nationally implemented programmes than in Brussels administered programmes for the non-profit sector. If you happen to have access to influential officials or your local MEP, you may be tempted to have a go at it, but this is risky and rash action may even backfire on you. The best investment in 'inside relations', certainly in the longer run, is to make sure that your work is of good quality and EU relevance, and that relevant politicians and officials know it. A pre-application visit to talk to the relevant official about your idea, although an investment of time and money, can pay dividends.

If your application is successful

- Be patient: your money won't arrive next week.
- Adjust your bookkeeping and activity reporting systems to those required by your application.
- For major changes in activities or expenses during the life of the project, consult the European Commission in good time.
- Hand in interim report, final report and evaluation on time, related clearly to the original application and budget.

If your application fails

- Don't assume it is your fault (it may, but may not be).
- Request an overview of successful applications and think why yours is not.

- Find out what percentage of 'eligible' applications was successful, according to which criteria.
- Seek feedback from the relevant officials, although they are not obliged to provide this to unsuccessful applicants.
- Try another source for the same or another aspect of your work.
- Try again next year.

Receiving your money and reporting on its use

Once your application has finally been accepted, you will sign a detailed contract defining your activities, rights and duties, and you will receive a first instalment of your grant. You will receive your remaining money after submitting a financial and narrative report. For larger projects, interim reports will be required.

It may be possible to include expenses made between the submission of your application and the signing of the contract, but only if the Commission has agreed to that beforehand. Unless you can safely pre-finance such expenses from other sources and are prepared to take the risk that your application fails, it is safer to wait, not only until you receive the good news that your application is successful, but also until the contract has been signed. After that it may still take several weeks (or longer) before the money arrives in your bank account: if your financial liquidity does not allow you to pre-finance expenses, you may have to wait a little more before starting the actual work.

You will only get the agreed financial support for expenses that were actually included in the project budget that you submitted and the Commission agreed to. You may have to refund the money that you have not spent or spent on items other than those agreed. If you feel such changes are inevitable, explain the reasons to the Commission in good time and ask their consent; don't wait until the project is over!

One final piece of advice is so obvious that you may forget it, possibly with disastrous results:

Submit your application in the required format.

Keep to the deadlines exactly to the minute.

Do not forget to sign the application.

SEARCH TOOLS

The full list of 1999 budget lines for which NGOs are eligible

INSIDE THE EUROPEAN UNION

B2-1	Regional policy structural funds			
B2-12	European Regional Development Fund – Community support frameworks	€15,646,000,000	£10,952,200,000	p 52
B2-13	European Social Fund – Community support frameworks	€9,611,000,000	£6,727,700,000	p 54
B2-14	**Community initiatives**			
B2-140	Pesca (restructuring of the fisheries sector)	€57,950,000	£40,565,000	p 60
B2-141	Interregional co-operation:			
B2-1410	Interreg II (border development, cross-border co-operation, and selected energy networks)	€1,063,770,000	£744,639,000	p 61
B2-1412	Special programme for regions in both parts of Ireland	€205,000,000	£143,500,000	p 62
B2-142	Employment and development of human resources:			
B2-1420	Now - New Opportunities for Women	€148,000,000	£103,600,000	p 63
B2-1421	Horizon	€91,000,000	£63,700,000	p 64
B2-1422	Integra	€193,000,000	£135,100,000	p 65
B2-1423	Youthstart	€127,000,000	£88,900,000	p 65
B2-1424	Adapt	€614,000,000	£429,800,000	p 66
B2-143	**Industrial restructuring**			
B2-1430	Rechar II (economic conversion of coal-mining areas)	€51,860,000	£36,302,000	p 67
B2-1431	Resider II (economic conversion of steel-making areas)	€166,770,000	£116,739,000	P 68
B2-1432	Konver (conversion of defence industries)	€80,540,000	£56,378,000	p 68
B2-1433	Retex (diversification of zones dependent on textiles & clothing industry)	€154,860,000	£108,402,000	p 69
B2-144	Regis II (most remote regions)	€216,850,000	£151,795,000	p 70
B2-145	Urban (urban areas)	€186,220,000	£130,354,000	p 70
B2-146	Leader II (rural development)	€567,000,000	£396,900,000	p 71
B2-147	SMEs Initiative (adaptation of SMEs to the internal market)	€332,180,000	£232,526,000	p 73
B2-180	European Agricultural Guidance and Guarantee Fund, Guidance Section	€25,250,000,000	£17,675,000,000	p 52
B2-181	Financial instrument for fisheries guidance	€23,000,000	£16,100,000	p 52
B2-182	European Regional Development Fund	€254,000,000	£177,800,000	p 52
B2-183	European Social Fund	€111,000,000	£77,700,000	p 54
B2-300	Cohesion Fund	€3,117,700,000	£2,182,390,000	p 51
General grants				
A-3021	Grants to organisations advancing the idea of Europe	€1,950,000	£1,365,000	p75
A-3022	Study and research centres	€1,500,000	£1,050,000	p76

A-3024	Associations and federations of European interest	€1,350,000	£945,000	p 77
A-3029	Support for international non-governmental youth organisations	€1,100,000	£770,000	p 78
A-3035	Preservation of Nazi concentration camp sites as historical memorials	€250,000	£175,000	p 79
A-3038	Other general grants	€300,000	£210,000	p 80
A-321	Town-twinning schemes in the European Union.	€10,000,000	£7,000,000	p 81

Education

B3-1000	Cooperation in the fields of education and youth policy	€4,500,000	£3,150,000	p 85
B3-1001	Socrates	€213,350,000	£149,345,000	p 87
B3-1002	Connect: Innovation and connection of Community programmes	€15,000,000	£10,500,000	p 91
B3-1006	Promotion and safeguard of regional and minority languages and cultures	p.m.		p 92

Youth

B3-1010	Youth for Europe	€31,800,000	£22,260,000	p 95
B3-1011	European Voluntary Service	€22,450,000	£15,715,000	p 98

Vocational training

B3-1021	Leonardo da Vinci	€139,900,000	£97,930,000	p 102

Culture

B3-2000	Raphael: Community action programme in the field of cultural heritage	€8,800,000	£6,160,000	p 110
B3-2001	Kaleidoscope: Programme to support artistic and cultural activities having a European dimension	€10,200,000	£7,140,000	p 112
B3-2002	Ariane: Support programme in the field of books and culture	€4,100,000	£2,870,000	p 114
B3-2004	Promotion of linguistic diversity in the Community in the information society	€4,000,000	£2,800,000	p 115
B3-2005	Experimental measures in relation to the cultural framework programme	€7,000,000	£4,900,000	p 117
B3-2006	Pilot projects on multicultural integration	€7,000,000	£4,900,000	p 118

Audiovisual media

B3-2010	Media: Measures to promote the development of the audiovisual industry)	€61,600,000	£43,120,000	p 120
B3-2016	Preparatory measures in the audiovisual sector	€4,000,000	£2,800,000	p 123

Sport

B3-2020	Sport in Europe	p.m.		p 124

Information and communication on the EU

B3-300	General information and communication work concerning the EU	€42,500,000	£29,750,000	p 127
B3-301	Information outlets	€7,000,000	£4,900,000	p 128
B3-302	Information programmes for non-member countries	€6,100,000	£4,270,000	p 128
B3-304	European integration in universities: Jean Monnet programme	€3,500,000	£2,450,000	p 129

B3-306	Information programme for European citizens (Prince):			
	Information activities in connection with specific policies	€38,000,000	£26,600,000	p 130
B3-309	Special annual events	€10,000,000	£7,000,000	p 131

Social dialogue and employment

B3-4000	Industrial relations and social dialogue	€7,300,000	£5,110,000	p 134
B3-4002	Information and training measures for workers' organisations	€9,000,000	£6,300,000	p 135
B3-4003	Information, consultation and participation of representatives of undertakings	€5,000,000	£3,500,000	p 136
B3-4011	Eures (European Employment Services)	€10,000,000	£7,000,000	p 137
B3-4012	Measures to achieve equality between men and women	€10,000,000	£7,000,000	p 138

Social protection and integration

B3-4101	Cooperation with charitable associations	€3,000,000	£2,100,000	p 140
B3-4108	Studies on the family, family policies and demographic trends	€2,425,000	£1,697,500	p 141
B3-4109	Daphne: Measures for combating violence against children, adolescents and women	€5,000,000	£3,500,000	p 142
B3-4110	Free movement of workers and coordination of social security systems	€2,500,000	£1,750,000	p 143
B3-4111	Preparatory measures combating and preventing discrimination	€7,000,000	£4,900,000	p 144
B3-4112	Preparatory measures combating and preventing social exclusion	€10,000,000	£7,000,000	p 145
B3-4113	Action to integrate refugees	€5,000,000	£3,500,000	p 146

Health

B3-4300	Public health, health promotion, information on health, health education and public health training	€4,800,000	£3,360,000	p 149
B3-4301	Combating cancer	€14,150,000	£9,905,000	p 150
B3-4302	Health aspects of drug abuse	€5,120,000	£3,584,000	p 151
B3-4303	Combating AIDS and certain other transmissible diseases	€10,450,000	£7,315,000	p 152
B3-4304	Health and well-being	€5,400,000	£3,780,000	p 153
B3-4306	Health surveillance	€2,700,000	£1,890,000	p 155
B3-4310	Health protection, hygiene and safety at work	€4,425,000	£3,097,500	p 156
B3-4313	SAFE: Actions for safety at work in Europe	€7,000,000	£4,900,000	p 157

Energy

B4-1030	Altener: Promotion of renewable energy sources	€15,400,000	£10,780,000	p 158
B4-1031	Save II: Encouragement of energy efficiency	€15,500,000	£10,850,000	p 159

Environment

B4-304	Legislation and other general action based on the Fifth Action Programme on the environment	€18,000,000	£12,600,000	p 161
B4-306	Awareness and subsidies	€6,650,000	£4,655,000	p 162
B4-3200	Life II - Part 1: Nature protection	€67,000,000	£46,900,000	p 163
B4-3201	Life II - Part 2: Environmental protection	€67,000,000	£46,900,000	p 164
B4-3300	Community cooperation on civil protection and environmental emergencies	€2,000,000	£1,400,000	p 166

THE EU IN THE WORLD: EXTERNAL MEASURES

B7-1	European Development Fund: Cooperation with ACP (African, Caribbean and Pacific) states			p 225

Food and humanitarian aid

B7-20	Food aid and support operations:			
B7-200	Products mobilised under the Food Aid Convention	€151,000,000	£105,700,000	p 227
B7-201	Other aid (products, support actions, early warning systems and storage)	€250,000,000	£175,000,000	p 227
B7-202	Transport, distribution, flanking measures and monitoring implementation	€104,000,000	£72,800,000	p 227
B7-21	Humanitarian aid (ECHO):			
B7-210	Aid, including emergency food aid to help the populations of developing countries after disasters	€162,850,000	£113,995,000	p 228
B7-214	Humanitarian aid to the people of central and eastern European countries	€98,000,000	£68,600,000	p 229
B7-215	Humanitarian aid to the people of the New Independent States and Mongolia	€45,000,000	£31,500,000	p 229
B7-217	Operations to help refugees, displaced persons and returnees	€18,000,000	£12,600,000	p 229
B7-219	Operational support and disaster preparedness	€7,000,000	£4,900,000	p 229
B7-910	Emergency aid reserve	€346,000,000	£242,200,000	p 229

Asian and Latin American developing countries; South Africa

B7-300	Financial and technical cooperation with Asian developing countries	€312,500,000	£218,750,000	p 231
B7-302	Aid to uprooted people in Asian countries	€37,950,000	£26,565,000	p 232
B7-303	Rehabilitation and reconstruction operations in developing countries in Asia	€5,000,000	£3,500,000	p 233
B7-310	Financial and technical cooperation with Latin American developing countries	€202,500,000	£141,750,000	p 234
B7-312	Aid to uprooted people in Latin American countries	€21,350,000	£14,945,000	p 235
B7-313	Rehabilitation and reconstruction operations in developing countries in Latin America	€4,250,000	£2,975,000	p 236
B7-320	Cooperation with South Africa	€127,500,000	£89,250,000	p 237

Mediterranean countries and the Middle East

B7-410	Meda: Measures to accompany reforms of the economic and social structures in the Mediterranean non-member countries	€976,000,000	£683,200,000	p 239
B7-420	Community operations connected with the Israel-PLO peace agreement	€50,000,000	£35,000,000	p 245

Central and eastern Europe, New Independent States and Mongolia

B7-500	Aid for economic restructuring of the countries of central and eastern Europe (Phare, including Lien and Tempus)	€1,243,190,000	£870,233,000	p 247
B7-502	Transfrontier cooperation in the field of structural operations (part of Phare with Interreg)	€180,000,000	£126,000,000	p 253
B7-520	Assistance to economic reform and recovery in the New Independent States and Mongolia (Tacis)	€402,550,000	£281,785,000	p 254

B7-521	Transfrontier cooperation in the field of structural operations (part of Tacis with Interreg)	€20,000,000	£14,000,000	p 256
B7-522	Rehabilitation and reconstruction operations in the New Independent States and Mongolia	€10,000,000	£7,000,000	p 257
B7-541	Measures for the reconstruction of the republics formerly part of Yugoslavia	€200,000,000	£140,000,000	p 258
B7-543	Measures for the rehabilitation of the republics formerly part of Yugoslavia	€42,000,000	£29,400,000	p 259

Support to development NGOs, training, information

B7-6000	Community contribution towards schemes concerning developing countries by non-governmental organisations	€200,000,000	£140,000,000	p 260
B7-610	Training and promotion of awareness on development issues including periods of training at the Commission for nationals of third counties	€4,500,000	£3,150,000	p 262
B7-611	Integrating gender issues in development cooperation	€3,300,000	£2,310,000	p 263
B7-612	Preparatory actions through NGOs against child discrimination	€5,000,000	£3,500,000	p 264

Environment, health, drugs and demography in developing countries

B7-6200	Environment in the developing countries	€16,000,000	£11,200,000	p 265
B7-6201	Tropical forests	€45,000,000	£31,500,000	p 266
B7-6210	North-South cooperation schemes in the context of the campaign against drug abuse	€9,800,000	£6,860,000	p 268
B7-6211	Health programmes and the fight against AIDS/HIV in developing countries	€16,500,000	£11,550,000	p 269
B7-631	Aid for population and reproductive health policies and programmes in developing countries	€8,000,000	£5,600,000	p 270

Specific aid in the field of development

B7-641	Rehabilitation and reconstruction measures for the developing countries, particularly ACP states	€15,000,000	£10,500,000	p 272
B7-643	Decentralised cooperation for the developing countries	€4,000,000	£2,800,000	p 273

Other cooperation: transatlantic relations, anti-personnel mines and sex tourism

B7-6601	Cooperation agreements with third countries	€1,600,000	£1,120,000	p 274
B7-6602	New Transatlantic Agenda	€6,000,000	£4,200,000	p 275
B7-661	Community participation in action concerning anti-personnel mines	€4,000,000	£2,800,000	p 276
B7-663	Campaigns against sex tourism in third countries	€1,000,000	£700,000	p 277

Democracy and human rights

B7-700	Support for democracy in the countries of central and eastern Europe, including the republics formerly part of Yugoslavia (Phare democracy programme)	€15,000,000	£10,500,000	p 281
B7-701	Support for democracy in the New Independent States and Mongolia	€10,000,000	£7,000,000	p 282
B7-7020	Human rights and democracy in the developing countries, in particular the ACP countries	€17,000,000	£11,900,000	p 283

Find your way

By using the following lists, you will find many budget lines that may be relevant to your work, but difficult to detect as such if you go by their official titles only. There are three different sections:

+ by activity (environment, training, human rights, etc.)
+ by target groups (disabled people, migrants, unemployed etc.)
+ by area where your activity takes place, inside or outside the European Union

When an incomplete number is given, the whole chapter with a number of budget lines is relevant: for instance B2-13⁰⁰ means all budget lines under the European Social Fund

Fields of activity

Your activities	*EU budget lines*
Culture	A-3021, 321
	B2-1410, 1423, 1430, 12⁰⁰, 182, 13⁰⁰, 183
	B3-1000, 1001, 1002, 1006, 1010, 1011, 1021, 2000, 2001, 2002, 2005, 2006, 2010, 4113
	B5-325, 330, 500, 501, 511, 512, 720
	B6-6121, 6141, 6142
	B7-410, 502, 541, 543, 6602
Education	B2-1421, 1422, 1423, 13⁰⁰, 183,
(*see also:* Training)	B3-1000, 1001, 1002, 1006, 1010, 1021, 2000, 2006, 2010, 304, 4002, 4113, 4300, 4301, 4302, 4303
	B5-100, 330, 336, 502, 702
	B4-306, 3300
	B6-6121, 6211, 6411
	B7-300, 310, 320, 410, 420, 500, 520, 541, 543, 6000, 6210, 631, 6602, 661, 704, 830
Environment	A-3021
	B2-1410, 1423, 1430, 1431, 1432, 1433, 145, 146, 147, 12⁰⁰, 182, 13⁰⁰, 183
	B3-1001, 1006, 1011, 309
	B3-4310, 4313
	B4-1030, 1031, 304, 306, 3200, 3201, 3300
	B5-100, 103, 325, 501, 511, 700, 720
	B6-6111, 6141, 6142
	B7-300, 310, 410, 420, 521, 543, 6000, 610, 6200, 6211, 810, 811

EU information, promotion, citizenship, NGO networking (general, not on specific topics)	A-3021, 3022, 3024, 3029, 3038, 321 B3-1000, 1001, 1002, 1010 B3-300, 301, 302, 304, 306, 4101
Health	B2-1410, 1422, 145, 13◊◊, 183 B3-2020 B3-43◊◊ B4-306 B5-103, 720 B6-6111 B7-1, 21, 320, 410, 420, 520, 543, 6000, 621, 6211, 631, 661, 704
Human rights and democracy	A-3021, 3024, 3028, 3035 B3-1000, 1002, 1010, 4111 B5-321 B7-320, 410, 543, 6601, 70◊◊
Information society	B2-12◊◊, 182, 13◊◊, 183 B3-2004 B5-100, 330, 331, 512 B6-6121
Research	A-3022, 3035, 3038 B2-147, 13◊◊, 183 B3-1001, 1002, 1020, 1021, 2000, 2002, 4000, 4108, 4110, 4301, 4306, 4313 B5-100, 321, 325, 330, 502, 511, 512, 800 B6-6◊◊ B7-410, 500, 6200, 631, 6601, 810, 830
Social integration	B2-1411, 1412, 1422, 1423, 12◊◊, 182, 13◊◊, 183 B3-1000, 1001, 1002, 1011, 1021, 2005, 2006, 4101, 4110, 4111, 4112, 4113 B5-500 B6-6411 B7-303, 313, 410, 520, 522, 541, 6000, 641, 661, 70◊◊
Sport	B3-1010, 2020, 300, 4111 B7-420
Training (*see also:* Education)	A-321 B2-1410, 1420, 1421, 1422, 1423, 1424, 1430, 1431, 1432, 1433, 145, 13◊◊, 183 B3-1000, 1001, 1002, 1006, 1010, 1021, 2000, 2002, 2005, 2006, 2010, 2016, 4002, 4012, 4109, 4110, 4113, 4300, 4301, 4302, 4303 B5-100, 300, 321, 325, 330, 336, 500, 502, 700, 702, 803 B4-306, 3300 B6-6121, 6211, 6411 B7-1, 20, 320, 410, 420, 500, 520, 541, 543, 6000, 610, 611, 6211, 7020, 704, 705, 709, 810, 830

Target groups

Your target group	*EU budget lines*
Children (*see also:* Youth)	B2-1412, 12⁰⁰, 182, 13⁰⁰, 183 B3-1001, 4109, 4112 B5-100, 336, 800 B7-300, 303, 310, 522, 6000, 612, 6211, 631, 641, 663, 703, 704, 705
Consumers	B5-100, 103, 300, 330, 336, 700 B6-6111, 6121 B7-300, 310, 320, 410, 500, 6000
Disabled people	B2-1421, 13⁰⁰, 183 B3- 2020, 4111, 4112, 4304 B5-700 B6-6111 B7-303, 313, 500, 522
Drug addicts	B3-4302 B5-800 B7-300, 310, 6210
Elderly people	B2- 12⁰⁰, 182, 13⁰⁰, 183 B3-4108, 4110, 4111, 4112 B6-6111, 6121 B7-500
Employees	B2-, 12⁰⁰, 182, 13⁰⁰, 183 B3-1021, 4000, 4002, 4003, 4011, 4012, 4110, 4310, 4313
Indigenous people	B3-1006 B7-6200, 6201, 703, 704
Migrants, refugees, displaced people	B2-1422, 13⁰⁰, 183 B3-1001, 2006, 4110, 4112, 4113 B5-800, 803 B7-1, 21, 302, 303, 312, 313, 520, 522, 541, 61, 641, 703, 705
Minorities (*see also:* Indigenous people)	B3-1000, 1006, 2006 B7-301, 310, 701, 704, 705, 7022
Small and medium sized enterprises	B2-140, 1410, 1420, 1430, 1431, 146, 147, 12⁰⁰, 182, 13⁰⁰, 183, B3-2004, 306, 4313 B5-325, 330, 500, 511, 512, 720 B6-6311 B7-410, 6602
Students	A-3022 B2-13⁰⁰, 183 B3-1001, 304, 4010, 4110 B5-330 B7-830

Unemployed	B2-1410, 1420, 1421, 1422, 1423, 1424, 12^{00}, 182, 13^{00}, 183
	B3-2005, 2006, 4011, 4012
	B5-330, 500, 502, 511
	B6-6141, 6412, 6411
	B7-320, 500
Volunteers	B2-1422, 13^{00}, 183
	B3-1010, 1011, 4101, 4109, 4304
	B5-321
	B7-500
Women, equality of men and women	B2-1411, 1420, 12^{00}, 182, 13^{00}, 183
	B3-1002, 1010, 1021, 306, 309, 4012, 4109
	B5-336, 500, 502, 800
	B7-20, 300, 303, 310, 313, 410, 500, 522, 6000, 611, 6211, 631, 641, 700, 7020, 7021, 7022, 703, 704, 705
Youth (*see also:* Children *and* Students)	A-3029
	B2-1411, 1423, 12^{00}, 182, 13^{00}, 183
	B3-1000, 1010, 1011, 1021, 2002, 2005, 300, 4109, 4302
	B5-512, 800
	B7-410, 500, 6000, 610

Area

Where does your activity take place?

Outside the European Union	EU budget lines
Africa (including South Africa, Nigeria)	B5-511
	B6-6211
	B7-1, 20, 210, 219, 320, 6000, 610, 611, 631, 641, 643, 7020, 7021, 7022
Asia (*for Central Asia, see:* Former Soviet Union)	B5-511
	B6-6211
	B7-20, 210, 219, 300, 302, 303, 6000, 610, 611, 612, 6200, 6201, 6210, 6211, 631, 641, 643, 661, 707, 830
Central and eastern Europe, including former Yugoslavia (**Note** This list focuses on central and eastern European countries as a primary target area or specifically mentioned as eligible. In the context of their forthcoming EU membership many other activities and budget lines are eligible.)	A-3022, 3024, 3035, 321
	B2-1410, 12^{00}, 182, 13^{00}, 183
	B3-1001, 1006, 1010, 2000, 2001, 2002, 2010, 2016, 4000, 4002, 4003, 4012
	B4-306, 3200, 3201
	B5-325, 511, 512, 800

Developing countries (general: ACP and others)	B5-331 B6-6211 B7-1, 20, 210, 219, 3, 4, 5, 6000, 610, 611, 612, 6200, 6201, 6210, 6211, 631, 641, 643, 663, 7020
Emergency, rehabilitation	B7-1, 20, 21, 303, 313, 420, 522, 541, 543, 643, 66, 70
Former Soviet Union	B2-1410 B3-1010 B5-511 B6-6211 B7-20, 215, 219, 520, 521, 522, 661
Latin America	B3-1010 B5-511 B6-6211 B7-210, 219, 310, 312, 313, 6000, 610, 611, 6210, 6211, 631, 641, 643, 661, 703, 830
Mediterranean (**Note** For EU applicant countries Cyprus and Malta, there may be more relevant budget lines. See: Central and eastern Europe, above.)	B2-1410 B3-1010 B5-511, 325 B6-6211 B7-210, 219, 4⁰⁰, 611, 612, 6200, 6210, 6211, 631, 661, 705, 810, 811

Inside the European Union	*EU budget lines*
Border areas	B2-1410, 12⁰⁰, 182, 13⁰⁰, 183 B3-4011, 4304 B5-100 B7-5, 810
Industrial areas in decline	B2-1410, 1424, 1430, 1431, 1432, 1433, 12⁰⁰, 182, 13⁰⁰, 183
Remote areas	B2-144, 12⁰⁰, 182, 13⁰⁰, 183 B5-700
Rural areas	B2-1410, 1411, 146, 12⁰⁰, 182, 13⁰⁰, 183 B3-2005, 301 B5-325 B6-6111, 6141
Urban areas	A-321 B2-1412, 145, 12⁰⁰, 182, 13⁰⁰, 183 B3-1011 B4-3201 B5-325 B6-6111, 6141 B7-1, 3, 4, 5, 62, 63, 64, 66, 810

INSIDE THE
EUROPEAN UNION

STRUCTURAL FUNDS: EUROPEAN SOCIAL FUND, COMMUNITY INITIATIVES

Economic and social cohesion among countries, regions, sectors, groups

Structural Funds and Community Initiatives

For decades, the European Union (EU) has implemented policies to reduce the disparities between its poorest and its richest countries and regions and to support economically and socially weak sectors and population groups. The principal way in which the EU tries to contribute to greater economic and social cohesion and uniformity of living standards is by granting financial assistance and resources to the poorer and declining regions of Europe through a series of inter-related funds, known as the Structural Funds.

They aim at helping regions to become competitive within the European single market, through infrastructure, training and employment projects, and to open up new opportunities for the benefit of marginalised communities and disadvantaged areas. This is achieved through a series of grants, as a complement to national or regional funding.

The Commission allocates 5% of the Structural Funds for the Community Initiatives, which are directed towards specific problems in economic sectors which are in difficulty across Europe and towards special training needs, mostly in relation to improving chances for employment.

Cohesion Fund

The Cohesion Fund is a separate special support programme for Greece, Spain, Portugal and the Irish Republic, as long as their economic performance is below 90% of the average of all member states taken together. €18 million will be available for the Cohesion Fund between 2000 and 2006, with Spain, the main beneficiary country, receiving nearly two-thirds. Ireland is expected to lose its eligibility in 2003, as its Gross Domestic Product (GDP) is approaching the 90% threshold (87% in 1999).

European Investment Bank

In addition to the Structural Funds and the Cohesion Fund, which are grant-giving instruments, economic assistance is also provided in the form of loans through the European Investment Bank.

General aspects of the Structural Funds

At the time of writing, the 1994–1999 Structural Funds were coming to an end and arrangements for the 2000–2006 implementation were still being worked out. The following overview focuses on aspects that are common to both periods and summarises the main guidelines and prospects for 2000–2006. The most important aims of the Structural Funds are:

- **European Regional Development Fund (ERDF)**: to reduce the gaps in development between different regions in the EU;
- **European Social Fund (ESF)**: to promote training and job opportunities;
- **European Agricultural Guidance and Guarantee Fund (EAGGF)**: to assist in the adaptation of agricultural structures and in developing and diversifying the EU's rural areas;
- **Financial Instrument for Fisheries Guidance (FIFG)**: to assist the restructuring of the fisheries sector.

Budget

Spending on the Structural Funds and the Cohesion Fund has increased considerably over the years, from only 4.8% of the EU budget in 1975, to 31% in 1993 and 40.5% in 1999, a little under 0.5% of the Gross National Product of all EU countries together. The total allocation for 1993–99 was €200 billion and the budgeted expenditure of €39 billion (£27.3 billion) for 1999 is nearly as much as expenditure for the Common Agricultural Policy. For the years 2000–2006, a total of €213 billion (£149 billion) has been allocated, starting with €32 billion in 2000 and gradually decreasing to €29.2 billion in 2006.

Eligibility

Funding for the non-profit sector is available through all of these funds, depending on the field of activity and concrete programmes or projects, but will be greatest in the European Social Fund (ESF) and the Community Initiatives, which deal with people-focused issues in which the non-profit sector is traditionally involved. In the other funds, the major beneficiaries will be public authorities, larger institutions and the private sector. The overview below therefore focuses on the general aspects of the Structural Funds and on ESF and the Community Initiatives in particular.

Beneficial areas

Priorities for the 2000–2006 Structural Funds are:

- improved financial management, simplified operation and administration of the funds;
- harmonious, balanced and sustainable development of economic activities;
- competitiveness and economic innovation, especially in small and medium-sized enterprises (SMEs);
- development of employment and human resources;
- protection and improvement of the environment;
- elimination of inequalities and the promotion of equality between men and women.

Compared to 1994–1999, funding is concentrated more strongly on areas of greatest need, and applicant EU countries in central and eastern Europe, Cyprus and Malta are also eligible.

Types of grants

In order to understand procedures and eligibility criteria, it is useful to keep in mind that most of the Structural Funds are allocated to specific regions in the EU for which national governments define the priorities on which they are spent, based on national or regional development plans. These are codified in long-term programmes called the Community Support Framework and Operational Programme or (if both are condensed into one) the Single Programming Document.

The basic principles that govern the operation of the Structural Funds are:
- concentration of resources on those regions, target groups and areas most in need of assistance, in order to make the most effective use of resources;
- emphasis upon a programme-based rather than a project-based approach to funding, with the EU providing cash for multi-annual programmes;
- a three-way partnership between the Commission, national governments, local or regional authorities and economic and social partners;
- consistency with the economic policies of member states (national, regional and local);
- additionality, to ensure that EU resources will supplement rather than replace resources already allocated at a national level.

As in the past, most of the Structural Funds are spent according to programmes and criteria, called Objectives, which are defined according to the level of economic development of a region or the specific problems of a certain economic sector. In any case, the priority for funding always goes to the poorest regions. There are 3 such Objectives, which combine the 6 Objectives of the period 1994–1999 and include some aspects of industrial reconversion that used to be dealt with through the Community Initiatives.

Objective 1 2000–2006: regions lagging behind economically

This section deals with all programmes for regions which are economically lagging behind (including the French overseas territories in the Caribbean) with a per capita GDP of less than 75% of the EU average, as well as the richer but remote areas in northern Sweden and Finland. During 2000–2006, €135.9 billion, nearly 70% of the total available for the Structural Funds, will be spent in this section.

Assistance to regions which used to be eligible but whose economic performance has risen above the 75% threshold is being phased out gradually. The percentage of the total EU population living in eligible areas is expected to be reduced accordingly, from 51% to 42%. This will affect the UK less than other countries, as it will be one of the two countries to increase rather than decrease the number of regions qualifying for Objective 1.

Between 1994 and 1999, the eligible areas in the UK were Merseyside, Northern Ireland and the Highlands and Islands of Scotland, for which €2.6 billion (£1.85 billion) was received. In 2000–2006, West Wales and the Valleys, Merseyside,

South Yorkshire and Cornwall and the Isles of Scilly qualify, with generous transitional packages (€1.166 billion, £816 million) for the regions losing that status: Northern Ireland, the Scottish Highlands and Islands. For Northern Ireland, the special Peace programme will remain in place under the Community Initiatives.

Objective 2 2000–2006: economic and social conversion

This section supports the economic and social conversion of areas facing structural difficulties (outside Objective 1 regions) in the industrial and service sectors and in rural, urban and fishery areas. A maximum of 18% of the total EU population will be covered by €22.5 billion for Objective 2 expenditure, 11.5% of the total Structural Funds. This section combines the 1994–1999 Objective 2 (industrial decline) and Objectives 5 and 5b (rural development, agricultural and fishery industries) programmes, and a number of Community Initiatives in the fields of urban development and reconversion of specific industries: coal mining, steel, defence and textiles.

Eligible UK areas for the 1994–1999 Objective 2 programmes included: Eastern Scotland, East London and the Lee Valley, East Midlands, Gibraltar, Greater Manchester, Lancashire and Cheshire, North East of England, Plymouth, Industrial South Wales, Thanet, West Cumbria and Furness, Western Scotland, West Midlands, Yorkshire and Humberside, to a total of €2.4 billion (£1.7 billion).

For the 1994–1999 Objective 5b programmes, 11 areas in the UK were eligible, including Grampian, Rural Stirling Uplands, Tayside, East Anglia and the Welsh Marches, to a total of €910 million (£637 million).

At the time of writing, eligible areas for the 2000–2006 period were not yet determined, but available funds will be €3.989 billion (£2.792 billion) plus €709 million (£496 million) for transitional measures.

Objective 3 2000–2006: human resource development

This section focuses on human resource development (education, training and employment) programmes in the whole of the UK outside Objective 1 areas, including activities which used to be covered by the 1994–1999 European Social Fund. Expenditure will be 12.3 % of the total (€24 billion). During 1994–1999, these subjects were dealt with in two sections (Objectives 3 and 4), under which €3.74 billion (£2.62 billion) were allocated to the UK.

Details on the 2000–2006 arrangements for Objective 3 and their consequences for the UK were not available at the time of writing, but available funds will be €4.568 billion (£3.198 billion) plus €121 million (£84.7 million) for transitional measures.

European Social Fund 2000–2006

The central aims of the fund will be:
+ developing and promoting active labour market policies to combat unemployment;
+ promoting equal opportunities and social inclusion for all in gaining access to the labour market;

- promoting and improving education, training and counselling, as part of lifelong learning policy;
- promoting a skilled, trained and adaptable labour force;
- improving women's access to and position in the labour market.

Eligible activities for financial assistance from ESF fall into 3 categories:
- assistance for persons: education and vocational training, aid for employment, higher education in science and research, new sources of employment;
- assistance for structures and systems: improving education and training systems, modernising employment services, developing systems to anticipate qualification needs;
- accompanying measures such as raising awareness and services.

It is the task of national governments to draw up their plans to implement these guidelines, on the basis of national Employment Action Plans to improve employability, to develop entrepreneurship, to encourage adaptability and to strengthen equal opportunities.

Information and applications

At the time of writing, only the general outlines of the Structural Funds had been agreed and published. Only after national governments have drawn up their own priorities and implementation plans and the Commission has agreed them, will it be the turn of local authorities, training institutions or NGOs in eligible fields to draw up and submit their plans. The European Commission's Directorate General on Social Affairs has estimated that this process might last well into the year 2000 before a start can be made with the implementation of the new Structural Funds.

Potential applicants in 1999 and early 2000 are advised not to wait that long before initiating the process of getting support for their activities. In contrast to applications for EU funding under other budget lines and programmes, projects under the Structural Funds, including Community Initiatives, are nearly exclusively dealt with by national, regional and local authorities. Therefore, expressing one's plans and prospects to those authorities in an early phase is a useful preparatory exercise before finalising your application. This time-consuming process of getting a project off the ground includes researching the answers to such questions as: Am I in an eligible region? Does my project fit into any of the priorities set out in the local Single Programming Document (which you can obtain from the relevant ministry in your country or from the Commission in Brussels)? Is it better to make an independent application for this project, to include it as part of a broader project with partners, or to include it in a package submitted by the regional authority?

It is, therefore, never too early to contact one of the addresses given below where you will also learn more about comparable projects financed by the funds, application procedures, etc. Browsing the Internet is also a good method of getting acquainted with the often complicated structures and procedures. It will introduce you to a wide variety of past and on-going activities in your field and may even introduce you to possibilities that you had not thought of.

UK contacts

ERDF

Department of Trade and Industry
1 Victoria Street
London SW1H 0ET
Tel: +44 171 215 5000
Fax: +44 171 215 6749
Internet: http://www.dti.gov.uk/public/frame10.html

Department of Finance and Personnel
Parliament Building
Stormont
Belfast BT4 3SW

For regional contacts in the UK and possibilities for grants, consult

http://www.inforegio.cec.eu.int/wbcont/gateways/gate_en.htm

ESF

Department for Education and Employment
ESF Unit, Caxton House, 6-12 Tothill Street
London SWIH 9NA
Tel: +44 171 273 5032
Fax: +44 171 278 5540

Training and Employment Agency
Clarendon House, 9–21 Adelaide Street
Belfast BT2 8DJ
Tel: +44 1232 257 650
Fax: +44 1232 257 646

ESF Internet sites:
general: http://www.esfnews.org.uk
in Yorkshire and the Humber: http://www.esf-yh.org.uk

EAGGF and FIFG

Ministry of Agriculture, Fisheries and Food
Nobel House (room 724 – for EAGGF, room 437 for FIFG)
17 Smith Square
London SW1P 3JR

The Scottish Executive
Agriculture and Fisheries Department
47 Robb's Loane
Edinburgh EH14 1TW

Department of Agriculture for Northern Ireland
Dundonald House, Upper Newtonards Road
Belfast BT4 3SB

The Welsh Office
Agriculture Department
Cathays Park
Cardiff CF1 3NE

For an overview of Structural Funds and Community Initiatives from a UK perspective, consult:

http://webserver.tag.co.uk/tagish/pubs/ukinfosoc/struct.htm

For non-profit organisations interested in ESF projects, it may be useful to consult:

NCVO – National Council for Voluntary Organisations
Regent's Wharf, 8 All Saints Street
London N1 9RL
Tel: +44 171 713 6161
Fax: +44 171 713 6300
Help desk: 0800 2 798 798
Minicom: 0800 01 88 111
E-mail: ncvo@ncvo-vol.org.uk
Internet: http://www.ncvo-vol.org.uk

NCVO has an EU section and will refer you to 8 ESF regional support offices if you need advice on funding.

EcoTec Research and Consulting Ltd.
Priestley House
28-34 Albert Street
Birmingham B4 7UD
Tel: +44 121 616 3671
Fax: +44 121 6616 3680
E-mail: http://www.employment.ecotec.co.uk

EU contacts

European Commission

DG V.C.3 – National employment monitoring and ESF operations, UK and Ireland
Mr George KINTZELE, Head of Unit
27 Rue Joseph II, B-1040 Brussels
Tel: +32 2 295 2539
Fax: +32 2 296 9905
E-mail: george.kintzele@dg05.cec.be
Internet: http://europa.eu.int/en/comm/dg05/esf/esf_home.htm

DG XVI.D.3 – Regional policy, UK
Mr Vittorio CURZI, Head of Unit
Cours Saint Michel 1, 23 Rue Père de Deken
B-1040 Brussels
Tel: +32 2 295 4686
Fax: +32 2 296 3277
E-mail: vittorio.curzi@dg16.cec.be
Internet: http://www.inforegio.cec.eu.int/dg16_en.htm

DG XVI.C.2 – Regional policy, Ireland, Northern Ireland
Mr Esben POULSEN, Head of Unit
Cours Saint Michel 1, 23 Rue Père de Deken
B-1040 Brussels
Tel: +32 2 295 0007
Fax: +32 2 296 3290
E-mail: esben.poulsen@dg16.cec.be
Internet: http://www.inforegio.cec.eu.int/dg16_en.htm

Community Initiatives

The 2000–2006 Community Initiatives consist of 4 activities:

Interreg: cross-border, transnational and interregional cooperation, like the previous Interreg programme, but now with a strong focus on cooperation with border regions in applicant countries and on coordination with Phare, Tacis and Meda programmes (which deal with support to central and eastern Europe, the former Soviet Union and the Mediterranean area respectively);

Equal: transnational cooperation to combat discrimination and inequalities in the labour market, including the social and vocational integration of asylum seekers; Equal will build on the experiences of and integrate the 1994–1999 Adapt and Employment programmes (see below);

Leader: rural development, as a follow-up programme of the 1994–1999 Leader programme;

Urban: inner city regeneration.

Funds allocated to the 2000–2006 Community Initiatives will be reduced to 5% (against 9% in 1994–1999) of the total for the Structural Funds, but this decline is offset by transferring the industrial conversion projects, which used to be part of the Community Initiatives, to the new Objective 2 programmes.

As a general rule, activities under 1994–1999 Community Initiatives which were not kept under the 2000–2006 Community Initiatives will be eligible under the 3 new mainstream Objectives.

For the whole period, the Community Initiatives in the whole of the EU will receive €10.5 billion (£7.35 billion) of which nearly half will be spent on Interreg, most of the other half for Equal and Leader and €700 million (£490 million) on

Urban. The division over member states and detailed programmatic and procedural guidelines were still undecided at the time of writing.

The special programme on the peace process in Northern Ireland (Peace) is kept in place for 5 years (2000–2004) with €500 million: €400 million to Northern Ireland and €100 million to the Irish Republic, in addition to the regular support under the Structural Funds and the EU contribution to the International Fund for Ireland (€15 million a year for 3 years).

To be eligible under the Community Initiatives programmes, projects must be guided by a few fundamental principles:

- transnationality: a project must operate in close cooperation with at least one other project in another member state to facilitate the exchange of information and know-how (such a transnational partnership is not necessary for projects under the mainstream Structural Funds);
- innovation: the aim of the Community Initiatives is to stimulate change in policies and practices so the projects are expected to be innovative in terms of content, tools and methodology or in the type of partners they involve;
- multiplier effect: the results of the projects are supposed to be disseminated at home and abroad amongst groups that have not been directly involved;
- complementarity: projects must not duplicate but complement other projects carried out under EU programmes.

As has been described above on the Structural Funds in general, much of 1999 and 2000 is a transitional phase between the old and the new regime. At the time of writing, the 'old style' Community Initiatives were in their last phase of implementation and specific information on the implementation of the 2000–2006 'new style' Community Initiatives was not yet available. Programme details and contacts for the 'old' Community Initiatives are given below in order to give you guidance on potentially eligible activities. You are advised to estimate, on that basis, where your activities appear to best fit in the old and new Community Initiatives and to liaise with the most appropriate units and contact people. As the Community Initiatives, like ESF and other mainstream Structural Funds, are primarily handled and implemented by UK authorities, we first give UK contact addresses and then central Commission contacts for each of the 1994–1999 Community Initiatives:

- Pesca: restructuring of the fisheries sector (B2-140);
- Interreg II: border development, cross-border cooperation, selected energy networks (B2-1410);
- Peace: special programme for regions in Northern Ireland and the Republic of Ireland (B2-1412);
- Employment – Now: new opportunities for women (B2-1420);
- Employment – Horizon: integration of disabled people into employment (B2-1421);
- Employment – Integra: integration of groups which are socially excluded (B2-1422);
- Employment – Youthstart: education and training for young people under the age of 20 years with no qualifications (B2-1423);

- Adapt: adjustment of the workforce to industrial change (B2-1424);
- Rechar II: economic conversion of coal mining areas (B2-1430);
- Resider II: economic conversion of steel areas (B2-1431);
- Konver: economic diversification of areas dependent on defence industries (B2-1432);
- Retex: economic diversification of areas dependent on textile and clothing industries (B2-1433);
- Regis II: for very remote regions (B2-144);
- Urban: city development (B2-145);
- Leader II: rural development (B2-146);
- SMEs Initiative: adjustment of SMEs to the internal market (B2-147).

For a general introduction to the 1994–1999 Community Initiatives, consult:

http://www.inforegio.org/wbpro/prord/prordc/prdc2_en.htm

For a comprehensive overview of 1994–1999 regional programmes in the UK under the Community Initiatives, consult:

http://www.inforegio.cec.eu.int/wbpro/prord/prordc/prordcuk.htm

B2-140

Pesca
Restructuring of the fisheries sector

Support for the fishing industry to cope with changes in the sector by training, diversification and job creation in coastal areas. Eligible applicants: public and private institutions such as regional and local authorities, chambers of commerce, SMEs, fishermen's cooperatives, training centres. Pesca will be included in the Objective 2 section of the 2000–2006 Structural Funds.

In the UK:

Ministry of Agriculture, Fisheries and Food
Nobel House (room 437), 17 Smith Square
London SW1P 3JR
Fax: +44 171 238 5951

European Commission

DG XIV.D.1 – Coordination and general questions on structural actions
Mr Stephanos SAMARAS, Head of Unit
99 Rue Joseph II, B-1040 Brussels
Tel: +32 2 295 8834
Fax: + 32 2 296 3033
E-mail: stephanos.samaras@dg14.cec.be

B2-1410

Interreg II
Border development, cross-border cooperation, selected energy networks

This large and varied Community Initiative supports internal and external border areas of the EU to overcome development problems caused by their relative isolation. It is subdivided into cross-border cooperation (Part A), energy networks (Part B) and cooperation in the area of regional planning, in particular management of water supply (Part C):

- support for SMEs;
- tourism;
- provision of public utilities, including water, gas, electricity and telecommunications;
- rural development;
- pollution prevention and control;
- rational use of energy and waste disposal;
- agricultural productivity and cross-border trade;
- education and culture;
- health;
- transport and communications infrastructure;
- training and employment measures;
- cross-border planning and administration.

Interreg II will be continued as a 2000–2006 Community Initiative.

In the UK:

Department of the Environment, Transport and the Regions
International Planning Division
4th Floor, Eland House, Bressenden Place
London SW1E 5DU
Tel: +44 171 890 3908
Fax: +44 171 890 3909
E-mail: Sean_Ryan@detr.gsi.gov.uk

All Interreg programmes have their own coordinating secretariat with contact addresses in each participating member state. For an overview, which includes all 1994–1999 programmes in which the UK is involved, consult:

http://www.inforegio.org/reg_prog/pay_them/themes/cip1/thci_all.htm

European Commission

DG XVI.D.3 – Regional policy, UK
Mr Vittorio CURZI, Head of Unit
Cours Saint Michel 1, 23 Rue Père de Deken
B-1040 Brussels

Tel: +32 2 295 4686
Fax: +32 2 296 3277
E-mail: vittorio.curzi@dg16.cec.be
Internet: http://www.inforegio.cec.eu.int/dg16_.htm

DG XVI.C.2 – Regional policy, Ireland, Northern Ireland
Mr Esben POULSEN, Head of Unit
Cours Saint Michel 1, 23 Rue Père de Deken
B-1040 Brussels
Tel: +32 2 295 0007
Fax: +32 2 296 3290
E-mail: esben.poulsen@dg16.cec.be
Internet: http://www.inforegio.cec.eu.int/dg16_en.htm

B2-1412

Peace

Special programme for regions in Northern Ireland and the Republic of Ireland

Peace aims at reinforcing the peace and reconciliation process in Northern Ireland and the 6 border counties of the Irish Republic. The aid is targeted in particular at local economic and social players and has a double strategic objective: to favour those on the margins of local economic and social life and to take advantage of the peace process to stimulate socio-economic revival and growth. Subject areas include:

◆ employment;
◆ urban and rural regeneration;
◆ cross-border development;
◆ social inclusion, particularly of women, children, young people and vulnerable social groups;
◆ productive investment and industrial development.

Peace will be maintained as a separate programme in the Objective 1 section of the 2000–2006 Structural Funds.

In the UK:

Department of Finance and Personnel
European Division
The Arches Centre, 11-13 Bloomfield Avenue
Belfast BT 5 5HD
Tel: +44 1232 526 938
Fax: +44 1232 526 932

European Commission: see Interreg II on Northern Ireland

B2-1420

Employment – Now

New opportunities for women

Reducing unemployment among women, improving the position of those already working, mainly by innovative and transnational measures for training and access to high-tech and management posts. Actions eligible for assistance include:

- the development of training, guidance, counselling and employment networks for women;
- the development of flexible training packages and programmes, including initial and continuing training, vocational training and training for trainers;
- job creation and support for the start-up of SMEs and cooperatives by women;
- measures to disseminate information and raise public awareness of the need for equal opportunities, including the creation of databases and the establishment of networks;

Employment will be included in the 2000–2006 Community Initiative Equal.

In the UK:

Department for Education and Employment
Caxton House, 6-12 Tothill Street
London SWIH 9NF
Tel: +44 171 273 3000
Fax: +44 171 278 5124

Training and Employment Agency
Clarendon House, 9-21 Adelaide street,
Belfast BT2 8DJ
Tel: +44 1232 257 650
Fax: +44 1232 257 646

The Employment Support Unit
Priestley House, 28-34 Albert Street
Birmingham B4 7UD
Tel: +44 121 616 3660
Fax: + 44 121 616 3680
E-mail: employment@ecotec.co.uk
Internet: http://www.employment.ecotec.uk

European Commission

DG V.B.4 Community Initiatives
Mr Michael LAINE, Head of Unit
27 Rue Belliard, B-1040 Brussels
Tel: +32 2 295 8138
Fax: +32 2 296 9770

E-mail: michael.laine@dg05@cec.be
Internet: http://www.europa.eu.int/comm/dg05/esf/en/index.htm

EUROPS, European Office for Programme Support
Mr Gerhard WELBERS,
2-3 Place du Luxembourg, B-1050 Brussels
Tel: +32 2 511 1510
Fax: +32 2 511 1960
E-mail: webmaster@europs.lrt.be
Internet: http://www.europs.be

B2-1421

Employment – Horizon
Integration of disabled people into employment

Improving the employment prospects of disabled people, partly by improving the quality of training and the development of new employment skills and qualifications and partly by action to create jobs through new forms of work organisation, employment aids and sheltered employment schemes:

- adaptation of buildings and transport to facilitate access to training or work;
- training for disabled or disadvantaged people, particularly in new technologies and skills;
- development of new types of employment, including sheltered employment and cooperatives;
- measures to disseminate information and raise public awareness.

Employment will be included in the 2000–2006 Community Initiative Equal.

In the UK: see Employment – Now.

But in Northern Ireland:

PROTEUS
Edgewater Office Road
8 Edgewater Road
Belfast BT3 9JQ
Tel: +44 1232 371 023
Fax: +44 1232 371 024
E-mail: michael.hegarty@proteus-ni.org
Internet: http://proteus-ni.org

The European Commission: see Employment – Now.

B2-1422

Employment – Integra
Integration of groups which are socially excluded

Improving employment prospects of groups which are socially excluded or at risk of exclusion such as immigrants, refugees, itinerants, single-parent families, the homeless and ex-prisoners. Eligible actions:

- development of model approaches and practices to improve access to quality public services and to develop grassroots capacities;
- development of community-based services for vulnerable groups within urban communities, combining information and advice on health, housing, social security benefits, legal problems, education, training, etc;
- action aimed at public service personnel and social partners to combat discrimination against vulnerable groups;
- training and support to empower local groups to play an active part in the decision-making process and stimulate dialogue between key actors in the public, private and voluntary sectors;
- cooperation and interaction between vocational schools, training and enterprises;
- assessment, counselling, training in basic skills and/or new skills;
- job creation, including development of social enterprises, self-employment, public-private partnerships
- awareness-raising and the development of self-help networks.

Employment will be included in the 2000–2006 Community Initiative Equal.

In the UK: see Employment – Now.
But in Northern Ireland: see Employment – Horizon.

European Commission: see Employment – Now.

B2-1423

Employment – Youthstart
Education and training for people under 20 with no qualifications

Encouraging the integration of young people under the age of 20 into the labour market, particularly those without adequate training or qualifications, as part of a much more ambitious long-term Youthstart scheme to guarantee every young person under 20 access either to full-time employment or to a recognised form of education or training. The more limited Employment - Youthstart scheme consists of pilot projects designed to ensure development of the innovative and transnational dimension of Youthstart. Eligible actions:

- the development of appropriate training guidance, counselling and employment systems (such as systems coordinating key actors: local and regional government, social partners, industry, youth organisations, recreation and training centres and associations);
- the provision of training and placements (including training of trainers);
- job creation in the context of local employment initiatives, particularly in the arts, cultural heritage, environmental protection, urban regeneration and the care sectors;
- measures to disseminate information and raise public awareness about the particular problems faced by young people and the opportunities that Youthstart offers.

Employment will be included in the 2000–2006 Community Initiative Equal.

In the UK: see Employment – Now.

European Commission: see Employment – Now.

B2-1424

Adapt

Adjustment of the workforce to industrial change

Helping European business and industry to adapt to industrial and technological change through training and other measures to improve qualifications and create new jobs. Adapt projects are targeted at men and women at risk of unemployment or workers who have recently lost their jobs as a result of industrial change or workers with prospects in newly created jobs:

- training, expert advice, guidance and counselling;
- sectoral or regional networks to monitor trends and anticipate employment opportunities;
- cooperation and exchanges between companies;
- dissemination of information and raising awareness.

Adapt will be included in the 2000–2006 Community Initiative Equal.

In the UK:
Government departments: see Employment – Now.

The Adapt Support Unit
Priestley House, 28-34 Albert Street
Birmingham B4 7UD
Tel: +44 121 616 3670

Fax: +44 121 616 3680
E-mail: adapt@ecotec.co.uk
Internet: http://www.adapt.ecotec.co.uk

But in Northern Ireland: see Employment – Horizon.

European Commission: see Employment – Now.

B2-1430

Rechar II
Economic conversion of coal mining areas

Helping designated coal-mining regions of the EU to overcome the economic and social consequences of major contraction in the industry. Priority is given to the environment, new economic activities and human resources:

- environmental improvement of areas seriously damaged by coal-mining activity, including reclamation of coal tips, cleaning up and conversion of disused coal-mining buildings and their surroundings, landscaping, road improvements, subsidence correction, etc;
- promotion of alternative economic activities, including support for SMEs and the construction of new factory units and industrial premises;
- improvement of community facilities, roads, water and electricity supplies in mining villages;
- promotion of tourism, particularly activities based on industrial heritage;
- vocational training and employment measures.

Rechar II will be included in the 2000–2006 Objective 2 section of the Structural Funds.

In the UK:

Department of Trade and Industry
1 Victoria Street
London SW1H 0ET
Tel.: +44 171 215 5517
Fax: +44 171 215 5634

European Commission: see Interreg II.

B2-1431

Resider II

Economic conversion of steel areas

Projects in regions seriously affected by steel closures:
- environmental improvements in areas seriously damaged by steel production, including the reclamation of derelict land and the conversion of disused buildings;
- job creation and training schemes;
- improvement of community facilities, roads, water and electricity supplies in steel areas;
- measures to promote SMEs, including advisory services;
- promotion of tourism.

Resider II will be included in the 2000–2006 Objective 2 section of the Structural Funds.

In the UK:

Department of Trade and Industry
Room 3120, 1 Victoria Street
London SW1H 0ET
Tel: +44 171 215 2572
Fax: +44 171 215 5634

European Commission: see Interreg II.

B2-1432

Konver

Economic diversification of areas dependent on defence industries

Assistance to regions heavily dependent on the defence sector which have been hard hit by reductions in military spending. Measures eligible for support include:
- advisory and business support services to improve know-how and encourage diversification;
- job creation and vocational training schemes;
- redevelopment of military sites for civilian use;
- environmental improvements;

- improvement of community facilities, including roads, water and electricity supplies;
- promotion of tourism.

The priorities addressed by Konver will be included in the 2000–2006 Objective 2 section of the Structural Funds.

In the UK: see Resider.

European Commission: see Interreg II.

B2-1433

Retex

Economic diversification of areas dependent on textile and clothing industries

Eligible measures include:
- improving know-how for businesses;
- formation of local business groupings and cooperatives;
- setting up of advisory teams to provide ideas and advice;
- vocational training;
- rehabilitation of industrial wasteland;
- aid to reduce pollution and facilitate recycling;
- improving access to venture capital and loans.

The Retex programme applies to Objective 1, 2 and 5b areas (see Structural Funds).
   Retex will be included in the 2000–2006 Objective 2 section of the Structural Funds.

In the UK: see Resider.

European Commission: see Interreg II.

B2-144

Regis II
For very remote regions

Promotion of the socio-economic integration of the most remote island regions of the EU, such as the Azores, Madeira, Guadeloupe, French Guyana, Martinique, Reunion and the Canary Islands by encouraging economic diversification and increased cooperation between these regions and other parts of the EU. Regis II will be included in the 2000–2006 Objective 1 section of the Structural Funds.

Note This programme is not applicable to the UK.

European Commission: see Interreg II.

B2-145

Urban
City development

Economic and social revitalisation and environmental improvement to find solutions to the serious socio-economic problems in many urban areas (a limited number of urban areas within cities and agglomerations with a population of more than 100,000). Support is focused on the following main areas:
- support for new economic activities;
- training, work experience and related schemes for local people;
- facilities in the health and safety fields;
- infrastructure and environmental improvement measures.

Most of the budget is spent in Objective 1 regions, the rest mostly in Objective 2 regions. Urban will be continued as a 2000–2006 Community Initiative.

In the UK:

Department of the Environment, Transport and the Regions
4/B6 Eland House, Bressenden Place
London SW1E 5DU
Tel: +44 171 890 3796
Fax: +44 171 890 3809

Department of Finance and Personnel
European Communities Branch
Room 213, Parliament Building
Stormont, Belfast
Tel: +44 1232 521 718
Fax: +44 1232 521 449

Department of the Environment
Orchard House, 40 Foyle Street
Londonderry BT48 6AT
Tel: +44 1504 319 900
Fax: +44 1504 319 700

European Funds Division
The Scottish Executive
Victoria Quay
Edinburgh EH6 6QQ

The Welsh Office, European Affairs Division
Cathays Park
Cardiff CF1 3NQ
Tel: +44 1222 823 127
Fax: +44 1222 823 900

European Commission: see Interreg II.

B2-146

Leader II
Rural development

Development of the rural economy by stimulating local action groups and other rural bodies to adopt innovative measures which contribute to rural development in a local area. Innovative measures in the following areas are supported:

- acquisition of skills, including technical support for the creation of local partnerships, analyses of local areas and the development of local development strategies;
- rural innovation programmes devised by local action groups, which might include assistance for training and recruitment, rural tourism, SMEs, craft enterprises and local services, the marketing of agricultural, forestry and fisheries products, environmental protection and conservation;
- assistance for the development of transnational cooperation projects and a rural development network.

Rural areas in Objective 1 and Objective 5b regions are eligible. Leader II will be continued as a separate 2000–2006 Community Initiative.

In the UK:

Department of Trade and Industry
1 Victoria Street
London SW1H 0ET
Tel: +44 171 215 2555
Fax: +44 171 215 5634

Department of the Environment, Transport and the Regions
4/B6 Eland House, Bressenden Place
London SW1E 5DU
Tel: +44 171 890 3796
Fax: +44 171 890 3809

Department of Agriculture for Northern Ireland
Rural Development Division
Dundonald House, Upper Newtownards Road
Belfast BT4 3SB
Tel: +44 1232 524 272
Fax: +44 1232 524 148

The Scottish Executive
Victoria Quay
Edinburgh EH6 6QQ
Tel: +44 131 244 0694
Fax: +44 131 244 0738

Welsh Office European Affairs Division
2 Cathays Park
Cardiff CF1 3NQ
Tel: +44 1222 823 514
Fax: +44 1222 823 900

European Commission: see Interreg II and:

DG VI.F.1.1 – Coordination of measures to aid rural society
Ms Irini PAPADIMITRIOU, Head of Unit
130 Rue de la Loi, B-1040 Brussels
Tel: +32 2 295 9127
Fax: +32 2 295 10 34
E-mail: irini.papadimitriou@dg06.cec.be
Internet: http://www.rural-europe.aeidl.be

Leader European Observatory
AEIDL
260 Chaussée St-Pierre
B-1040 Brussels
Tel.: +32 2 736 4960
Fax: +32 2 736 0434
E-mail: leader@aeidl.be
Internet: http://www.rural-europe.aeidl.be

B2-147

SMEs Initiative

Adjustment of SMEs to the internal market

Adjustment of SMEs to the single market and to becoming competitive in international markets by improving their business skills and the business environment within which they operate. Eligible measures include:

+ improvement of production systems and internal organisation;
+ schemes involving the environment and rational use of energy;
+ strengthening participation and cooperation in research;
+ improving access to new markets;
+ developing SME cooperation and networks;
+ upgrading professional qualifications;
+ improving SME access to finance and credit.

Various aspects of the SMEs initiative will be included in the 2000–2006 Structural Funds.

In the UK:
Business Link Directorate
Department of Trade and Industry
1 Victoria Street
London SW1H 0ET
Tel.: +44 171 215 3922
Fax: +44 171 215 3935

European Commission: see Interreg II.

GENERAL GRANTS

A-3021	Grants to organisations advancing the idea of Europe	€1,950,000	£1,365,000
A-3022	Study and research centres	€1,500,000	£1,050,000
A-3024	Associations and federations of European interest	€1,350,000	£945,000
A-3029	Support for international non-governmental youth organisations	€1,100,000	£770,000
A-3035	Preservation of Nazi concentration camp sites as historical memorials	€250,000	£175,000
A-3038	Other general grants	€300,000	£210,000
A-321	Town-twinning schemes in the European Union	€10,000,000	£7,000,000

These grants are intended to contribute to the financing of organisations or projects advancing the idea of European civil society, while respecting the following criteria:

◆ promotion of European integration;

◆ development of networks throughout Europe;

◆ encouragement of partnerships with organisations in the public and private sector;

◆ ability to attract co-financing from external sources: at least 15% of the budget must come from sources other than the European Union; if a higher co-financing percentage is required, it is indicated in the grant description;

◆ budget transparency and annual accountability.

The application procedure under these budget lines is relatively straightforward. You can expect an answer from the Commission about 3 months after sending in your application. The *Vademecum on Grant Management for Applicants and Beneficiaries* explains the common application and payment procedures applying to this chapter.

Further information and the *Vademecum* can be obtained from:

European Commission
Secretariat general, Unit C.2, Europe and the citizen
Mr Adam BUICK
9 Avenue des Nerviens, B-1040 Brussels
Tel: +32 2 295 7696/296 7328
Fax: +32 2 296 7242
E-mail: adam.buick@sg.cec.be
Internet: http://europa.eu.int/comm/sg/subvention/en/subv.htm

A-3021

Grants to organisations advancing the idea of Europe

Budget 99 €1,950,000 (£1,365,000)

Eligibility Non-profit organisations without political affiliations, preferably established or active in more than one member state, which are committed to furthering the cause of European integration.

Beneficial areas Creation and re-enforcement of European networks to raise European awareness and European integration in general.

Partners needed No.

Types of grant Annual grant for running costs (co-financing needed) for a maximum period of 3 years.

Note Most of this budget heading is earmarked for organisations working for European integration. Therefore, only €285,000 remain available for public-law and non-profit organisations involved in advancing and raising awareness of the European ideal, particularly those seeking to establish transnational networks.

Grant range: €5,000–80,000

Earmarked support in 1999: grants of €50,000–300,000 for the International Secretariat of the European Movement, the International Secretariat of the Union of European Federalists, the Council of European Municipalities and Regions, the European Citizens' Action Service, the Centre for European Studies in Strasbourg, the College of Europe in Hamburg, the Global Legislators Organisation for a Balanced Environment (Globe), the European Council of Artists, the European Forum for the Arts and Heritage, the European Informal Theatre Meeting, Europa Nostra, the Congress of European Writers, EU Net Art and the Pegasus Foundation.

Examples
– Fair Trials Abroad Trust (1998): third and final year grant to start up a European network of lawyers that appear in court and a data bank to support them;
– Federal Trust for Education and Research: grant for conferences, publications, European policy briefings, networking with other organisations carrying out similar research and analysis.

Information and applications
Application deadlines: 1 March, 1 June or 1 October.

European Commission
Secretariat general, Unit C.2, Europe and the citizen
Mr Adam BUICK
9 Avenue des Nerviens, B-1040 Brussels
Tel: +32 2 295 7696/296 7328
Fax: +32 2 296 7242
E-mail: adam.buick@sg.cec.be
Internet: http://europa.eu.int/comm/sg/subvention/en/subv.htm

A-3022

Study and research centres

Budget 99 €1,500,000 (£1,050,000)

Eligibility Universities or equivalent institutes established in a member state or an applicant country, national or European networks for research or teaching in the field of European studies or other non-profit bodies designed to further knowledge of the process of European integration, such as non-governmental teachers' organisations which are working to bring together teaching bodies in the EU.

Beneficial areas Develop new courses, research or teaching programmes in the field of European integration.

Partners needed No.

Types of grant Grants for universities and networks organising courses on European integration and projects such as series of meetings, conferences, seminars.

Grant range and maximum: €5,000–30,000. Can be up to €100,000 for large European institutes. In general the EU grant will not exceed 50% of total project costs.

Examples
– Royal Institute of International Affairs: support for its European programme of policy research, networking meetings and dissemination of information and for a conference coinciding with the British Presidency in January 1998;
– Universities of Birmingham and Essex: support for their European programmes.

Information and applications
Application deadlines: 1 March, 1 June or 1 October.

European Commission, DG XXII.A.1, Cooperation on education
Mrs Yolanda VILLAR, Desk Officer
7 Rue Belliard, B-1040 Brussels
Tel: +32 2 296 8055
Fax: +32 2 299 4152
E-mail: yolanda.villar@dg22.cec.be

A-3024

Associations and federations of European interest

Budget 99 €1,350,000 (£945,000)

Eligibility Non-profit organisations without political affiliations in the member states or in the applicant countries.

Beneficial areas Any event, activity or programme organised specifically to further the cause of European integration and raise public awareness of and commitment to the objectives pursued by the European institutions.

Partners needed Yes: preference is given to organisations established in more than one member state or working in close cooperation with organisations in other member states.

Types of grant Grants for projects such as conferences, hearings, workshops, events.

Grant range: €5,000–40,000

Examples
– Fontainebleau Youth Foundation: a grant for a week-end conference in Oxford on 'Europe 2020' with workshops, debates, plenary sessions;
– Christianity and the Future of Europe: support for a seminar in Budapest for clergy on minorities; twinning of religious communities; spreading to other regions in the UK; meeting of theological students; research on church/state relations in Europe;
– Islamic Foundation: a grant for a conference in Leicester;
– Leo Baeck College: a grant for 25th annual Jewish-Christian-Muslim student conference at Bendorf, Germany;
– Hindu Council of Birmingham;
– West Midlands European Centre.

Information and applications
Application deadlines: 1 March, 1 June or 1 October.

European Commission, DGX.A, Information
MrTheo HUSTINX
120 Rue de Trèves, B-1040 Brussels
Tel: +32 2 295 4008
Fax: +32 2 299 9205
E-mail: theo.hustinx@dg10.cec.be

A-3029

Support for international non-governmental youth organisations

Budget 99 €1,100,000 (£770,000)

Eligibility Non-governmental and non-profit international organisations involving young people and/or contributing to their welfare.

Beneficial areas The grants are intended primarily to help cover general expenses associated with the organisation and execution of activity programmes in a European context.

Partners needed Yes: the organisation must have members in at least 6 member states.

Types of grant Funding is granted on an annual basis and will generally not exceed €25,000 for 1 year, and not more than 50% of the general annual overheads of the organisation.

Grant average: €10,000 in 1998.

Information and applications Applications must be submitted on a standard form. Application deadlines: end of February.

European Commission
DG XXII.C.2, Actions in the field of youth
Mr Alexandros TSOLAKIS, Head of Unit
7 Rue Belliard, B-1040 Brussels
Tel: +32 2 299 9981
Fax: +32 2 299 4158
E-mail: ingyo@dg22.cec.be
Internet: http://europa.eu.int/en/comm/dg22/youth/ingyoen.html

A-3035

Preservation of Nazi concentration camp sites as historical memorials

Budget 99 €250,000 (£175,000)

Eligibility Non-profit bodies established in the member states or in applicant countries whose main objective is to keep alive the memory of the victims of the Nazi concentration camps, or to study the phenomenon from a historical perspective.

Beneficial areas Projects designed to improve the understanding of present and future generations of what took place in the camps and why. They may relate to specific sites or to the preservation and study of archive material.

Partners needed Not necessary but preference is given to projects involving more than one European country.

Types of grant Most grants are awarded to German and to international organisations for projects such as installations in museums and at the site of the camps, conferences, ceremonies, CD-ROMs, publications, films and interviews of survivors, making lists of deportees, etc.

Grant range: €5,000–50,000

Information and applications
Application deadlines: 1 March, 1 June or 1 October.

European Commission
Secretariat general, Unit C.2, Europe and the citizen
Mr Adam BUICK
9 Avenue des Nerviens, B-1040 Brussels
Tel: +32 2 295 7696/296 7328
Fax: +32 2 296 7242
E-mail: adam.buick@sg.cec.be
Internet: http://europa.eu.int/comm/sg/subvention/en/subv.htm

A-3038

Other general grants

Budget 99 €300,000 (£210,000)

Eligibility Non-profit organisations.

Beneficial areas Projects not covered by the other items in chapter A 30.

Partners needed No.

Types of grant This budget heading is a reserve for the Commission to support projects or organisations which it finds interesting but which do not meet the conditions for the other budget lines in chapter A-30, for example projects outside the member states.

Examples

– European Institute in the US (1997): €40,000 for administrative costs associated with programmes featuring European dignitaries and meetings with US leaders on issues of current interest to EU;

– Institut Agronomique Méditerrannéen de Montpellier (1997): €50,000 to support its 1997/1998 programme of assistance to academics from non-member states working on problems of Mediterranean agriculture.

– International Press Centre in Brussels: which hosts the press correspondents to the EU.

Information and applications

European Commission, DGX.A Information
Mr Theo HUSTINX
120 Rue de Trèves, B-1040 Brussels
Tel: +32 2 295 4008
Fax: +32 2 299 9205
E-mail: theo.hustinx@dg10.cec.be

A-321

Town-twinning schemes in the European Union

Budget 99 €10,000,000 (£7,000,000)

Eligibility
- exchanges between citizens: local authorities and associations of local authorities;
- conferences and meetings;
- training seminars: the above and other public institutions, associations and organisations.

Beneficial areas Strengthening existing links between twin towns and the development of new twinning initiatives in the 15 member states, the countries of central and eastern Europe, the Baltic states, Cyprus or Malta.

Partners needed Yes: projects must involve at least 2 towns in different countries.

Types of grant Priority is given to new partnership projects involving regions where twinning is not common.

The European Commission uses its available budget to promote various European-scale twinning activities:

Action 1: exchanges between citizens from twinned towns; the planned exchanges must be focused on a clearly defined European theme (the Amsterdam Treaty, the euro, Europe and culture, accession of new member states, employment, etc.) in an appropriate form (debates, workshops, information meetings or competitions);

Action 2: conferences, meetings and activities designed to give fresh impetus to the twinning concept;

Action 3: training seminars for organisers of town-twinning schemes.

Grant range: €1,000–50,000, for no more than two-thirds of the total costs. The local authorities involved in the project must provide some matching funding (in kind or in cash).

Information and applications Local authorities must apply on the special application form (different for Actions 1, 2 or 3) at least 3 months before starting the project. *A Europe of Towns and Cities: A practical guide to town-twinning* can be obtained from the Commission.

European Commission
DG X.D.1 – Centre for citizens and the media – Town-twinning
Ms Anne-Blanche HARITOS, Head of Unit
2 Rue Van Maerlant, B-1040 Brussels
Tel: +32 2 295 2685/296 3223
Fax: +32 2 296 2389
E-mail: anne.blanche.harritos@dg 10.cec.be

You may contact your local authority town twinning officer and:

Twinning Officer, Local Government International Bureau
35 Great Smith Street, London SW1P 3BJ
Tel: +44 171 222 1636
Fax: +44 171 233 2179

The Council of European Municipalities and Regions can provide general information, information about town twinning in different countries and help you find partner towns:

Council of European Municipalities and Regions (CEMR)
Mrs Sybille WEBER
14 Rue de Castillon, F-75001 Paris
Tel: +33 1 4450 5959
Fax: +33 1 4450 5960
E-mail: cemrpar@ccre.org

Education, Youth and Training

Education

B3-1000	Cooperation in the fields of education and youth policy	€4,500,000	£3,150,000
B3-1001	Socrates	€213,350,000	£149,345,000
B3-1002	Connect: Innovation and connection of Community programmes	€15,000,000	£10,500,000
B3-1006	Promotion and safeguard of regional and minority languages and cultures	p.m.	

Youth

B3-1010	Youth for Europe	€31,800,000	£22,260,000
B3-1011	European Voluntary Service	€22,450,000	£15,715,000

Vocational Training

B3-1021	Leonardo da Vinci	€139,900,000	£97,930,000

There will be a major recasting of EU programmes in the fields of youth, education and training over the period 2000-2004, with changes in both practical arrangements and longer-term planning. The Commission envisages an integrated policy for a 'Europe of Knowledge': future programmes will have a larger budget and there will be links, switches and complementarity between them. More detailed information is given under the chapter sub-headings.

The objective of the Commission is to double the level of movement in exchange schemes in education, training, the voluntary sector or youth programmes. Between 2000 and 2004, 2.5 million people should directly benefit: students, teachers, trainees and other young people.

These programmes are all managed by the European Commission, DG XXII, Education, Training and Youth.

EDUCATION

New Socrates programme 2000-2004

Phase II of the main EU education programme, called Socrates, will run 2000–2004. There will be more continuity and innovation than in the current Socrates programme (see B3-1001, p 87). The structure of the programmes and the application and selection procedures will be simplified, to allow easier access. The European Commission will try to have more regional and local cooperation, and cooperation between all the people involved in education, including parents.

The description of the current Socrates programme is a good introduction to the main lines of activities that can be funded through the programme, which is so large that it would take a whole book to describe in full. The basic information which is provided here should guide you to finding the sections of particular interest to you.

The main Commission contact for education policies and programmes is:

European Commission, DG XXII.A, Education
Mr Domenico LENARDUZZI, Director
7 Rue Belliard, B-1040 Brussels
Tel: +32 2 295 4185/295 5881
Fax: +32 2 299 4150
Internet: http://europa.eu.int/en/comm/dg22/socrates.html

In the UK, general information is available from:

Central Bureau for Educational Visits and Exchanges
The British Council
10 Spring Gardens, London SW1A 2BN
Tel: +44 171 389 4157

The importance of multimedia and the information society
The information society in general and the integration of this dimension in education is a priority for the Commission. There will be a new education and multimedia programme called Atlas in the next phase of Socrates.

If you have a project using or developing multimedia, you may contact the

European Commission
DGXXII.A.4 – Multimedia Educational Task Force
Ms Corinne HERMANT, Desk Officer
7 Rue Belliard, B-1040 Brussels
Tel: +32 2 296 3455
Fax: +32 2 299 6321

Themes

Many other EU programmes can provide funding for education projects with a specific or geographical theme:

- about Europe: most budget lines under *General Grants*, p 74, in particular, A-3021, A-3022, A-3024, A-3038; also see the Jean Monnet programme on European integration in universities, B3-304, p 129
- culture: see *Culture*, p 108
- audiovisual media education: see Media, B3-2010, p 120
- equal opportunities for men and women: see B3-4012, p 138
- combating social exclusion and discrimination, violence against children and adolescents, see *Social Welfare*, p 133
- health: see *Health*, and in particular B3-4300, p 149
- environment: see *Environment*, p 161
- consumer interest: B5-100, p 167
- the information society: see *Information Society*, p 176
- research: see *Research and Technological Development*, p 202

Outside the EU

If your education project includes partnership/exchanges with non-member states, look at the chapter on cooperation with third countries. Most EU agreements with third countries include educational exchange arrangements.

See in particular USA and Canada, B7-830, cooperation with third countries on education and vocational training, p 296 and the Tempus programme for central and eastern Europe and the New Independent States, p 250.

B3-1000

Cooperation in the fields of education and youth policy

Budget 99 €4,500,000 (£3,150,000)

Eligibility
- universities, schools and education centres in the member states;
- cultural organisations;
- youth organisations.

Beneficial areas
- European activities in the field of education and youth policy, using new information technologies;
- actions to promote and safeguard regional or minority languages and culture in the EU;
- youth parliaments of the union.

Partners needed Yes: projects must have a strong European dimension, e.g. involve at least 3 member states.

Types of grant

European activities in the field of education and youth policy

These are in addition to the measures covered by the Socrates and Youth for Europe programmes, with priority given to activities related to the development and use of the new information technologies, for example:

- national networks linking educational and training institutions promoting the use of inter-active multimedia technologies for educational purposes;
- development of inter-active educational multimedia programmes;
- promotion of educational software products and services;
- studies on the adaptability and effectiveness of multimedia technologies in the educational field.

Actions to promote and safeguard community regional or minority languages and culture

€2,500,000 are earmarked for actions promoting regional languages and cultures as well as minority languages, such as Yiddish, Roma and Sinti, etc. See description of B3-1006, p 92 for further details.

Youth parliaments of the union

A minimum amount of €320,000 is set aside for the youth parliaments of the union: €120,000 to finance the European Youth Parliament based in the United Kingdom ; €60,000 for the Model European Parliament Foundation based in the Netherlands ; and €140,000 for the 'Parliaments representing the Youth of Europe' in various regions of the European Union, i.e. projects in secondary schools throughout the school year which culminate in model parliamentary sessions on a local, regional, national or European level.

Priority is given to projects which involve young people from disadvantaged backgrounds.

Grant maximum: €30,000; financial support may not exceed 50% of the total costs.

Information and applications There are different procedures and deadlines depending on the type of activities. Ask the Commission for further information.

European Commission, DG XXII.A.1 Education
Mr Anders Joest HINGEL, Head of Unit
7 Rue Belliard, B-1040 Brussels
Tel: +32 2 296 0555
Fax: +32 2 299 4150
E-mail: anders.hingel@dg22.cec.be

B3-1001

Socrates

Budget 99 €213,350,000 (£149,345,000)

Eligibility Educational institutions of all kinds, teaching staff of all categories, learners of all ages.

Beneficial areas Developing the European dimension of education: European languages; mobility of teachers and students; academic recognition of diplomas, study periods and other qualifications; distance learning in the European context; exchanges of information and experience about educational systems and educational politics.

In the member states, the European Economic Area (Iceland, Liechtenstein, Norway), Cyprus and applicant countries of central and eastern Europe.

Partners needed This varies considerably from one action to the other.

Types of grant The Socrates programme is divided into 3 chapters, each of which has different kinds of actions.

Chapter I: Higher education (Erasmus)
Action 1: Promotion of the European dimension in universities: organisation of student mobility, mobility of teaching staff (who can provide tuition in other participating countries), intensive short teaching programmes, joint development of university curricula, etc.

Action 2: Encouragement of the mobility of students and the granting of Erasmus scholarships.

Grant range: €300 for a period of 3 to 6 months or €50 monthly for a period of 6 to 12 months. The maximum is €5,000 per student for a stay of 12 months in another country.

Chapter II: School education (Comenius) European cooperation between schools at all levels: pre-school, primary, secondary.
Action 1: Partnership between at least 3 schools form 3 different countries, to develop activities around themes of European interest such as cultural heritage, environmental protection, arts and crafts, science and technology, literary tradition, European citizenship, local and regional identity, media studies, equal opportunities between men and women.

Grants of €3,000 for coordinating establishments and €2,000 for each partner school cover visits to prepare partnerships, exchanges or in-service placements for teachers or education staff and study visits for headteachers.

Action 2: Education of children of migrant workers, occupational travellers, intercultural education: at least 3 countries must be involved. Developing cooperation networks is a priority.

Action 3: In-service training for education staff: grants for developing European training projects and individual grants to teachers.

Example
A network of 15 teacher-training establishments which have produced a set of 12 modules to assist headteachers in strengthening the European dimension of their schools.

Chapter III: Horizontal actions

◆ Promotion of language learning (Lingua), for all levels of education: European cooperation projects for the training of language teachers, in-service training, assistantships for future language teachers, development of instruments for language learning and teaching, assessment of language proficiency.

Example
Training institutions from the UK, Italy and Flanders jointly developed material for the training of teachers of English, Italian and Dutch, to show teachers that learning another language can be made easier by highlighting the many similarities between languages in everyday speech.

◆ Open and distance learning (ODL), especially through multimedia. This includes partnership projects (at least 3 countries), such as the joint development of new teaching methods and materials, and observation projects, for example a European database on multimedia supplies, studies and research on trends in ODL, etc.

◆ Adult education to promote knowledge of Europe (culture, language and traditions of European countries, political, economic and administrative aspects of the EU) and European cooperation between adult education establishments (at least 3 partners form 3 different countries).

◆ Exchange of information and experience, including Eurydice (Information network on education in Europe), Arion (study visits for decision-makers in education), NARIC (Network of National Academic Recognition Information Centre) and other measures such as studies, scientific analyses, conferences, exchanges of experts on education policies.

Grant maximum: €25,000 for a maximum period of 3 years and not more than 50% of total costs for European continuing training projects; €1,500 for participation of individuals in training courses.

Information and applications The application procedure and deadlines vary considerably depending on whether the project is run by the Commission or by the national agencies designated by the member states.

A Guide for Applicants that contains all the necessary details and other information is available from the Technical Assistance Bureau in Brussels and in the member states (see contacts below).

European Commission, DG XXII.A, Education
Mr Domenico LENARDUZZI, Director
7 Rue Belliard, B-1040 Brussels
Tel: +32 2 295 4185/295 5881
Fax: +32 2 299 4150
Internet: http://europa.eu.int/en/comm/dg22/socrates.html

Technical Assistance Office Socrates and Youth
70 Rue Montoyer, B-1040 Brussels
Tel: + 32 2 233 0111
Fax: + 32 2 233 0150
E-mail: info@socrates-youth.be

Eurydice European Information Unit
15 Rue d'Arlon, B-1050 Brussels
Tel: +32 2 238 3011
Fax: +32 2 230 6562
e-mail: eurydice@infoboard.be

In the UK:

General information about Erasmus, ODL, common education policy:

The University of Canterbury
UK Socrates Erasmus Student Grants Council
Research and Development Building
Canterbury, Kent CT2 7PD
Tel: + 44 1227 762 712
Fax: + 44 1227 762 711
E-mail: erasmus@ukc.ac.uk
Internet: http://www.ukc.ac.uk/ERASMUS/erasmus

General information about Comenius, Lingua, Arion, adult education:

Central Bureau for Educational Visits and Exchanges
British Council
10 Spring Gardens, London SW1A 2BN
Tel.: +44 171 389 4157
Tel.: +44 171 389 4460 (Comenius)
Tel.: +44 171 389 4852 (Lingua)
Tel.: +44 171 389 4648 (Arion)
Fax: +44 171 389 4426
E-mail: socrates@centralbureau.org.uk
Internet: http://www.britcoun.org/cbeve/

Specific contact for open and distance learning and adult education:

EC Education Policy Team
Department for Education and Employment
Caxton House, 6-12 Tothill Street
London SW1H 9NF
Tel: +44 171 273 4751
Fax: +44 171 273 5217
E-mail: ecet.dfee.ch@gtnet.gov.uk

NARIC
ECCTIS 2000 Ltd
Mr Christopher WEST
Oriel House, Oriel Road
Cheltenham, Gloucestershire GL50 1XP
Tel.: +44 1242 252 627 / 260 010
Fax: +44 1242 258 611
E-mail: 101472.22542@compuserve.com

Eurydice
Eurydice Unit for England, Wales and Northern Ireland
Mr Gill HOLT, Mrs Jenny LOOSE
National Foundation for Education Research
The Mere, Upton Park
Slough, Berkshire SL1 2DQ
Tel.: +44 1753 574 123
Fax: +44 1753 531 458
E-mail: eurydice@nfer.ac.uk

Eurydice Unit Scotland
The Scottish Office Education and Industry Department
International Relations Branch SOIED
Mrs Sue MORRIS
Floor 1, Area B
Victoria Quay, Edinburgh EH6 6QQ
Tel.: +44 131 244 0914
Fax: +44 131 244 5581
E-mail: sm@irb.soeid.gov.uk

B3-1002

Connect

Innovation and connection of Community programmes

Budget 99 €15,000,000 (£10,500,000)

Eligibility No precise information available at the time of writing.

Beneficial areas Preparatory actions for a 'Europe of Knowledge' to develop synergies between education, culture, training, innovation, research and new technologies, aimed at reducing the gap which currently exists between these fields.

Partners needed No precise information available at the time of writing

Types of grant In the field of innovative ideas, actions must be prepared in:
◆ musical training using multimedia technologies;
◆ studies of the cultural and architectural heritage at schools;
◆ school competitions for inventions;
◆ civic studies and democracy, comparative studies;

It also covers:
◆ measures to promote access by young people, especially women, to technological training courses;
◆ measures to support parental involvement in education at a European level;
◆ measures to combat violence in schools and academic failure.

Priority is given to initiatives which involve young people from disadvantaged backgrounds.

Information and applications This is a new budget line introduced by the European Parliament in 1999: no precise information was available at the time of writing. Contact the European Commission.

European Commission, DG XXII.A.1 Education
Mr Anders Joest HINGEL, Head of Unit
7 Rue Belliard, B-1040 Brussels
Tel: +32 2 296 0555
Fax: +32 2 299 4150
E-mail: anders.hingel@dg22.cec.be

B3-1006

Promotion and safeguard of regional and minority languages and cultures

Budget 99 p.m. There is no budget allocated to this line in 1999 but the activities can be funded through B3-1000, p 85. Up-to-date information is available from the contact below.

Eligibility Non-profit organisations, legal entities.

Beneficial areas Exchanges and visits, pilot projects, seminars, symposia, reports, study grants and didactic material to promote and safeguard the EU's regional languages and culture and minority languages. The countries of central and eastern Europe are eligible.

Partners needed At least 2 language communities or eligible countries have to be involved, or a transfer of experience from one region to another should be the result.

Types of grant

- support for actions intended to promote and safeguard the EU's regional languages and cultures, such as Gaelic, Welsh, Catalan, Basque, Irish, Corsican, Frisian, Sardinian, etc. This also applies to minority languages which do not belong to a specific region, e.g. Yiddish, Roma and Sinti;
- co-financing of exchanges and activities between minority culture groups in the countries of central and eastern Europe;
- co-financing of exchanges and visits, pilot projects, seminars, symposia, reports, study grants, and didactic material;

Grant maximum: financial support for the projects may not exceed 50% of the actual costs.

Information and applications A call for proposals is usually published in the first half of the year in the Official Journal; deadline for applications will be approximately 2 months after publication.

European Commission
DG XXII.A.4 Regional or minority languages
Mrs Caroline LOUP, Desk Officer
7 Rue Belliard, B-1040 Brussels
Tel: +32 2 299 5655
Fax: +32 2 299 6321
E-mail: caroline.loup@dg22.cec.be

YOUTH

New youth programme from 2000 onwards

From 2000 to 2004, the 2 programmes described below – Youth for Europe and European Voluntary Service – will be incorporated into one called Youth. It has a budget of €600 million for the period 2000–2004 (an increase on the previous 4-year period).

The emphasis is on innovation in methods and collaboration between people from different backgrounds. The new programme aims to promote amongst young people:

- a greater sense of solidarity;
- active involvement in the European ideal;
- a spirit of initiative and enterprise.

The programme will be made up of 5 actions:

Action 1: European Voluntary Service (see description on p 98): Young people can volunteer to work on a public service scheme in one of the participating countries or in a third country for a period of between 3 weeks and a year.

Action 2: Youth for Europe: Groups of young people can take part in exchange projects in participating countries or in a third country on a subject of interest, e.g. cultural diversity, the environment, discovering Europe (see p 95).

Action 3: Opportunity for youth: Young people devise and take responsibility for projects such as setting up a small business, organising neighbourhood activities, or taking up training. They are given financial aid and the requisite back-up.

If they wish, volunteers can meet and work together beyond national borders (see Youth for Europe).

Action 4: Joint actions: This concerns action on matters which affect young people without any barriers between different sectors: e.g. education, training, etc.

Action 5: Accompanying measures: Better information for young people, training for youth workers, to improve mutual cooperation and to try out new methods.

Further information can be obtained from:

European Commission, DG XXII.C.2, Youth
Mr Alexandros TSOLAKIS, Head of Unit
7 Rue Belliard, B-1040 Brussels
Tel: +32 2 295 9981
Fax: +32 2 295 4158

In the UK:

The British Council, Youth Exchange Centre
10 Spring Gardens, London SW1A 2BN
Tel: +44 171 389 4030
Fax: +44 171 389 4033

Themes
Many other EU programmes can provide funding for projects by or/and for young
people with a specific or geographical theme:
- about Europe: most budget lines under *General Grants*, p 74; in particular, A-
  3029, Support for international youth organisations, and A-3024, Associations
  and federations of European interest
- in deprived areas and for social integration projects look at *Structural Funds*,
  p 51
- culture: see *Culture*, p 108
- sport: see *Sport*, p 124
- helping young people to start their working life or integrate into society:
  Employment – Youthstart, p 65, Now, p 63 (women), Horizon, p 64 (disabled
  people), Integra, p 65 (vulnerable and disadvantaged people such as the homeless,
  ethnic minorities, migrants, refugees, drug or alcohol dependants, ex-offenders,
  lone parents)
- organising training: look at *Vocational Training*, p 100
- equal opportunities for men and women: see B3-4012, p 138
- combating social exclusion and discrimination, violence against children and
  adolescents: see *Social Welfare*, p 133
- health: see *Health*, in particular B3-4300, p 149
- environment: see *Environment*, p 161
- consumer interests: B5-100, p 167
- the information society: see *Information Society*, p 176
- research: see *Research and Technological Development*, p 202

Outside the EU
Third countries are eligible for youth projects under Youth for Europe and European
Voluntary Service.

B3-1010

Youth for Europe

Budget 99 €31,800,000 (£22,260,000)

Eligibility
- youth organisations;
- organisations/structures operating at local, regional, national or European level;
- governmental and non-governmental organisations with responsibilities for youth-related matters;
- young people who get together for the purpose of a project (e.g. youth clubs, social or cultural organisations, youth services).

Beneficial areas Young people age 15–25 participating in European projects, in the member states, Iceland, Liechtenstein and Norway. Participation in the programme is also open to young people from Cyprus, the Czech Republic, Hungary, Poland, Romania and the Slovak Republic. The programme also has an action for cooperation with third countries.

Partners needed Yes: a minimum of 4 different eligible states on average.

Types of grant Projects aiming at:
- developing the capacities of youth workers, governmental and non-governmental bodies to act and to cooperate on a European level;
- allowing young people to view the European Union as part of their historical, political, cultural and social environment and to see themselves as active citizens taking part in the construction of this union;
- increasing awareness of the importance of democracy in the organisation of society and thus encouraging young people to play an active role in its institutions;
- allowing young people to express their opinions on the organisation of society and encouraging public authorities to listen to them;
- underlining the importance of equal opportunities and encouraging women to lead an active life in all sectors of society;
- activities and events in the field of sport;
- measures involving disadvantaged young people in open-air projects and sporting activities.

The programme supports 5 main actions:

Action A: Intra-Community activities directly involving young people
Action A.I: Youth exchanges and mobility
  Example
  Eurocamp brought together 59 disadvantaged young people from 6 countries in Hawkshead, UK (1997).

Action A.II: Spirit of initiative, creativity and solidarity among young people

Action A.II.1: Youth initiatives

> *Example*
>
> An informal group of 9 young people runs a series of workshops on the theme of European performance traditions, and reach 20 other young people participating in the activities.

Action A.II.2: Periods of voluntary service

> *Example*
>
> An anti-racist organisation in the UK has brought in a German volunteer in order to develop the European dimension of its work.

Action B: Youth workers

Action B.I.1: General support for Action A: Activities aimed at partner-finding and launching exchange and cooperation projects. Youth workers can receive financial support for short study visits, feasibility visits, practical training, seminars and contacts visits.

Action B.I.2: Youth training in relation to projects in Action A: Youth worker training projects, mainly focusing on intercultural learning, and linguistic preparation projects.

Action B.II: Direct support for European cooperation on training youth workers: This heading provides support to activities intended to exchange know-how between those responsible for youth worker training and leaders of youth organisations working in European networks.

> *Example*
>
> A joint training project of group organisers from 6 different countries on adapting their work to a multicultural Europe.

Action C: Cooperation between member states' structures

Support for governmental and non-governmental structures in member states. Special attention will be paid to projects involving those responsible for youth matters at regional or local level, because they have fewer opportunities to make European contacts.

Action D: Exchanges with non-member countries

Central and eastern Europe, the Confederation of Independent States, the Mediterranean countries and Latin America.

Action E: Information for young people and youth research

Action E.I: Information for young people

> *Examples:*
>
> – A British association prepared a training manual in several languages to make media targeted at young people aware of the need to provide information against racism;
>
> – A network of information on European opportunities for young people was created by 16 partners from 13 different countries.

Action E.II: Youth research

   Example

   A partnership between 3 universities in 3 different member states which examines the increasing problem of marginalisation and disaffection amongst a specific age cohort of young people.

Grant maximum: may not exceed 50% of the budget for each project, but a higher rate of funding can be requested for projects concerning young people from deprived backgrounds.

Information and applications Application deadlines vary depending on the action and on the period of the activities, but in general applications must be submitted 2–5 months before the activities start. The programme Youth for Europe III follows 3 procedures for the presentation and selection of projects, depending on whether the actions are centralised or decentralised.

   The Technical Assistance Office in Brussels will provide further information on the whole programme. A brochure *Guidelines for applicants* can be ordered or obtained electronically on the web-site below.

European Commission
DG XXII.C.2, Actions in the field of youth
Mr Alexandros TSOLAKIS, Head of Unit
7 Rue Belliard, B-1040 Brussels
Tel: +32 2 295 9981 / 295 2327
Fax: +32 2 295 4158
E-mail: YFE@dg22.cec.be
Internet: http://europa.eu.int/en/comm/dg22/youth/youth.html

Technical Assistance Office – Socrates and Youth
70 Rue Montoyer, B-1000 Brussels
Tel: + 32 2 233 0111
Fax: + 32 2 233 0150
E-mail: youth@socrates-youth.be

In the UK:

The British Council
Youth Exchange Centre – National Agency
Indra BAHADUR, Information officer
10 Spring Gardens, London SW1A 2BN
Tel: +44 171 389 4030
Fax: +44 171 389 4033
E-mail: indra.bahadur@britcoun.org

B3-1011

European Voluntary Service

Budget 99 €22,450,000 (£15,715,000)

Eligibility NGOs, local authorities, non-profit associations of all kinds, youth organisations, voluntary organisations, cooperatives and so on from one or more of the 15 member states, Iceland, Liechtenstein and Norway. Project initiators need not have any experience in transnational programmes.

Beneficial areas Complementary voluntary service by young people age 18–25, to broaden their horizons, to familiarise themselves with a different social and cultural environment, and to develop self-confidence. Multilateral and third country projects (see below) may involve partners from outside the EU.

Partners needed There needs to be a solid partnership between the young volunteer, a sending organisation and a hosting organisation in order to provide for the ambitious objectives of a project within the EVS programme.

Types of grant Projects under this programme can be:
- long-term voluntary service projects (6-12 months);
- short-term voluntary service projects (3 weeks to 3 months);
- special event projects (a number of volunteers may be hosted);
- multilateral projects (organisations from at least 4 countries and at least 6 volunteers participating);
- third country projects (hosting organisation outside the EU);
- future capital programme (support for start-up activities or participation in educational activities).

Hosting organisations can offer opportunities in numerous fields, including: assistance to the elderly, sick or disabled, creation of a drop-in centre for the homeless, development of a multi-purpose youth centre in an urban area, environmental projects to prevent pollution, develop local facilities (hiking or cycle paths etc.), intercultural activities to promote integration and the fight against racism, sporting activities and events. These types of actions can be combined.

Grant maximum: co-financing will be awarded to selected projects, up to a maximum of 50% of the total costs. Additional funding may be available in exceptional circumstances in order to promote the participation of volunteers from disadvantaged backgrounds.

Example
A small association in Italy which provides the local community with different types of services (first aid, help to the elderly, school help, etc.) received a Scottish volunteer who was very active in his youth club, especially in street work with drug addicts. He shared his knowledge with his Italian hosting organisation,

which now wants to develop a similar scheme and the 2 organisations are developing contacts and planning study visits in order to exchange good practice. They are also planning to work on an exchange of elderly and young people.

During the Pilot Action (1996/97) over 2,500 volunteers participated in more than 1,000 local projects across Europe and around the world.

Information and applications There are different calls for proposals and deadlines during the year for various activities. Priorities and strategies vary from one country to another. Up-to-date information can be found on the web-site and through the contact in the UK.

European Commission, DG XXII.C.2, Actions in the field of youth
Mr Alexandros TSOLAKIS
7 Rue Belliard, B-1040 Brussels
Tel: +32 2 295 9981 / 295 2327
Fax: +32 2 295 4158
E-mail: vol@dg22.cec.be
Internet: http://europa.eu.int/comm/volunt/index.html
(to download *User's Guide*)

Structure for Operational Support SOS – Technical assistance office
Mrs C. FITZSIMONS
35 Rue des Drapiers, B-1050 Brussels
Tel: +32 2 549 5590
Fax: +32 2 549 5599
E-mail: EVS@SOSforEVS.org

In the UK:

The British Council
Youth Exchange Centre
Mr Ian PAWLBY
Mrs Dorothy SAUNDERS, Information Unit
The British Council
10 Spring Gardens, London SW1A 2BN
Tel: +44 171 389 4030
Fax: +44 171 389 4033
E-mail: dorothy.saunders@britcoun.org

VOCATIONAL TRAINING

EU funding programme for training: a new phase 2000–2004

A second phase of the main EU training programme Leonardo will run from 2000 to 2004. It will be simpler than the current programme described below, with more concentrated objectives, more clearly defined measures and simpler practical arrangements.

There will be one general call for proposals at the beginning of the programme, and another one mid-term. The projects will be selected at a decentralised level in each EU country, thus giving the member states more responsibility for the actual implementation.

The 3 main objectives are:
- to improve and strengthen the social and vocational integration of young people, especially by way of apprenticeships;
- to broaden and develop access to high-quality continuing training and lifelong access to skills, particularly to keep up with technological and organisational innovation. This should be achieved by investing in training and by seeking a better balance between men and women in all trades, occupations and sectors of the economy;
- to support vocational training systems which contribute to (re)integration in the job market of people with inadequate or obsolete skills.

The type of activities that will be supported will remain the same as those described for the current programme (B3-1021, p 102), but they will be restructured and reduced from 23 to 6 measures, which can be combined:
- physical mobility;
- virtual mobility;
- transnational pilot projects;
- European training networks;
- improving language skills;
- EU terms of reference.

For further details read the description of the current Leonardo programme (B3-1021) on p 102, look on the Internet or call the UK contact below for updates on the new 2000–2004 programme.

Internet: http://europa.eu.int/en/comm/dg22/leonardo.html

UK National Co-ordination Unit
Department for Education and Employment
EC Education and Training Division
Mr Gordon PURSGLOVE and Mr Roger LANGDON
Moorfoot, Sheffield S1 4PQ
Tel: +44 114 2594359
Fax: +44 114 2594103
E-mail: eurotrain.ed@gtnet.gov.uk

For general information on vocational training in Europe, contact:

CEDEFOP - the European Centre for the Development of Vocational Training (abbreviation from the French: Centre européen pour le développement de la formation professionnelle)
Marinou Antipa 12, GR-55102 Thessaloniki
Greece
Tel: +30 3149 0111
Fax: +30 3149 0102
E-mail: info@cedefop.gr
Internet: http://www.cedefop.gr

Themes

Many other EU programmes can provide funding for training projects depending on the subject or means of training:

- about Europe: most budget lines under *General Grants*, p 74
- in deprived areas and for social integration projects: *Structural Funds*, p 51
- culture: see *Culture*, p 108
- helping young people start their working life or integrate in society: Employment – Youthstart, p 65
- if your target group is women, see Employment – Now, p 63
- for disabled people: B2-1421, Employment – Horizon, p 64
- for vulnerable and disadvantaged people (homeless, ethnic minorities, migrants, refugees, drug or alcohol dependants, ex-offenders, lone parents) see Employment – Integra, p 65
- training for youth workers: see Youth for Europe, p 95
- equal opportunities for men and women: see B3-4012, p 138
- combating social exclusion and discrimination, violence against children and adolescents, see *Social Welfare*, p 133
- health: see *Health*, and in particular B3-4300, p 149
- environment: see *Environment*, p 161
- consumer interest: B5-100, p 167
- the information society: see *Information Society*, p 176
- research: see *Research and Technological Development*, p 202

Outside the EU
If your training project includes partnerships/exchanges with non-member states, look at the chapter on cooperation with third countries. Most EU agreements with third countries include opportunities for joint training projects. See in particular USA and Canada, B7-830, cooperation with third countries on education and vocational training, p296 and the Tempus programme for central and eastern Europe and the New Independent States (p250).

B3-1021

Leonardo da Vinci

Budget 99 €139,900,000 (£97,930,000)

Eligibility
- business;
- establishments from the public or private sectors;
- training organisations;
- universities, public bodies, research institutes;
- social partners organisations;
- regional, local authorities, etc.

Beneficial areas Support for improving quality and innovation, while advancing the European dimension in vocational training, in the member states, Iceland, Liechtenstein, Norway and more recently in the Czech Republic, Cyprus, Hungary, Romania, Poland and the Slovak Republic. As soon as a formal decision is taken the programme will also be open to other central and eastern European countries.

Partners needed Yes: you must have one or more partners from at least 3 participating countries. Under Strands I.1.2.a,b,c, III.1.a, III.1.b (see below), proposals bringing together partners from only 2 countries can be considered. All partnerships must include at least one EU member state. Particular attention will be given to partnerships of different types of organisations. A partner database on the Internet can be accessed through: http://www.leonardocentre.fi/psd/

Types of grant Subsidies can be granted for 3 kinds of activities:
- pilot projects for transnational training run by an international partnership, diffusion and experimenting with diffusion and transfer of professional training methods, creating ways to anticipate training needs.;
- placements and transnational exchange programmes for young people undergoing initial vocational training or in the transition to working life; similar programmes for people involved in policy development, planning and delivery in human resource development, including social partners;
- surveys and analysis for developing knowledge in the field of vocational training.

The programme is divided into 4 sections on different subjects:

Strand I: Support for the improvement of vocational training systems and arrangements in the member states

I.1.1 Transnational pilot projects (design and implementation):
- improving the quality of initial vocational training and the transition of young people to working life;
- improving the quality of arrangements in the member states on continuing vocational training
- vocational information and guidance;
- promotion of equal opportunities for men and women in vocational training;
- improving the quality of vocational training arrangements for persons who are so disadvantaged on the labour market that they are at risk of social exclusion; this may, for instance, be due to socio-economic, geographical or ethnic factors, physical or mental disabilities or insufficient qualifications.

Example
A transnational project on improving access for women to innovatory small industry professions in the ecological field. Training contents and suitable teaching methods have been jointly designed by British, Danish, Dutch and German partners.

I.1.2 Transnational placements and exchange programmes:
- transnational placement programmes for young people receiving initial vocational training;
- transnational placement programmes for young workers;
- transnational exchange programmes for instructors.

Strand II: Improvement of vocational training, including university/enterprise cooperation, concerning enterprises and workers

II.1.1. Transnational pilot projects design and implementation on:
- innovation in vocational training, taking into account technological change, its impact on work and the necessary qualification and skills;
- investment in continuing vocational training for workers;
- transfer of technological innovation in the context of cooperation between enterprises and universities on vocational training;
- promotion of equal opportunities for men and women in vocational training by projects to develop women's career prospects, in particular where women are under represented.

II.1.2. Transnational placements and exchange programmes:
- placements in enterprises for young people receiving university training and for graduates;
- exchanges between enterprises and universities and/or training bodies;
- exchanges of people in charge of training.

Strand III: Support for the development of language skills, knowledge and the dissemination of innovation in the field of vocational training

III.1. Cooperation to improve language skills:
- transnational pilot projects;
- transnational exchange programmes.

III.2. Development of knowledge in the field of vocational training:
- surveys and analyses in the field of vocational training;
- exchange of comparable data on vocational training.

III.3. Dissemination of innovation in the field of vocational training:
- multiplier-effect projects;
- transnational exchange programmes.

Example

Under Strand III.1.b the University of Bristol coordinated an exchange project of language trainers in different European countries. The aim was to improve transfer of innovatory techniques and assessment systems in this area.

Strand IV: Support measures

IV.1 Cooperation network between the member states;

IV.2 Information, monitoring and assessment measures.

Grant maximum: Transnational pilot projects may receive up to 75% of the total project costs to a maximum of €100,000 annually and for a period of up to 3 years. Exchange and placement programmes may receive up to €5,000 per person for an exchange or placement for a period of no more than 12 months. Surveys and analyses may receive 50–100% of expenses.

Information and applications From 2000, the selection of Leonardo projects will be done in each member state. The EU web-site and DG XXII of the Commission can update you on UK contacts if necessary.

European Commission, DG XXII.B, Training
Mr Klaus DRAXLER, Director
7 Rue Belliard, B-1040 Brussels
Tel: +32 2 296 3171
Fax: +32 2 299 5325
E-mail: leonardo@dg22.cec.be

Or:

Mr Timo WILKKI
Tel: +32 2 299 6381
Fax: +32 2 295 5704
E-mail: timo.wilkki@dg22.cec.be
Internet: http://europa.eu.int/en/comm/dg22/leonardo.html

In the UK:

National Co-ordination Unit
Department for Education and Employment
EC Education and Training Division
Mr Gordon PURSGLOVE
Mr Roger LANGDON
Moorfoot, Sheffield S1 4PQ
Tel: +44 114 259 4359
Fax: +44 114 259 4103
E-mail: eurotrain.ed@gtnet.gov.uk

(Strand I.1.1.c)

Department for Education and Employment
EC Education and Training Division
Mrs Judith GRANT
Mr John GOODWIN
Level 4 Caxton House, Tothill Street
London SW1H 9NF
Tel: +44 171 273 5660
Fax: +44 171 273 5195
E-mail: etp@depemp.demon.co.uk

(Strands I.1.1.a, I.1.2.a, I.1.2.b, I.1.2.c, III.1.a, III.1.b, III.3.a)

Central Bureau for Educational Visits and Exchanges
The British Council
Ms Subha RAY
10 Spring Gardens, London SW1A 2BN
Tel: +44 171 389 4389
Tel: +44 171 389 4509 (Ms Subha RAY)
Fax: +44 171 389 4626
E-mail: sray@centralbureau.org.uk

(Strands I.1.1.b, I.1.1.d, I.1.1.e, II.1.1.a, II.1.1.b, II.1.1.d, II.1.2.c)

Centre for Training Policy Studies
The University of Sheffield
Mr Philip EDMEADES
1 Northumberland Road, Sheffield S10 2TT
Tel: +44 114 222 1380/222 1381/222 1382
Fax: +44 114 275 5682
E-mail: leonardo@sheffield.ac.uk

(Strands II.1.1.c, II.1.2.a, II.1.2.b)

Department for Education and Employment
Higher Education and Employment Divisions
Ms Jean NICHOL
Mr Martin PIPER
Sanctuary Buildings
Great Smith Street, London SW1P 3BT
Tel: +44 171 925 5306 (Ms Jean NICHOL)
Tel: +44 171 925 5254 (Mr Martin PIPER)
Fax: +44 171 925 5310
E-mail: eurotrain.ed@gtnet.gov.uk

(Strand III.2.a, b)

Department for Education and Employment
EC Education and Employment Division
Mr Brian WALKER
Room N710 – Moorfoot, Sheffield S1 4PQ
Tel: +44 114 259 4258
Fax: +44 114 259 4531
E-mail: eurotrain.ed@gtnet.gov.uk

Culture, Audiovisual Media and Sport

Culture

B3-2000	Raphael: Community action programme in the field of cultural heritage	€8,800,000	£6,160,000
B3-2001	Kaleidoscope: Programme to support artistic and cultural activities having a European dimension	€10,200,000	£7,140,000
B3-2002	Ariane: Support programme in the field of books and culture	€4,100,000	£2,870,000
B3-2004	Promotion of linguistic diversity in the Community in the information society	€4,000,000	£2,800,000
B3-2005	Experimental measures in relation to the cultural framework programme	€7,000,000	£4,900,000
B3-2006	Pilot projects on multicultural integration	€7,000,000	£4,900,000

Audiovisual media

B3-2010	Media: Measures to promote the development of the audiovisual industry	€61,600,000	£43,120,000
B3-2016	Preparatory measures in the audiovisual sector	€4,000,000	£2,800,000

Sport

B3-2020	Sport in Europe	p.m.	

CULTURE

Until 1999, there were 3 main EU culture programmes: Raphael for cultural heritage, Ariane for books and reading, and Kaleidoscope for artistic and cultural activities. They will continue for the period 2000–2004, and will be incorporated into a single framework programme of support for cultural projects with a European dimension.

Culture 2000 will support 3 types of activities:
- activities based on structured and multiannual cooperation agreements;
- major activities with a European and/or international effect;
- specific and/or innovative activities in the EU and/or third countries.

This programme will also support cooperation agreements with the countries which have applied to joint the EU: Czech Republic, Estonia, Hungary, Poland, Slovenia.

See the Raphael, Kaleidoscope and Ariane programmes, pp 110–115 for details about the specific funding criteria for projects on cultural heritage, artistic and cultural activities and books, reading and translation.

The Commission also wants culture to be reflected in other EU policies by:
- a legislative framework favourable to culture and exchanges, for example on copyrights, free movement of professionals, cultural goods and services, audiovisual policy, state aid and taxation;
- emphasising the cultural dimension in other support programmes: the structural funds and regional policy, employment, research, education and training, etc. This means that from now on, cultural projects should be welcomed by the other DGs if you can highlight, for example, that your project contributes to the main aims of a policy field such as job creation, innovative training methods, regional development, etc;
- taking account of the special nature of culture in the EU's external relations.

For further information, contact:

European Commission,
DG X.C.5, Culture
Ms Enrica VARESE, Head of Unit
Mr Richard GRANVILLE, Deputy Head of Unit
120 Rue de Trèves, B-1040 Brussels
Tel: +32 2 299 9419
Fax: +32 2 299 9283
Internet: http://europa.eu.int/en/comm/dg10/culture/index-en.html

The Commission has also established national contact points for culture throughout the member states and the EEA countries to provide information and assistance.

National contact point in the UK:

Euclid
Mr Geoffrey BROWN
1st Floor, 46-48 Mount Pleasant
Liverpool L3 5SD
Tel: +44 151 709 2564
Fax: +44 151 709 8647
E-mail: euclid@cwcom.net

Themes
Almost any EU programme might provide funding for projects with a cultural aspect, if they fit into one of the themes and priorities described, such as:

- A-3021 Grants to organisations advancing the idea of Europe, p 75
- A-321 Town-twinning schemes, p 81
- *Structural Funds*, p 51
- all budget lines in *Education, Youth and Training*, p 83
- programmes under *Social Welfare*, in particular those with a specific target group: disabled persons, women, minorities, etc, p 133; and some of the health budget lines such as Combating cancer, p 150, Health aspects of drug abuse, p 151, and Combating AIDs and certain other transmissible diseases, p 152
- *Environment*, Life II – Part 2, p 164
- *Information Society* programmes, p 176
- *Labour Market Initiatives/SMEs*, pp 184–196
- *Research and Technological Development*, p 202
- cooperation with third countries: Asia, p 231; Latin America, p 234; Southern Africa, p 237; Mediterranean countries, p 239; central and eastern Europe, the Confederation of Independent States and Mongolia, p 247; training and promotion of development issues, p 262; environment, health and the fight against drugs in developing countries, p 268

B3-2000

Raphael

Community action programme in the field of cultural heritage

Budget 99 €8,800,000 (£6,160,000)

Eligibility Cultural institutions, European networks, non-governmental organisations, companies.

Beneficial areas Conservation, protection and development of the European cultural heritage in the member states. Organisations from Iceland, Liechtenstein, Norway and the countries of central and eastern Europe can be partners.

Projects cannot be profit making.

Partners needed Yes: at least 3 partners from 3 different member states except for action 2.1. (exchange of professionals, see description below), for which 2 partners in 2 member states are the minimum.

Types of grants The programme provides grants, in addition to national co-funding, for 4 types of activities:

Action 1: Conservation, safeguarding and enhancement of the European cultural heritage through European cooperation. Grants for the establishment and activities of cooperation networks which aim at studying, protecting and enhancing the cultural heritage, and dealing with themes and problems common to several European countries.

The type of heritage concerned varies from one year to another: in 1998 the focus was on building and cultural sites; in 1999 on the movable heritage. Grant maximum: €250,000.

Action 2: Cooperation for the exchange of experiences and the development of techniques applied to cultural heritage. Grants for strengthening transnational cooperation between institutions and/or operators in the field of cultural heritage by pooling skills and developing best practice, as well as professional mobility.
2.1. Support for projects aiming at the mobility and training of professionals:
  • exchange of professionals, not necessarily reciprocal, for a period of 1 to 12 months; the grant covers travel expenses and accommodation;
  • transnational projects for training professionals in the new technologies and communication services applicable to the cultural heritage sector.
  Grant maximum: €150,000.
2.2. Support for the exchange of experience and information: Projects implemented by transnational networks or partnerships to collect, exchange and disseminate information on cultural heritage through advanced information and communication technologies, seminars or special events. Specific themes vary from one action and one year to another.

Action 3: Public access to and participation in awareness-raising activities. Transnational cooperation projects or events with a European dimension to raise awareness and to improve public access to cultural heritage, based on a multilingual and multimedia approach, e.g. transnational cooperation between museums, interactive education activities, transnational cultural itineraries.

Action 4: Cooperation with third countries: Support for projects as above, with non-member countries, the Council of Europe or UNESCO. In 1999, such cooperation will not be supported, but it might be again from 2000.

Whatever the type of action chosen, the EU contribution cannot cover more than 50% of the total cost of the project and you must show evidence of matching funding – from your own, public or private sources.

Examples

In 1997, 92 projects were selected from the 841 requests submitted. Workshops brought together specialists from all over Europe on general themes such as the dangers and threats to the European architectural heritage, or on more specific themes such as:

- developing the restoration and conservation of film, using digital technology;
- creating an Internet facility for illustrated humanist manuscripts;
- promoting the Viking maritime heritage;
- discussing the production and consumption of olives, considered as an aspect of European culinary heritage (no, this is not a joke, but a real example: do not be afraid to be creative);
- keeping traditional music alive.

One call for proposals concerned the development of thematic networks between European museums; another concerned the preservation and enhancement of decorated facades and could provide co-financing for restoring specific buildings in Europe, always through a transnational partnership which would pool and disseminate knowledge and skills.

Information and applications Calls for proposals are published annually in the Official Journal. The 1999 call for proposals was published in November 1998 with a deadline to submit applications by the end of March 1999. Project promoters and heritage professionals may ask to go on the mailing list for future information.

Application forms and further information can be obtained from:

European Commission, DG X.C.5, Culture
Ms Enrica VARESE, Head of Unit
Mr Richard GRANVILLE, Deputy Head of Unit
Mr Theo MASTROMINAS, Desk Officer
120 Rue de Trèves, B-1040 Brussels
Tel: +32 2 299 9334
Fax: +32 2 299 9283

B3-2001

Kaleidoscope

Programme to support artistic and cultural activities having a European dimension

Budget 99 €10,200,000 (£7,140,000)

Eligibility Transnational networks and transnational partnership of national, regional and local organisations in the member states, Norway, Liechtenstein and Iceland. Organisations from Bulgaria, Cyprus, Czech Republic, Estonia, Latvia, Lithuania, Hungary, Malta, Poland, Romania, the Slovak Republic and Slovenia may also participate under certain conditions.

Beneficial areas Cultural projects with a European dimension.

Partners needed Yes: for Action 1 at least 3 partners from 3 different member states or other eligible countries, and for Action 2 at least 4 partners from 4 member states or other eligible countries (see description below).

Types of grant Projects should either involve creative work for public display or dissemination in Europe or help to promote greater cultural exchanges and public access to culture.

Areas covered by the programme are:
◆ the performing arts (e.g. dance, music, theatre, opera);
◆ visual or spatial arts (e.g. painting, sculpture, carving, engraving);
◆ the applied arts (e.g. architecture, photography and design);
◆ multimedia as a from of artistic expression

Funding is granted through 2 main actions:

Action 1: Support for events and cultural projects carried out in partnerships or through networks. In 1998, about €6,000,000 were shared between the 135 selected projects (about 15% of the total of submitted projects).

Example
Projects co-ordinated from the UK include:
– the 1998 Brouhaha International Street Theatre Festival;
– Colours of the Chameleon, a training workshop for young European playwrights;
– the Three Opera House Project aimed at the creation and production of 3 operas by young European composers and musicians.

Many other projects included festivals, training projects, seminars and meetings aimed at strengthening European cooperation or public access to culture.

Grant range: never less than €5,000 and generally not more than €50,000, representing a maximum of 25% of the total budget of the project. More funding might be available for a project to improve professional skills (training and courses) or to increase public access to culture.

Action 2: Large scale European projects with a major cultural and socio-economic impact. Only very few and very large projects are covered under this action: in 1998 only 12 large projects were selected, receiving EU support of €100,000–200,000.

> *Example*
>
> The Spoleto Festival, coordinated by an Italian organisation in partnership with cultural organisations from 6 other eligible states, including Intermusica Music Management in the UK.

Activities funded under this budget line also include the organisation of the cultural and artistic events in each year's European City of Culture, which in 1999 will be Weimar. For 2000, 9 cities have exceptionally been chosen: Avignon, Bergen (Norway), Bologna, Brussels, Cracow, Helsinki, Prague, Reykjavik and Santiago de Compostela. The European Culture Month, held once every 2 years in cities of central and eastern Europe (1999: Plovdiv, Bulgaria), is also supported under Kaleidoscope.

In future years the European Cities of Culture and Culture Month will be:
2001: Rotterdam and Porto; Culture Month: Riga
2002: Bruges and Salamanca
2003: Graz; Culture Month: Saint-Petersburg
2004: Genoa and Lille

Information and applications Calls for proposals are published annually in the Official Journal. Potential applicants may ask to go on the mailing list for future information.

Application forms and further information can be obtained from:

European Commission, DG X.C.5, Culture
Ms Enrica VARESE, Head of Unit
Mr Richard GRANVILLE, Deputy Head of Unit
Ms Trine BERGGREN, Desk Officer
120 Rue de Trèves, B-1040 Brussels
Tel: +32 2 296 9663
Fax: +32 2 299 9283
Internet: http://www.europa.eu.int/en/comm/dg10/culture/en/action/kaleidos-gen.html

B3-2002

Ariane

Support programme in the field of books and culture

Budget 99 €4,100,000 (£2,870,000)

Eligibility
- publishers, with priority given to small publishing houses;
- theatre managers or producers;
- universities, research centres;
- networks, associations or organisations of professionals, non-profit foundations in the field of books;
- library networks and translation schools.

Beneficial areas The programme seeks to encourage cooperation between those working in the field of books and reading, and seeks to provide incentives for further training in the member states, Norway, Liechtenstein and Iceland. Organisations from Bulgaria, Czech Republic, Cyprus, Estonia, Latvia, Lithuania, Malta, Hungary, Poland, Romania, the Slovak Republic and Slovenia may also participate under certain conditions.

Partners needed Not for Action 1 (see below); for Actions 2 and 3: partners from at least 3 member states or other eligible countries or European networks, associations or professional organisations.

Types of grant Three types of actions:

Action 1: Translation
- grants for the translation of contemporary literary works (novels, short stories, literary essays, literary histories, biographies, poetry, etc.) that are representative of the culture of their country and likely to appeal to a broad European audience. Priority is given to books translated into or from less widely used languages. In other cases, the original book must already have been published in 2 European languages to receive support for a further translation ;
- grants for the translation of plays with a view to public performance: the plays must already have received some popular acclaim and the project must include the translation into 2 European languages;
- grants for the translation of reference works relating to European culture into at least 2 European languages.

Grant range: up to 100% of translator's fees; for theatrical or reference works not intended for commercial publication, translator's grants of up to €3,500 per work.

Action 2: Partnership projects which improve access by the citizen (including young people) to books and reading. Examples would include: European meetings on literary topics, residence for writers or translators from different European countries, festivals, libraries.

Grant maximum: €50,000, and not, as a general rule, exceeding 25% of total costs. An additional contribution of up to €20,000 can be given for wider dissemination of the results among the general public.

Action 3: Training for literary translators and advanced training. This should supplement the training provided by the competent authorities in the member states.

Grant maximum: €50,000 to cover travelling expenses and further training costs. A part of this budget line is earmarked for the Aristeion Prizes: the European Literary Prize and the European Translation Prize.

Information and applications Calls for proposals will be published in the Official Journal once a year, with a fixed deadline (7 May in 1999). You may ask to go on the mailing list for future information.

Application forms and further information can be obtained from:

European Commission, DG X.C.5, culture
Ms Enrica VARESE, Head of Unit
Mr Richard GRANVILLE, Deputy Head of Unit
120 Rue de Trèves, B-1040 Brussels
Tel: +32 2 295 8492
Fax: +32 2 299 9283
Internet: http://europa.eu.int/en/comm/dg10/culture/en/action/ariane-gen.html

B3-2004

Promotion of linguistic diversity in the Community in the information society

Budget 99 €4,000,000 (£2,800,000)

Eligibility
- language professionals (translators, terminologists, editors);
- public sector organisations dealing with language matters;
- publishers of language resources, tools and standards;
- computer service companies and software publishers in the field of language processing tools;
- private and public sector users of language tools.

Beneficial areas Technologies, tools and methods which reduce the costs of transferring information between languages and the development of multilingual services; strengthening of the language industries, development of multilingual services and of the linguistic diversity in the information society.

Partners needed Yes: transnational partnership is required, at least 2 independent organisations from different EU countries, Iceland, Liechtenstein and/or Norway.

Types of grant This programme, also called MLIS (Multilingual Information Society), is aimed at:
- creating favourable conditions for the expansion of the language industries;
- reducing the costs of transferring information between languages, particularly for small and medium sized companies;
- promoting the linguistic diversity of the EU, including regional and less-used languages (€500,000).

The EU financial contribution to the shared-cost projects will, as a general rule, be 50%. Universities and other institutes which do not have a cost accounting system will be reimbursed at 100% of their additional costs.

Examples
Summary information on the projects can be found on the web-site:

http://www2.echo.lu/projects

Information and applications See note below.

European Commission, DG XIII.E.4, Linguistic applications
Mr Erwin VALENTINI, Desk Officer
Euroforum 1267, 10 Rue Stumper
L-2557 Luxembourg
Tel: +352 4301 34117
Fax: +352 4301 34655
E-mail: Erwin.valentini@dg13.cec.be or MLIS@lux.dg13.cec.be

Internet: http://www2.echo.lu/info2000/midas/MLIS.html
UK: http://www.midas-net.org.uk/mlishome/

Note The MLIS programme was adopted for 3 years (1996–1999) and it will not be continued as an independent (follow-up) programme, but the objectives and main activities will be pursued in other programmes:
- the 5th Research and Technological Development programme, in particular User-friendly information society, B6-6121, p 208; the Human Language Technologies sub-programme includes Full Multilinguality as one of its action lines and supports projects aimed at developing and demonstrating multilingual products and services which are nearly ready for commercial introduction;
- Info 2000, B5-330, p 177: the Commission is currently (autumn 1999) discussing a proposal for a follow up programme. This proposal emphasises multilinguality as an essential component of cultural heritage and thus for the multimedia content industry. See contact above for further information on if and how these proposals are approved.

B3-2005

Experimental measures in relation to the cultural framework programme

Budget 99 €7,000,000 (£4,900,000)

Eligibility
- operators in the cultural sector (event organisers, theatre workers, etc.), artists and creative people;
- disadvantaged sections of the population and young people.

Beneficial areas Experimental actions to test the new Culture 2000 programme (see introduction to this chapter, p 108).

Partners needed Yes: partners from at least 3 member states or at least 2 member states and 1 non-member state amongst eligible countries must be involved or a European network/organisation.

Types of grant There are 3 types of actions:

Action 1: Cooperation agreements:
- measures to improve knowledge;
- cooperation agreements between cultural operators to produce works and to organise events in a given sector;
- cooperation agreements linking different cultural fields.

Action 2: Major projects with a European and/or international influence:
- a new approach to symbolic measures with a European dimension;
- making events and works available through television and the new media;
- operations to publicise European cultures outside the EU.

Action 3: Specific measures to improve social integration. Projects dealing with the emergence of more popular new cultural forms and social integration, which are also:
- promoting participation by young people, particularly with underprivileged and multicultural backgrounds;
- raising the profile of the EU;
- providing training to enhance employment opportunities;
- based in regions rather than in capital cities.

The organisations, foundations or groups must have a demonstrated experience in the project area. The projects must be large scale and have a maximum impact.

Grant maximum: up to 60% of the total cost of the projects.

Nearly 40% of this budget heading (€2,712,500) is earmarked for the Yehudi Menuhin Foundation, the European Union Youth Orchestra, the European Union Baroque Orchestra, the European Chamber Orchestra, the European Choral

Academy, the European Opera Centre in Manchester, the European Union Youth Opera and the European Union Jazz Youth Orchestra (Swinging Europe). It also funds the European City of Culture (see B3-2001, Kaleidoscope).

Information and applications
European Commission, DG X.C.5, Culture
Enrica VARESE, Head of Unit
Richard GRANVILLE, Deputy Head of Unit
120 Rue de Trèves, B-1040 Brussels
Tel: +32 2 2999444
Fax: +32 2 2962686

Note   This is a new item in the budget so there are no examples of previously approved projects. Contact DGX for further information.

B3-2006

Pilot projects on multicultural integration

Budget 99 €7,000,000 (£4,900,000)

Eligibility NGOs, charities.

Beneficial areas Pilot projects which promote multicultural integration.

Partners needed Yes: at least 3 partners from 3 member states or project proposed by a European/international organisation.

Types of grant Grants for pilot projects which:
• develop new models for integrating ethnic minorities, in particular in education and training;
• promote information and communication through European networks against racism, xenophobia and anti-Semitism;
• heighten public awareness of discrimination on cultural, ethnic or religious grounds;
• promote the principle of solidarity and social cohesion;
• publicise the benefits of integration policies in the fields of education, training, sport, housing and employment;
• facilitate the creation of forums to discuss the need to combat all discrimination on grounds of race, religion or ethnic origin;
• promote 'action to prevent the public forgetting', including 27 January as an annual day of remembrance of the Holocaust;
• support the activities of the Starting Line Group and increase awareness about ethnic minorities such as the Roma and Sinti.

The European Centre for Research into Racism and Anti-Semitism will be supported by a grant of €400,000. €50,000 are also earmarked for the *Migration News-sheet*, a magazine published in French and English.

Grant maximum and range: up to 90% of the costs directly linked to the transnational activities. Small-scale projects requiring less than €50,000 EU funding will not be considered. The average EU subsidy will be €70,000. Between 50 and 60 projects are selected every year.

Information and applications Calls for proposals are published in the Official Journal (2 calls in 1999). Fax DGV.D.4 for an update.

European Commission
DGV.D.4 – Free movement of workers, integration of migrants and anti-racism
Mr Robertus CORNELISSEN
37 Rue Joseph II, B-1040 Brussels
Tel: +32 2 2957667
Fax: +32 2 295 1899
Internet: http://europa.eu.int/comm/dg05/tender_en.htm

Note On the fight against discrimination, see also Preparatory measures combating and preventing discrimination, B3-4111, p 144.

AUDIOVISUAL MEDIA

The main audiovisual EU programme is Media, whose second phase (Media II, 1995–1999) is coming to an end. There is therefore a new budget line B3-2016, Preparatory measures in the audiovisual sector, to test what should be developed next.

In general, many EU programmes provide funding for multimedia or audiovisual schemes as a tool:

- education: see *Education*, p 84
- training: see *Vocational Training*, p 100
- see *Research and Technological Development*, p 202 and in particular B6-6121 on User-friendly information society, p 208
- culture: see *Culture*, p 108
- about the EU: see *Information and Communication on the EU*, B3-30⁰⁰, p 126
- in or about developing countries: see *The EU in the World*, for instance the information and awareness raising projects under B7-6000 and 610, pp 260 and 262

B3-2010

Media

Measures to promote the development of the audiovisual industry

Budget 99 €61,600,000 (£43,120,000)

Eligibility Companies, institutions, organisations, training institutes, etc. in the audiovisual field.

Beneficial areas Strengthening the competitiveness of the European audiovisual industry by supporting the training of professionals, the development of production projects and companies and the distribution of cinematographic works and audiovisual programmes. The EEA countries – Iceland, Liechtenstein, Norway – and Bulgaria, the Czech Republic, Hungary, Poland, Romania, the Slovak Republic, Estonia, Latvia, Lithuania and Slovenia, as well as Cyprus and Malta may participate.

Partners needed Yes: at least 3 member states must be involved.

Types of grant Media II is divided into 3 sections: training, development, distribution.

Training
Subsidies for the training of professionals based on a close cooperation and an exchange of knowledge and skills between partners working in the training area, such as cinema and television schools, universities, specialised training centres, production and distribution companies.

Grant maximum: up to 50% of the total costs, with maximum €200,000 per year for initial training and €300,000 per year for continuing vocational training.

Development

- development of new production projects: fiction – feature films and television, documentaries, cartoons, multimedia. EU support takes the form of loans (maximum 50% of the budget and ranging from €10,000–80,000). In the case of multimedia products (entertainment or educational), the EU support can be a subsidy for the design of the project (maximum: €20,000) and advances against receipts (maximum: €250,000) for further development up to the making of the master copy;
- development of independent European production companies: co-financing (maximum: 50%) for 2 complementary types of support: a maximum of €10,000 for the establishment of a business plan, and company loans of €30,000–150,000 for investment in the development of the company;
- networking of companies in the animation sector ('Cartoon').

Distribution

- distribution and broadcasting of audiovisual works (fiction, documentary, animation, interactive programmes) and of European films in movie theatres, on video, on digital disc and on television;
- promotion and access to the market of European works by supporting independent producers and distributors in audiovisual markets and at festivals;
- support to cinema networks with a common strategy for the promotion and marketing of European films.

There are nine different types of support available (subsidies, loans, advance on receipts), but in all cases the amount to cover dubbing and subtitling costs is regarded as a subsidy:

- automatic support scheme for cinema distribution (subsidies);
- selective support for the transnational distribution of European films;
- video publishing and distribution;
- support for TV broadcasting of projects (fiction, documentary, animation) of independent producers, with participation of at least 2 broadcasters from 2 member states of different languages;
- marketing of licensing rights;
- multi-media distribution (advance on receipts of maximum €100,000 per title);
- subsidies to independent European production initiatives in large trade markets and audiovisual festivals or specialised markets, both inside and outside the EU;
- cooperation schemes between European audiovisual events (in at least 8 member states or 2 associated countries and 7 member states) and festivals carried out in partnership;
- networking of cinemas with a common strategy for promoting and marketing European films (currently supported by the Media Programme: Europa Cinémas and Euro Kids Network).

For details on the conditions and the amounts available, check with the contacts and web-site below.

Examples

– support to festivals such as the Bradford Film Festival and the Animation Festival in Cardiff;

– 'Fastlane – Training programme for film professionals' on management; Webshields Ltd, Euroscript, First Film Foundation, all in London, for training on script writing;

– projects for training on new technologies, such as CITE – A-EMMA (European media masters degrees);

– the distribution of films such as *The English Patient, Secrets and Lies, Brassed off.*

Information and applications For each section and type of action, a call for proposals is published in the Official Journal, with different guidelines and deadlines. Information may be sent to you directly if you have asked to be on the appropriate mailing list. You can obtain general information and specific addresses for each type of activity (media training, media development, media distribution, animation platform, etc.) from the web-site and the contacts below.

European Commission, DG X.C.2 – Audiovisual Media
Jacques DELMOLY, Head of Unit
120 Rue de Trèves, B-1049 Brussels
Tel: +32 2 295 8406/299 0314
Fax: +32 2 299 9214
E-mail: jacques.delmoly@dg10.cec.be
Internet: http://europa.eu.int/en/comm/dg10/avpolicy/index.html

In Scotland:

Media Antenna Glasgow
Louise Scott, c/o Scottish Screen
74 Victoria Crescent Road, Glasgow G12 9JN
Tel: +44 141 302 1700
Fax: +44 141 357 2345
E-mail: louise.scott@dial.pipex.com

In Wales:

Media Antenna Cardiff
Gethin While, c/o SGRÎN
The Bank, 10 Mount Stuart Square
Cardiff CF1 6EE
Tel: +44 1 222 333 304
Fax: 44 1 222 333 320
E-mail: antenna@sgrinwales.demon.co.uk
Internet: http://www.sgrinwales.demon.co.uk

In England:

A new antenna is planned; further information is available from the European Commission or the other UK antennae.

B3-2016

Preparatory measures in the audiovisual sector

Budget 99 €4,000,000 (£2,800,000)

Eligibility Companies, institutions, organisations, training institutes, etc. in the audiovisual field.

Beneficial areas Audiovisual production, distribution, events, and training which contribute to the development of the European audiovisual industry. Partners from the EEA countries, the applicant countries of central and eastern Europe, Malta and Cyprus can also participate.

Partners needed Yes: at least 3 member states must be involved.

Types of grant

Action 1: Support for jointly organised audiovisual events. This action aims at overcoming the technological deficit in Europe, in particular in the field of digital technology, and at encouraging the creation of European networks of professionals. For example, film distribution by electronic means (cable, satellite, etc.), networking between audiovisual companies to pool resources in developing digital and new technologies, in particular European cartoon networks, broadcasting networks for cultural events (operas, ballet, plays, etc.) to facilitate more widespread distribution throughout the EU, and networks to promote European cinema at local and regional level. There will also be support for the exchange of programmes between non-commercial radio broadcasters.

Action 2: Support for new initiatives in the field of advanced services, such as digital radio and the creation of multilingual television programmes. This is mainly aimed at consulting professionals to prepare for the future Media programme and EU audiovisual policy.

It will also fund a radio called Radio Europa 2000, which will broadcast information about the economic, political and cultural aspects of Europe.

Information and applications

European Commission
DG X.C.3, Advanced audiovisual services
Mr Costas DASKALAKIS, Head of Unit
120 Rue de Trèves, B-1040 Brussels
Tel: +32 2 296 3596 / 299 0327
Fax: +32 299 9214
E-mail: constantin.daskalakis@dg10.cec.be
Internet: http://europa.eu.int/en/comm/dg10/avpolicy/index.html

SPORT

B3-2020

Sport in Europe

Budget 99 p.m.

Eligibility Associations, non-profit organisations.

Beneficial areas European sport events.

Partners needed Yes: projects must have the broadest possible participation and involvement by ordinary citizens, sportsmen or administrators from at least 3 member states.

Types of grant
- the Eurathlon programme, which is to contribute to a better understanding between citizens of Europe through sport, and to promote the essential role of sport as a factor contributing to social integration, health education and human solidarity;
- sport for the disabled, in addition to exchange programmes for participants in popular sports, school sports competitions;
- sectoral conferences, training courses and informative meetings to help sporting bodies understand the EU and the impact of EU legislation on sport.

Information and applications There is no budget under this line in 1999, so there is nothing to apply for. See the contact below and the note for guidance on finding EU funding for sport.

European Commission, DG X.C.6, Sport
Mr Jaime ANDREU, Head of Unit
102 rue de la Loi, B-1040 Brussels
Tel: +32 2 299 9252 / 295 0356
Fax: +32 2 295 7747
Internet: http://europa.eu.int/comm/dg10/sport/index.html

Note There is no budget in 1999 under this heading because it has no legal basis: the Council of Ministers never approved any decision and the budget line has been introduced by the European Parliament only. However, this problem might be solved by 2000, in which case funding will become available.

In the meantime, you might get funding for sports projects from another EU fund:

- Eurathlon is financed through B3-300, General information and communication work concerning the European Union, p 127
- for disadvantaged people and in deprived areas: see the European Social Fund and the European Regional Development Fund, most Community Initiatives of the Structural Funds, p 51
- see Town twinning, A-321, p 81 and Other general grants, A-3038, p 80
- sport for youth and international exchanges: see *Youth*, p 93
- sport for multicultural integration: see B3-2006, p 118
- sport to promote the EU: see *Information and Communication on the EU*, p 126
- highlighting social integration aspects: see *Social Protection and Integration*, p 140: sport with women, refugees, disabled people, minority groups.
- sport and health: see *Health*, p 148

With some imagination, many of the budget lines in this book could fund a sport project, if not with sport as the main activity, at least with it as a means to something else.

INFORMATION AND COMMUNICATION ON THE EU

B3-300	General information and communication work concerning the EU	€42,500,000	£29,750,000
B3-301	Information outlets	€7,000,000	£4,900,000
B3-302	Information programmes for non-member countries	€6,100,000	£4,270,000
B3-304	European integration in universities: Jean Monnet programme	€3,500,000	£2,450,000
B3-306	Information programme for European citizens (Prince): Information activities in connection with specific policies	€38,000,000	£26,600,000
B3-309	Special annual events	€10,000,000	£7,000.000

Most of these budget lines are not directly relevant to non-government organisations (NGOs). They are meant to ensure the effective flow of information and communication between the European Union (EU) and the general, or more targeted, public. The EU has its own communication and information plans (which do not always reach the outreached) and outside organisations are more likely to be companies replying to a call for tender than independent NGOs having submitted a proposal. However, the Commission uses external organisations which have contacts with target groups that it can not reach from Brussels or through its official representations: the Commission aims to get closer to the citizen.

B3-300

General information and communication work concerning the EU

Budget 99 €42,500,000 (£29,750,000)

Eligibility Companies or organisations specialised or involved in providing information and communication about Europe.

Beneficial areas This budget is mainly for the Commission to produce and distribute its own information.

Partners needed Not necessarily.

Types of grant Most of this budget heading is spent on information and communication measures implemented by the Commission itself and through its representations, e.g. opinion surveys, colloquiums, conferences, publications by the representations in the member states, production and distribution of EU information by the Commission itself, visiting programmes for the media and VIPs. However, a part of it can be of direct interest to NGOs and the non-profit sector:

◆ its direct communication measures, carried out by the representations in the member states (see addresses in the UK at the end of this book, p 308), include for example Eurojus, which gives free advice on your rights as a European citizen, or information on the organisation of European events, including sport.

The Commission headquarters also develop and disseminate information through civil society, for example:

◆ to and through trade unions;
◆ in sporting events at European level (Eurathlon);
◆ information aimed specifically at young people or women.

Information and applications Contact the Commission if you have something to propose.

European Commission
DG X.A.5, Information of trade unions, women, young people
Mr Franco CHITTOLINA, Head of Unit
120 Rue de Trèves, B-1040 Brussels
Tel: +32 2 299 9036
Fax: +32 2 299 9302
Internet: http://europa.eu.int/en/comm/dg10/infcom.html

B3-301

Information outlets

Budget 99 €7,000,000 (£4,900,000)

Eligibility Not open to NGOs or external organisations.

Beneficial areas
- International Federation of Europe Houses (€1,700,000), the European Movement;
- information and documentation outlets (European Documentation Centres, Info Points and Rural Information Forums), the European Journalism Centre in Maastricht, which backs up the work of the representation offices;
- large national information centres such as Source d' Europe in Paris.

Contact

European Commission
DGX.B.3 Information relays
Mr Claudio GUIDA, Head of Unit
Tel: +32 2 299 9425
Fax: +32 2 299 9014

B3-302

Information programmes for non-member countries

Budget 99 €6,100,000 (£4,270,000)

Eligibility Official delegations; associations and NGOs are not directly eligible.

Beneficial areas Information and communication about the EU outside the EU.

Types of grant Some programmes are conducted from Brussels, such as the European Union Visiting programme (for special guests from outside the EU) and radio and television news services for broadcasting in non-member countries. Others are carried out by one of the 164 European Community delegations worldwide: information material, seminars, conferences, visits, communicating with political decision-makers and the press.

Contact

European Commission, DGX.B.2, Information for non-member countries
Mr Jacques VANTOMME, Head of Unit
120 rue de Trèves, B-1040 Brussels
Tel: +32 2 295 4933
Fax: +32 2 296 0227

B3-304

European integration in universities

Jean Monnet programme

Budget 99 €3,500,000 (£2,450,000)

Eligibility Universities and higher education establishments.

Beneficial areas Development of European courses in EU universities.

Partners needed No.

Types of grant Funding on a co-financing basis for a start-up period of 3 years for universities to create and develop courses on European integration – economic monetary and political union. The Jean Monnet programme includes: Jean Monnet chairs (grant range: €4,000–20,000 for a full-time member of the teaching staff); Jean Monnet permanent courses; Jean Monnet modules in European law, European economy, political studies of European construction, and the history of European integration; Jean Monnet centres of excellence (grant maximum: €20,000).

Funding maximum is awarded in exchange for a commitment on the part of the university to maintain the teaching activities thus created for a period of at least 4 years following the period of EU co-financing, that is a total period of 7 years.

Examples in 1998
– Jean Monnet European Centres of Excellence were set up in the University of Bath, the Queen's University Belfast, the University of Birmingham, the University of Sussex and the University of Leeds;
– Jean Monnet chairs were awarded to 10 UK universities;
– another 30 launched permanent courses or European modules.

Information and applications
Application deadlines: generally February, with a call for proposals published at the end of the year.

The Commission makes a final selection on the advice of European University Council for the Jean Monnet Project (a group of independent academics).

European Commission
DG X.C.4 – European integration in universities
Ms Jacqueline LASTENOUSE, Head of Unit
120 Rue de Trèves, B-1040 Brussels
Tel: +32 2 299 9453 / 9454
Fax: +32 2 296 3106
E-mail: Jacqueline.Lastenouse@dg10.cec.be
Internet: http://europa.eu.int/comm/dg10/university/ajm

An external body is in charge of following up actions during the 4-year period after EU financial support has ended and can also provide general information about the programme:

European University Council for the Jean Monnet Project
Ms Béatrice MIEGE
67 Rue de Trèves, B-1040 Brussels
Tel: +32 2 286 9460
Fax: +32 2 230 5608

Note See also B3-1001, Socrates, p 87

B3-306

Information programme for European citizens (Prince)

Information activities in connection with specific policies

Budget 99 €38,000,000 (£26,600,000)

Eligibility Trans-European non-profit organisations with proven experience in European information or communication campaigns.

Beneficial areas Information campaigns on EU policies.

Partners needed Not compulsory, but in practice necessary: actions proposed must have a direct impact in at least 3 member states.

Types of grant Prince is the communications programme for informing citizens about the building of Europe. In 1999 it is centred on 2 main subjects:
- the euro – a currency for Europe;
- Agenda 2000 (on new EU issues beyond the year 2000, see *The European Union: a Short Introduction*, p 16).

These measures should serve as an effective channel of information and dialogue between the citizens and institutions of the EU. These campaigns must take account of specific national and regional characteristics, in close cooperation with the member state authorities, and target strategic audiences such as small and medium-sized enterprises, local authorities, women, young people, vulnerable groups (elderly, illiterate, people with physical or mental disabilities, people living in poverty, etc.). It can include publications, conferences, seminars and congresses, audio-visual and production material, pilot schemes, support for specific outlets and networks in the areas concerned and the organisation of training for specialists and opinion-leaders.

Grant range and maximum: €50,000–300,000 for maximum 1 year. Financial assistance will not cover more than 50% of total costs.

Most of this budget will go for campaigns about the euro. There wi be a very small amount available for informing and communicating with young people about Agenda 2000.

Information and applications

European Commission, DG X.D.4, Priority actions
Mr Gérard LEGRIS, Head of Unit
2 Rue Van Maerlant, B-1040 Brussels
Tel: +32 2 299 9406
Fax: +32 2 296 3350
E-mail: gerard.legris@dg10.cec.be
EURO@dg10.cec.be

Mr Derek PULLINGER, Desk Officer
Tel: +32 2 299 9337

B3-309

Special annual events

Budget 99 €10,000,000 (£7,000,000)

Eligibility Not really open to NGO projects.

Beneficial areas EU presence at Expo 2000 in Hanover and a European communication campaign to combat violence against women.

Partners needed Not necessarily.

Types of grant This is a new budget line to finance the EU presence at notable events.

Examples

– Expo 2000 held in Hanover from 1 June to 30 October on the theme of 'Humankind, nature technology and the environment'.

– a European campaign to combat violence against women: In 1999, there was a call for proposals from NGOs and public authorities to conduct an information awareness campaign on violence against women. NGOs operating in one of the member states were eligible for funding from the total budget of €1,900,000.

Grant average: €50,000, rbut never more than 50% of total project costs.

Information and applications

European Commission, DG X.D.4, Priority actions
Mr Gérard LEGRIS, Head of Unit
2 Rue Van Maerlant, B-1040 Brussels
Tel: +32 2 299 9406
Fax: +32 2 296 3350
E-mail: gerard.legris@dg10.cec.be

European Commission, DGX.A.5, Women's information sector
Mr Franco CHITTOLINA, Head of Unit
120 rue de Trèves, B-1040 Brussels
Tel: +32 2 299 9036
Fax: +32 2 299 3891
E-mail: infofemmes@dg10.cec.be

Social Welfare

Social Dialogue and Employment

B3-4000	Industrial relations and social dialogue	€7,300,000	£5,110,000
B3-4002	Information and training measures for workers' organisations	€9,000,000	£6,300,000
B3-4003	Information, consultation and participation of representatives of undertakings	€5,000,000	£3,500,000
B3-4011	Eures (European Employment Services)	€10,000,000	£7,000,000
B3-4012	Measures to achieve equality between men and women	€10,000,000	£7,000,000

Social Protection and Integration

B3-4101	Cooperation with charitable associations	€3,000,000	£2,100,000
B3-4108	Studies on the family, family policies and demographic trends	€2,425,000	£1,697,500
B3-4109	Daphne: Measures for combating violence against children, adolescents and women	€5,000,000	£3,500,000
B3-4110	Free movement of workers and coordination of social security systems	€2,500,000	£1,750,000
B3-4111	Preparatory measures combating and preventing discrimination	€7,000,000	£4,900,000
B3-4112	Preparatory measures combating and preventing social exclusion	€10,000,000	£7,000,000
B3-4113	Action to integrate refugees	€5,000,000	£3,500,000

All these budget lines are the responsibility of DGV of the Commission, Employment, Industrial Relations and Social Affairs.

Information can be found on the Internet at:

http//europa.eu.int/comm/dg05/index_en.htm.

DG V also produces many free publications – magazines, news, reports – explaining European policies and concerns in your field of activity. For information on what is available in your field, contact:

European Commission
DGV-2 Information and publications
Tel: +32 2 295 4988
Fax: +32 2 296 2393
E-mail: info@dg5.cec.be

SOCIAL DIALOGUE AND EMPLOYMENT

B3-4000

Industrial relations and social dialogue

Budget 99 €7,300,000 (£5,110,000)

Eligibility Social partner organisations or organisations dealing with industrial relations issues, e.g. universities, research centres, magistrates' associations, labour inspectors' associations.

Beneficial areas Activities to develop or create a social dialogue between representative organisations in Europe. Social partners from countries of central and eastern Europe are eligible.

Partners needed Yes: organisations from at least 3 member states.

Types of grant Subsidies for meetings, negotiations and other measures to promote social dialogue at inter-professional and sectoral level and for seminars, conferences, round-table talks, exchanges of experience and networks of interested parties and/ or industrial relations specialists.

These activities must contribute to:
+ developing European social dialogue;
+ improving knowledge of industrial relations in Europe;
+ promoting financial participation by workers.

Grant maximum: 80% of the total costs; the rest must be provided by the applicant, preferably in cash.

Information and applications Application deadlines: mid-March, mid-April, mid-May, mid-August and mid-September.

A guide for applicants, the application form and the *Vademecum on Grant Management* are available in electronic form by e-mail on request.

European Commission
DG V.D.1 – Relations with management and labour and organisation of the social dialogue
Dr Walter FABER, Head of Unit
Mr Jean-François LEBRUN, Deputy Head of Unit
37 Rue Joseph II, B-1040 Brussels
Tel: +32 2 299 2274
Fax: +32 2 299 2466
E-mail: line.B3-4000@dg5.cec.be

B3-4002

Information and training measures for workers' organisations

Budget 99 €9,000,000 (£6,300,000)

Eligibility Workers' organisations:
* European organisations: European Confederation of Trade Unions (ECTU), European Trade Union Federations of the ECTU, Council for European Professional and Managerial Staff, European Managers' Confederation and other European organisations;
* national, regional or local organisations.

Beneficial areas Information and training of workers' representatives, in the EU and the countries of central and eastern Europe.

Partners needed The transnational or EU dimension of the project is one of the selection criteria but this does not need to be fulfilled through a specific number of partner countries.

Types of grant Information and training measures for workers' organisations, including representatives from the social partners of the countries of central and eastern Europe.

A part of the budget is earmarked as a core grant for the European Trade Union Institute (€3,100,000), the European Trade Union Academy (€2,400,000) and the European Workers' Centre (€1,600,000). Therefore, €1,900,000 are not pre-allocated, of which at least 80% will be used for projects submitted by European organisations (see Eligibility heading). This leaves €380,000 for projects proposed by national, regional or local organisations.
Maximum grant: 90% of total costs.

Information and applications Application deadlines: spring for projects starting before autumn and autumn for projects starting later in the year.

Send a written request to the Commission to receive the application guidelines. Application forms are available in electronic form by e-mail on request.

European Commission
DG V.D.1 – Relations with management and labour and organisation of the social dialogue
Dr Walter FABER, Head of Unit
Mr Jean-François LEBRUN, Deputy Head of Unit
37 Rue Joseph II, B-1040 Brussels
Tel: +32 2 299 2274
Fax: +32 2 299 2466
E-mail: line.B3-4002@dg5.cec.be

B3-4003

Information, consultation and participation of representatives of undertakings

Budget 99 €5,000,000 (£3,500,000)

Eligibility Representatives of workers and of employers in multinational companies.

Beneficial areas Transnational cooperation between worker and employer representatives in respect of information, consultation and participation in the EU and in central and eastern Europe.

Partners needed Yes: partners from at least 3 eligible countries.

Types of grant Projects to strengthen transnational cooperation between worker and employer representatives and to ensure that employees in multinational companies are correctly informed and consulted by management when decisions affecting them are taken in a member state other than the one in which they work.

It also covers exchanges of experience to prepare workers' representatives to participate in the decision-making bodies of European companies (European Company Statutes).

Grant maximum: 80% of the costs. The co-funding (20%) can consist of a contribution in kind.

Information and applications Application deadlines: a selection committee meets in April, June, September and October to examine applications received no later than 15 days previously. More details can be obtained from:

European Commission
DG V.D.2 – Industrial relations and Labour Law
Mr Rosendo GONZALEZ DORREGO, Head of Unit
37 Rue Joseph II, B-1040 Brussels
Tel: +32 2 295 3048
Fax: +32 2 299 0890
E-mail: b3-4003@bxl.dg5.cec.be
Internet: http://europa.eu.int/comm/dg05/tender_en.htm

B3-4011

Eures (European Employment Services)

Budget 99 €10,000,000 (£7,000,000)

Eligibility Employment services in the member states and the EEA (Iceland, Liechtenstein and Norway).

Beneficial areas Job seekers willing to work in another country and employers recruiting abroad.

Partners needed Yes.

Types of grant There are no grants but Eures can help organisations to recruit abroad and workers to work abroad:
- employment services of the member states exchange job vacancies and applications at EU level and across borders. They also exchange information concerning labour market trends and living and working conditions.

The Eures network is organised through:
- basic and continuing training of about 450 Euro-advisors in the EU and the EEA and contacts amongst them. Their job is to inform job seekers and companies about opportunities for finding a job or recruiting in another country;
- a constantly updated database of about 20,000 jobs available in Europe;
- a database on applications and living and working conditions in each country.

Information and applications

European Commission
DG V.D.4 – Free movement of workers, integration of migrants and anti-racism
Mr Robertus CORNELISSEN, Head of Unit
37 Rue Joseph II, B-1040 Brussels
Tel: +32 2 295 7667
Fax: +32 2 295 1899
E-mail: eures@dg5.cec.be
Internet: http://europa.eu.int/comm/dg05/elm/eures/index.htm

Contact in the UK:

Mr Trevor Arnold
Employment Service
Eures Coordinator
Overseas Placing Unit
123 West Street - Rockingham House
Sheffield S1 4ER

B3-4012

Measures to achieve equality between men and women

Budget 99 €10,000,000 (£7,000,000)

Eligibility Non-profit organisations, the social partners (workers' and employers' representative organisations), local and regional authorities.

Beneficial areas Exchange, development and transfer of information and experience on good practice, in the member states, the EEA and the applicant countries: Czech Republic, Estonia, Hungary, Lithuania, Romania, Slovenia.

Partners needed Yes: projects must involve partner organisations from at least 3 member states and/or from EEA countries (Iceland, Liechtenstein, Norway). Specific conditions apply to the participation of applicant countries.

Types of grant Measures to change the status of women in society and to promote *de facto* equality. The programme is implemented in partnership with NGOs. The 4th medium-term EU action programme on equal opportunities for women and men (1996-2000) has 6 objectives:

- integration of the equal opportunities dimension in all policies and activities;
- mobilising all those involved in the economic and social spheres to achieve equality of opportunity for women and men;
- promoting equal opportunities in a changing economy, particularly regarding education, vocational training and the labour market;
- striking a balance between family and working life for women and men;
- fostering the balanced participation of women and men in decision making;
- making conditions more favourable for exercising equal rights.

Funding is available for exchanging information and experience, transferring good practice from one organisation to another, or cooperation on designing and implementing equal opportunity measures, in the areas of:

- integration of the equal opportunities for women and men dimension in all policies and activities (mainstreaming): promoting and developing methods, strategies and models.
- employment and working life: education, training and continuing training; access to employment and conditions for employment; promotion of economic independence; equal pay for equal work; organisation of working life; the working environment and sexual harassment; entrepreneurism; reconciliation of professional and parental responsibilities;
- gender balance in decision making: promoting and developing methods, strategies and models;
- information to promote equal opportunities.

Grant range and maximum: €30,000–150,000. The project must be co-financed by non-Commission sources for at least 40% of the total costs. The EU will not finance small-scale projects.

Projects can last for a maximum of 1 year; if they are part of a multiannual work programme, co-financing by the Commission will be re-negotiated each year.

Information and applications Contact the Commission, the technical assistance office or the local contact below for deadlines and for the application form and guidelines for applicants.

European Commission
DG V.D.5. – Equal Opportunities for women and men and matters regarding
families and children
Ms Soledad BLANCO, Head of Unit
37 Rue Joseph II, B-1040 Brussels
Tel: +32 2 299 5182
Fax: +32 2 296 3562

Technical assistance office:

ANIMA
61 Rue de Spa, B-1000 Brussels
Tel: +32 2 230 9031
Fax: +32 2 230 7511

There is an advisory committee on equal opportunities for women and men. The UK member is:

Ms Esther ABSALOM,
Department for Education and Employment
4F Caxton House, 6-10 Tothill Street
London SW1H 9NF

You may also contact the Sex and Race Equality Division of the same department:

Dianna Cunliffe,
Fax: +44 171 273 5476

SOCIAL PROTECTION AND INTEGRATION

B3-4101

Cooperation with charitable associations

Budget 99 €3,000,000 (£2,100,000)

Eligibility
- European networks of NGOs and other civil society organisations operating at a European level;
- National NGOs operating in partnership with organisations from other member states;
- NGOs in partnership with other bodies such as foundations, research institutes, local authorities, social partners and other organisations.

Beneficial areas Tackling social exclusion with the help of NGOs and voluntary organisations working in the field of social exclusion, or with charitable associations which represent, or whose members are, people facing social exclusion.

Partners needed Yes: proposals must come from partners in at least 4 member states.

Types of grant Projects which aim to:
- improve knowledge of the current experience in member states in tackling social exclusion, including evaluating actions and policies;
- exchange experience and information on current approaches to promoting social inclusion;
- promote networking between NGOs on best practice and the impact of civil dialogue on tackling exclusion and promoting social inclusion.

An allocation of €600,000 is reserved for the Platform of European Social NGOs and €2,000,000 are to be used for grants to NGO projects.

Information and applications Detailed information including application forms, procedures and eligibility criteria are available from the address below.

European Commission
DGV.E.2, Social protection, social inclusion and civil society
Mr Kevin WALSH, Desk Officer
27 Rue Joseph II, B-1040 Brussels
Tel: +32 2 299 4914
Fax: +32 2 299 0509

B3-4108

Studies on the family, family policies and demographic trends

Budget 99 €2,425,000 (£1,697,500)

Eligibility Non-profit bodies which can carry out research on demographic trends.

Beneficial areas Mainly research, studies, statistics on demography.

Partners needed Yes: partners from at least 2 member states must be involved.

Types of grant Support for studies on and research into the family and family policies (for example comparative studies of family policies in the member states and research into new lifestyles and social trends affecting families) and on demographic trends.

The Commission will also finance:
- a report on the social situation, including demographic aspects;
- demographic studies and research;
- research to assess the consequences of an ageing population;
- methodological work to establish a system of social indicators for the study of society.

Information and applications Contact the Commission for further information.

European Commission
DG V.E.1 – Analysis of and research on the social situation
Mr Paolo BACCHIELLI, Head of Unit
27 Rue Joseph II, B-1040 Brussels
Tel: +32 2 296 0495
Fax: +32 2 299 3890

Note Further information on the subject is available from:

The European Observatory on National Family Policies
c/o Austrian Institute for Family Studies
Gonzagagasse 19 / 8, A-1010 Vienna, Austria
Tel: +43 1 535 1454 0
Fax: +43 1 535 1455
E-mail: team@oif.ac.at
Internet: www.oif.ac.at

B3-4109

Daphne

Measures for combating violence against children, adolescents and women

Budget 99 €5,000,000 (£3,500,000)

Eligibility NGOs and voluntary organisations with appropriate qualifications and experience.

Beneficial areas Action for the rights and the protection of children, adolescents and women in the EU, in particular victims of trafficking for sexual exploitation and victims of sexual abuse.

Partners needed Actions which involve organisations from at least 2 member states have priority.

Types of grant Funding is available for projects such as training and exchanges for the personnel of NGOs and private associations, pilot projects, setting up or reinforcement of European networks, studies and research, dissemination of information, cooperation between NGOs and public authorities.

The aims of Daphne are:
- to set up or reinforce networks at European level, between NGOs, voluntary organisations, authorities involved in the protection of children, young people and women;
- prevention of, and protection of children, young people and women from, all kinds of violence and commercial sexual exploitation;
- pilot projects and subsidies for NGOs working for the rights and protection of victims of trafficking for sexual exploitation and victims of sexual abuse;
- to help introduce instruments for the reporting of violence against children, young people and women and for of trafficking in women for the purpose of sexual exploitation.

Grant range and maximum: €10,000–250,000, and generally not exceeding 80% of total budget, exceptionally 100%.

Examples

Successful projects cover a wide range of programmes in prevention, protection, rehabilitation and reintegration. In the UK, organisations such as the National Society for the Prevention of Cruelty to Children, Childline UK, The Bridge Childcare Development Service, The Crime Concern Trust Limited, 'End Child Prostitution, Child Pornography and the Trafficking of Children for Sexual Abuse Purposes', the National Children's Bureau, the Methodist Association of Youth Clubs within the Methodist Church of Britain and Childnet International have received funding under this budget line.

Information and applications Application forms and guidelines for applicants are available from the Commission contact below.

Application deadlines: calls for proposals are published in the Official Journal in March and the final selection is announced in September or October each year.

European Commission
General Secretariat, Justice and Home Affairs Task Force
Mr Anthony SIMPSON
9 Avenue des Nerviens, B-1040 Brussels
Tel: + 32 2 296 6933
Fax: +32 2 295 0174
Internet: http://europa.eu.int/comm/sg/daphne/en/index.htm

Note Project sponsors are encouraged to share information, which the Daphne Initiative encourages through *Daphne News*, available from the Commission. The Commission can also provide the final reports submitted by each project and examples of previously approved projects.

B3-4110

Free movement of workers and coordination of social security systems

Budget 99 €2,500,000 (£1,750,000)

Eligibility
- representative associations of migrant workers from both the EU and non-member countries and other NGOs focusing on migrant workers;
- other democratically run bodies and associations representing migrant workers or operating for their benefits, such as local, regional and national authorities or social partners.

Beneficial areas The rights of migrants in the EU (right to establishment, social security, working conditions and so on).

Partners needed Enquire of the Commission.

Types of grant Funding for innovative projects and information campaigns to:
- improve the reception of migrant workers and their living and working conditions;
- improve their economic, social and legal conditions;
- facilitate their participation at all levels of social and administrative life in the host country;

- evaluate, help implement and disseminate the results of the above measures;
- promote the free movement of migrant workers.

For example, projects for the care and integration of immigrants from third countries and resettlers (services, conferences, debates, information campaigns on the rights of migrant workers, training, the renovation and construction of housing, the provision of social centres, and so on).

For the purposes of the budget the term migrant is applied to any person who leaves his/her country of nationality, in order to take up permanent or temporary residence in the territory of member states (excluding tourists, students, asylum seekers, and so on). Migrants include ethnic minorities, naturalised migrants, second generation migrants, refugees, gypsies, and so on.

Part of this budget (€840,000) is earmarked for the European Migrants' Forum.

Information and applications A document with the selection criteria and an application form can be obtained upon written request to the Commission.

European Commission
DGV.D.4 – Free movement of workers, integration of migrants and anti-racism
Mr Robertus CORNELISSEN, Head of Unit
37 Rue Joseph II, B-1040 Brussels
Tel: +32 2 295 7667
Fax: +32 2 295 1899

B3-4111

Preparatory measures combating and preventing discrimination

Budget 99 €7,000,000 (£4,900,000)

Eligibility NGOs, associations and networks working for disabled and elderly people and children.

Beneficial areas Cooperation, improving knowledge, developing exchange of information and best practice, promoting innovative approaches and evaluating experiences in order to combat discrimination based on disability and age in the EU.

Partners needed Partners from at least 2 member states must be involved.

Types of grant Transnational activities of EU interest, and contributing significantly to the further development and implementation of EU policy on the fight against discrimination of elderly and/or disabled people:
- identification of the needs of disabled people on access to EU programmes;

- sport for disabled people as a factor of social integration;
- organisations of disabled people or parents of disabled people (i.e. the European Disability Forum and European NGOs working in the field of disability, projects to raise awareness of the rights of disabled people, the European Day of Disabled Persons);
- activities to promote full citizenship, participation and equality of opportunity for older people;
- the UN International Year 'Towards a society for all ages', including the promotion of inter-generational solidarity, the situation of older people in the labour market, their role in society and their quality of life.

Grant size: average €80,000. The total cost of any proposed action should not be less than €50,000. The EU financial contribution will not exceed 70% of the total costs, which may include the counter value of contributions in kind.

Actions eligible under other EU programmes such as the Structural Funds or Community Initiatives (see p 51) will not be considered.

Information and applications Calls for proposals are regularly published in the Official Journal, with various deadlines and conditions. Further information is available from the Commission.

European Commission, DG V.E.4 – Integration of disabled persons
Mrs Antonella SCHULTE-BRAUCKS, Head of Unit
27 Rue Joseph II, B-1040 Brussels
Tel: +32 2 295 7159 / 295 4274
Fax: +32 2 295 1012
Internet: http://www.europa.eu.int/comm/dg05/soc-prot/disable/callprop9902/call_en.htm

Note See also B3-2006, Pilot projects on multicultural integration, p 118

B3-4112

Preparatory measures combating and preventing social exclusion

Budget 99 €10,000,000 (£7,000,000)

Eligibility NGOs, associations and networks working for the poor and socially excluded, disabled and older people and children.

Beneficial areas Combating social exclusion in Europe.

Partners needed Yes: at least 4 partners from different member states must be involved.

Types of grant Subsidies for projects which involve cooperation, improving knowledge, developing exchanges of information and best practice, innovative approaches and evaluating experiences in combating social exclusion.

Part of this budget heading is earmarked for the European Anti-Poverty Network and the European Federation of National Organisations Working with the Homeless (FEANTSA).

€7,000,000 are available for grants.

Information and applications Calls for proposals are published in the Official Journal. Further information is available from the Commission.

European Commission
DGV.E.2, Social protection, social inclusion and civil society
Mr Kevin WALSH, Desk Officer
27 Rue Joseph II, B-1040 Brussels
Tel: +32 2 299 4914
Fax: +32 2 299 0509

B3-4113

Action to integrate refugees

Budget 99 €5,000,000 (£3,500,000)

Eligibility NGOs and other organisations working for refugees.

Beneficial areas Integration of refugees in the EU.

Partners needed Yes: projects must be transnational.

Types of grant Funding for pilot projects which look at factors conducive to the integration of refugees, such as education and vocational training (including language courses), housing, access to services, social protection, culture and leisure, etc.

Projects can consist of:
+ improving public awareness and understanding of refugees;
+ analysis and evaluation of the situation of refugees in the EU and member states' policies on refugees;
+ disseminating and exchanging information, experience and good practice at European level;
+ creating and developing networks between activists, projects and/or academics working towards integrating refugees.

Grant maximum: up to 50% of the total costs.

Information and applications Calls for proposals are published once or twice a year. Contact the Commission for information.

European Commission
DG V.D.4 – Free movement of workers, integration of migrants and anti-racism
Mr Robertus CORNELISSEN, Head of Unit
37 Rue Joseph II, B-1040 Brussels
Tel: +32 2 295 7667
Fax: +32 2 295 1899

Note See also B3-2006, Pilot projects on multicultural integration, p 118

HEALTH

B3-4300	Public health, health promotion, information on health, health education and public health training	€4,800,000	£3,360,000
B3-4301	Combating cancer	€14,150,000	£9,905,000
B3-4302	Health aspects of drug abuse	€5,120,000	£3,584,000
B3-4303	Combating AIDS and certain other transmissible diseases	€10,450,000	£7,315,000
B3-4304	Health and well-being	€5,400,000	£3,780,000
B3-4306	Health surveillance	€2,700,000	£1,890,000
B3-4310	Health protection, hygiene and safety at work, including a subsidy for European Trade Union Technical Bureau for Health and Safety	€4,425,000	£3,097,000
B3-4313	Safe: Actions for safety at work in Europe	€7,000,000	£4,900,000

The EU has a number of multi-annual (1996–2000) public health programmes, implemented with funds from the budget lines above and dealing with:

+ AIDS and other communicable diseases;
+ drug dependence;
+ cancer;
+ health promotion;
+ health monitoring;
+ pollution-related diseases (started in 1999);
+ rare diseases (started in 1999);
+ injury prevention (started in 1999);
+ health and safety at work.

Other activities, outside these action programmes and not specifically covered by dedicated budget lines include:

+ electromagnetic fields;
+ preparation of health status reports;
+ strategy for blood safety and self-sufficiency;
+ annual reports on the integration of health requirements in other EU policies;
+ a network on the surveillance and control of communicable diseases.

Note that treatment and care, the core activities of public health, remain the responsibilities of the member states and are outside EU competence. EU involvement is limited to adjacent and supportive activities such as research, prevention, cooperation, exchange of information, pilot projects, etc.

Most activities are covered by the summaries of budget lines below. Potential applicants are strongly recommended to consult the web-site of DG.V.F of the European Commission. Further details can be obtained from the units mentioned below or from the general DG.V.F address.

EU programmes to support research in the field of health are dealt with by DG XII – Science, Research and Development, Directorate B – Life Sciences, which implements chapter B6 of the EU budget on research. For details, see p 206.

Other aspects are covered by budget line B5-103 on consumer health and safety, which is implemented by DG XXIV – Consumer Protection and Consumer Health Protection, see p 169.

Mr DGV.F – Public health and safety at work
EUROFORUM Building
Rue Robert Stumper, L 2920 Luxembourg
Tel: +352 4301 32719
Fax: +352 4301 34511
Internet: http://europa.eu.int/comm/dg05/phealth/sitemap.htm

For NGOs, a useful contact is:

European Public Health Alliance
33 Rue de Pascale, B-1040 Brussels
Tel: +32 2 230 3056
Fax: +32 2 233 3880
E-mail: epha@epha.org
Internet: http://www.epha.org

B3-4300

Public health, health promotion, information on health, health education and public health training

Budget 99 €4,800,000 (£3,360,000)

Eligibility Specialised NGOs and NGO networks, professional organisations, universities, research institutions.

Beneficial areas Projects in the fields mentioned in the title which contribute to a high level of health protection and aim to:
- encourage the health promotion approach in member states' health policies (exchanges of experience, pilot projects, networks, etc.);
- encourage the adoption of healthy lifestyles and behaviour;
- promote awareness of risk factors and health-enhancing factors;
- encouraging intersectoral and multidisciplinary approaches to health promotion with particular attention to disadvantaged groups.

Partners needed Not specified.

Types of grant Priority will be given to large-scale projects, which must have an EU dimension and be likely to produce an added value for the EU, in particular through involving the participation of more than one member state. Check (co-)financing conditions with the Commission.

Information and applications Calls for proposals are published in the Official Journal. Application deadline: usually 15 September, for funding in the following year.

European Commission
Mr DG V.F.3 – Health promotion, health monitoring and injury prevention
Matti RAJALA, Head of Unit
EUROFORUM Building
Rue Robert Stumper, L 2920 Luxembourg
Tel: +352 4301 38502
Fax: +352 4301 32059
E-mail: matti.rajala@lux.dg5.cec.be
Internet: http://europa.eu.int/comm/dg05/phealth/sitemap.htm

B3-4301

Combating cancer

Budget 99 €14,150,000 (£9,905,000)

Eligibility Mostly specialised research institutes, universities and so on, some NGOs.

Beneficial areas Prevention of cancer, through subsidies, studies, public information campaigns, raising awareness, training of health workers.

Partners needed Yes: see under Types of grant.

Types of grant The Commission co-finances projects (percentage not specified in available documentation) which must have an EU dimension and be likely to produce an added value for the EU, in particular through involving the participation of more than one member state.

Priority is given to large-scale projects. Overlapping with activities by other Commission services and national or international organisations (WHO, Council of Europe, ILO, OECD, etc.) must be avoided.

The main fields of activity are:
+ data collection and research;
+ information and health education;
+ early detection and screening;
+ training and quality control.

The annual priorities within these fields can be found on the DG V.F web-site, which also has overviews of projects and organisations funded previously.

Information and applications Calls for proposals are published in the Official Journal. Application deadline: usually 15 September, for funding in the following year.

European Commission
DG V.F.2 – Prevention of cancer, drugs dependence and pollution related diseases
Mr Yves MORETTINI, Head of Unit
EUROFORUM Building
Rue Robert Stumper, L 2920 Luxembourg
Tel: +352 4301 32737
Fax: +352 4301 34975
E-mail: yves.morettini@lux.dg5.cec.be
Internet: http://europa.eu.int/comm/dg05/phealth/sitemap.htm

B3-4302

Health aspects of drug abuse

Budget 99 €5,120,000 (£3,584,000)

Eligibility Specialised NGOs and NGO networks, professional organisations, universities, research institutions, public bodies.

Beneficial areas Prevention of drug addiction by: exchanges between member states, pilot schemes, networks, cooperation with third countries and international organisations, public information and awareness campaigns, especially towards young people, training of health workers.

Partners needed Bringing together public-sector and/or NGOs and multi-disciplinary cooperation are encouraged.

Types of grant Priorities for 1999:
◆ new usage trends, multiple drug dependence and young people;
◆ prevention of drug addiction relapses.

Priority will be given to large-scale projects, which must have an EU dimension and be likely to produce an added value for the EU, in particular through involving the participation of more than one member state. Overlapping with activities by other Commission services and national or international organisations (WHO, Council of Europe, ILO, OECD, etc.) must be avoided.

   For details on the 1999 workplan and an overview of projects and organisations funded earlier, see the DG V.F web-site. Check (co-)financing conditions with the Commission.

Information and applications Calls for proposals are published in the Official Journal. Application deadline: usually September, for funding in the following year.

European Commission
DG V.F.2 – Prevention of cancer, drugs dependence and pollution related diseases
Mr Yves MORETTINI, Head of Unit
EUROFORUM Building
Rue Robert Stumper, L 2920 Luxembourg
Tel: +352 4301 32737
Fax: +352 4301 34975
E-mail: yves.morettini@lux.dg5.cec.be
http://europa.eu.int/comm/dg05/phealth/sitemap.htm

On content, it may be useful to liaise with the Commission's own specialised body:

European Monitoring Centre for Drugs and Drug Addiction (EMCDDA)
23-25 Rua Cruz de Santa Apolonia
P-1149-045 Lisbon, Portugal
Tel: +351 1 811 3000
Fax: +315 1 813 1711
Internet: http://www.emcdda.org

B3-4303

Combating AIDS and certain other transmissible diseases

Budget 99 €10,450,000 (£7,315,000)

Eligibility Projects involving public bodies and/or NGOs with sufficient evidence of competence have priority.

Beneficial areas
* surveillance and monitoring of communicable diseases;
* combating transmission;
* information, education and training;
* support for people with HIV/AIDS and combating discrimination.

Partners needed Not specified.

Types of grant The EU co-finances projects (percentage not specified in available documentation) which produce real added value for the EU, for example by:
* the participation of several member states;
* activities conducted jointly in several member states;

- pilot projects applicable to other member states if adapted to their conditions and cultures.

Priority will be given to large-scale projects which are methodologically relevant and are likely to make a genuine contribution towards the attainment of the programme's objectives. Overlapping with activities by other Commission services and national or international organisations (WHO, Council of Europe, ILO, OECD, etc.) must be avoided.

For an overview of projects and organisations funded earlier, see the DG V.F web-site.

Information and applications Calls for proposals are published in the Official Journal. Application deadline: usually 15 September, for funding in the following year.

European Commission
DG V.F.4 – Communicable, rare and emerging diseases
Mr Ronald Haigh, Head of Unit
EUROFORUM Building
Rue Robert Stumper, L 2920 Luxembourg
Tel: +352 4301 32734
Fax: +352 4301 33241
E-mail: ronald.haigh@lux.dg5.cec.be
Internet: http://europa.eu.int/comm/dg05/phealth/sitemap.htm

B3-4304

Health and well-being

Budget 99 €5,400,000 (£3,780,000)

Eligibility Includes the non-profit sector, see details below.

Beneficial areas Injury prevention, pollution-related diseases, rare diseases, new areas under the Treaty of Amsterdam, policy analysis and proposals, reactions to emergencies, support of representative patients' groups.

Partners needed Check with Commission services on different subjects.

Types of grant Selection of supported issues and activities, relevant for the non-profit sector:
- representative European NGOs, supporting patients' interests;
- injury prevention: creation of networks of those active in the field; dissemination of information on injury prevention campaigns; collaboration between expert centres on investigating risk factors;

- pollution-related diseases: networks to improve understanding of the role of pollutants in causing and aggravating diseases; information on pollution-related health risks and their perception, assessment and management;
- rare diseases: providing information to patients and their families, health professionals and researchers; improving knowledge and transnational cooperation between voluntary and professional support groups to handle and monitor disease clusters more effectively; voluntary organisations supporting affected people, including organisations of disabled people and parents of disabled children;
- Alzheimer's disease: cross-border activities to improve the quality of life of Alzheimer patients and those who help them on a non-professional basis. Examples of projects funded in 1997 and 1998 are on the DG V.F web-site: http://europa.eu.int/comm/dg05/phealth/sitemap.htm
- Creutzfeldt-Jacob disease: pilot projects and preparatory measures to assist organisations supporting victims of new variant C-J disease and/or their relatives.

For most subjects and activities, check with the DG V.F units below for details on co-financing, eligibility, priorities for subjects and activities, etc.

Information and applications Calls for proposals are published in the Official Journal. Application deadline: usually 15 September, for funding in the following year.

European Commission, EUROFORUM Building
Rue Robert Stumper, L 2920 Luxembourg
Internet: http://europa.eu.int/comm/dg05/phealth/sitemap.htm

Pollution related diseases:

DG V.F.2 – Prevention of cancer, drugs dependence and pollution related diseases
Mr Yves MORETTINI, Head of Unit
Tel: +352 4301 32737
Fax: +352 4301 34975
E-mail: yves.morettini@lux.dg5.cec.be

Injury prevention:

Mr DG V.F.3 – Health promotion, health monitoring and injury prevention
Matti RAJALA, Head of Unit
Tel: +352 4301 38502
Fax: +352 4301 32059
E-mail: matti.rajala@lux.dg5.cec.be

Rare diseases, Alzheimer's, Creutzfeldt–Jacob:

DG V.F.4 – Communicable, rare and emerging diseases
Mr Ronald Haigh, Head of Unit
Tel: +352 4301 32734
Fax: +352 4301 33241
E-mail: ronald.haigh@lux.dg5.cec.be

B3-4306

Health surveillance

Budget 99 €2,700,000 (£1,890,000)

Eligibility NGOs, research institutions, consultants, and so on, may be involved in specific actions. The main actors are the Commission, member states with their specialised institutions, and international organisations.

Beneficial areas Establishing a health monitoring system to measure health status, trends and determinants in the EU, to facilitate planning, monitoring and evaluation of EU policy, to provide member states with information to compare and support national health policies.

Partners needed Priority will be given to projects involving most if not all member states.

Types of grant The Commission co-funds projects with an EU dimension and added value, through involving more than one member state. Priority will be given to large-scale projects involving bodies and associations which are able to offer sufficient evidence of competence.

Fundable activities at local, regional or national level include:
- establishment of EU health indicators including the selection of relevant information and data for exchange
- development of an EU-wide network for sharing and transferring health data
- development of methods and tools for analysis and on health status, trends, determinants and the effect of policies on health.

For details of the 1998-99 workplan and an overview of projects and organisations funded previously, see the DG V.F website.

Information and applications Calls for proposals are published in the Official Journal. Application deadline: usually 15 September, for funding in the following year.

European Commission
Mr DG V.F.3 – Health promotion, health monitoring and injury prevention
Matti RAJALA, Head of Unit
EUROFORUM Building
Rue Robert Stumper, L 2920 Luxembourg
Tel: +352 4301 38502
Fax: +352 4301 32059
E-mail: matti.rajala@lux.dg5.cec.be
Internet: http://europa.eu.int/comm/dg05/phealth/sitemap.htm

B3-4310

Health protection, hygiene and safety at work

Budget 99 €4,425,000 (£3,097,500)

Eligibility Check with the Commission.

Beneficial areas Application of the EU directives on health and safety in the workplace and effective participation of both sides of industry in the design and implementation of policies in this area.

Partners needed Check with the Commission.

Types of grant Information and public awareness campaigns, training measures for health workers, pilot projects on environmental training for workers in small and medium-sized businesses. NGO involvement appears to be limited (absent in 1998). Check with the Commission on possibilities for 1999 and beyond, both for this budget line and the SAFE programme (B3-4313).

Information and applications

European Commission
DG V.F.5 – Health, safety and hygiene at work.
Mr José Ramon Biosca de Sagastuy, Head of Unit
EUROFORUM Building
Rue Robert Stumper, L 2920 Luxembourg
Tel: +352 4301 34988
Fax: +352 4301 34259
Internet: http://europa.eu.int/comm/dg05/h&s/index_hs.htm

Specialised agencies of the European Commission:

European Foundation for the Improvement of Living and Working Conditions
Wyattville Road, Loughlinstown, Co Dublin, Ireland
Tel: +353 1 204 3100
Fax: +353 1 282 6456 / 282 4209
E-mail: postmaster@eurofound.ie
Internet: http://europa.eu.int/efilwc/index.htm

European Agency for Health and Safety at Work
33 Gran Via, E-48009 Bilbao, Spain
Tel: +34 94 479 4360
Fax +34 94 479 4383
E-mail: information@eu-osha.es

B3-4313

SAFE

Actions for safety at work in Europe

Budget 99 €7,000,000 (£4,900,000)

Eligibility Mostly government agencies, universities and specialised institutes, professional organisations, trade unions and employers' organisations.

Beneficial areas Workplace-related research, information dissemination, training and seminars (SAFE – Safety Action for Europe). Spending is targeted at small and medium sized undertakings and concerns EU health, safety and environmental legislation, to improve awareness of environmental risks at workplaces.

Partners needed Check with the Commission.

Types of grant For details about projects and participation possibilities, contact the Commission.

Information and applications

European Commission
DG V.F.5 – Health, safety and hygiene at work.
Mr José Ramon Biosca de Sagastuy, Head of Unit
EUROFORUM Building
Rue Robert Stumper, L 2920 Luxembourg
Tel: +352 4301 34988
Fax: +352 4301 34259
Internet: http://europa.eu.int/comm/dg05/h&s/index_hs.htm

Specialised agencies of the European Commission:

European Foundation for the Improvement of Living and Working Conditions
Wyattville Road, Loughlinstown,
Co Dublin, Ireland
Tel: +353 1 204 3100
Fax: +353 1 282 6456 / 282 4209
E-mail: postmaster@eurofound.ie
Internet: http://europa.eu.int/efilwc/index.htm

European Agency for Health and Safety at Work
33 Gran Via, E-48009 Bilbao
Spain
Tel: +34 94 479 4360
Fax: +34 94 479 4383
E-mail: information@eu-osha.es

ENERGY

B4-1030	Altener: Promotion of renewable energy sources	€15,400,000	£10,780,000
B4-1031	Save II: Encouragement of energy efficiency	€15,500,000	£10,850,000

B4-1030

Altener
Promotion of renewable energy sources

Budget 99 €15,400,000 (£10,780,000)

Eligibility Legal entities, regional and local authorities, organisations, individuals, public and private enterprises and existing EU-wide networks or temporary groupings of organisations or enterprises formed to accomplish the projects.

Beneficial areas Promote renewable energy sources in the member states and the EEA countries.

Partners needed Depends on the type of action.

Types of grant The budget line covers expenditure to:
- help create the necessary conditions for the implementation of an EU action plan for renewable energy sources, in particular the legal, socio-economic and administrative conditions;
- encourage private and public investment in the production and use of energy from renewable sources.

Categories of measures:
- studies and other actions to develop the potential of renewable energy sources. For example the development of sectoral and market strategies, the development of norms and standards, grouped procurements and the analysis of the legal, socio-economic and administrative conditions which are more favourable to the penetration of renewable energies and the preparation of appropriate legislation;
- pilot measures aimed at creating and extending infrastructures and instruments for the development of renewable energies in local and regional planning; tools for planning, conception and evaluation; new financial and market instruments;
- development of information, education and training structures which could exchange experience and skills and improve coordination between international,

EU, national, regional and local activities; creation of a centralised system for gathering and disseminating information on renewable energies;
- actions facilitating the market penetration of renewable energy and relevant skills.

Information and applications

European Commission
DG XVII.C.2 – Rational use of energy and renewable sources of energy
Mr Ronan HARBISON, Desk Officer
226 Avenue de Tervuren, B-1040 Brussels
Tel: +32 2 295 6319
Fax: +32 2 296 6283
Internet: http://europa.eu.int/en/comm/dg17/altener.htm

B4-1031

Save II

Encouragement of energy efficiency

Budget 99 €15,500,000 (£10,850,000)

Eligibility Legal entities, regional and local authorities, organisations, individuals, public and private enterprises and existing EU-wide networks or temporary groupings of organisations or enterprises formed to accomplish the projects.

Beneficial areas Improve energy efficiency in the member states and the EEA countries. The applicant countries of central and eastern Europe, Cyprus and Malta may also participate.

Partners needed Yes: at least 2 partners from different member states or the EEA.

Types of grant Fields of activities:
- rational use of energy and buildings, equipment, transport, industry, demand-side management and integrated resource planning, combined heat and power. Grant maximum: 50% of total costs;
- studies, monitoring operations, information and dissemination activities Grant maximum: up to 100% of total costs;
- creation of local and regional energy agencies Grant maximum: up to 40% of total costs.

Information and applications

European Commission
DG XVII.C.2 – Rational use of energy and renewable sources of energy
Mr Ronan HARBISON, Desk Officer
226 Avenue de Tervuren, B-1040 Brussels
Tel: +32 2 295 6319
Fax: +32 2 296 6283
Internet: http://europa.eu.int/en/comm/dg17/save.htm

ENVIRONMENT

B4-304	Legislation and other general action based on the Fifth Action Programme on the environment	€18,000,000	£12,600,000
B4-306	Awareness and subsidies	€6,650,000	£4,655,000
B4-3200	Life II – Part 1: Nature protection	€67,000,000	£46,900,000
B4-3201	Life II – Part 2: Environmental protection	€67,000,000	£46,900,000
B4-3300	Community cooperation on civil protection and environmental emergencies	€2,000,000	£1,400,000

In addition to containing Commission services in DG XI (see details in each budget line description), a useful contact for the voluntary sector is the EU umbrella network of environment NGOs:

European Environment Bureau
34 Boulevard de Waterloo
B-1060 Brussels
Tel: +32 2 289 1090
Fax: + 32 2 289 1099
E-mail: info@eeb.org
Internet: http://www.eeb.org

B4-304

Legislation and other general action based on the Fifth Action Programme on the environment

Budget 99 €18,000,000 (£12,600,000)

Eligibility Non-profit organisations or non-profit projects of commercial organisations.

Beneficial areas A broad range of activities and aspects of EU policy on environmental protection. See the DG XI web-site for documentation on the Fifth Action Programme on the environment:

http://europa.eu.int/comm/dg11/actionpr.htm

Partners needed Not specified.

Types of grant Spontaneous, ad hoc proposals on any of the subjects of the Fifth Environmental Action Plan may be submitted at any time by non-profit organisations, independently of the ongoing calls for proposals. A commercial company must demonstrate that the immediate objective of the project is non-commercial and definitely not profit-making. The Commission gave co-financing grants of approximately €2,000,000 in total to 50 projects in 1999.

Information and applications

European Commission
DG XI.3 – Budget, finance and contracts
Mr Brendan SINNOTT, Head of Unit
Avenue de Beaulieu 5, B-1160 Brussels
Tel: +32 2 295 8688
Fax: + 32 2 99 4449
E-mail: brendan.sinnott@dg11.cec.be
Internet: http://europa.eu.int/comm/dg11/funding/general/call_en.htm

B4-306

Awareness and subsidies

Budget 99 €6,650,000 (£4,655,000)

Eligibility Mostly non-profit organisations.

Beneficial areas Education and awareness raising on environmental problems and effects on public health, promotion of representative European NGOs (EU and applicant states), information and documentation resources, developing indicators on awareness of public authorities and economic operators about sustainable development.

Partners needed Not specified.

Types of grant No call for proposals is being issued in 1999. Contact the Commission for details of later years, the implementation of this budget line in general and possibilities for NGO involvement. For co-financing possibilities, see budget line B4-304.

Information and applications

European Commission, DG XI.3 – Budget, finance and contracts
Mr Brendan SINNOTT, Head of Unit
Avenue de Beaulieu 5, B-1160 Brussels
Tel: +32 2 295 8688
Fax: + 32 2 99 4449
E-mail: brendan.sinnott@dg11.cec.be
Internet: http://europa.eu.int/comm/dg11/funding/envinfo.htm

B4-3200

Life II

Part 1: Nature protection

Budget 99 €67,000,000 (£46,900,000)

Eligibility Applicants may be all natural persons and legal entities in the EU.

Beneficial areas
- nature conservation actions required to maintain or restore the natural habitats and the population of species of wild fauna and flora to a favourable status;
- establishment of the European network of protected areas – Natura 2000, on-site management and conservation of the most valuable fauna and flora species and habitats in the EU.

Partners needed Partnerships are possible, including from applicant EU countries.

Types of grant The EU co-finances up to 50% (exceptionally 75%) of activities on priority natural habitats or priority species, except when they are fundable from the Structural Funds, Cohesion Fund, etc.

Examples
Projects supported in 1998 and 1997, most of them run by NGOs and NGO networks, can be found on the Life website.

Information and applications Application deadlines: usually from end-November to end-December, but vary from country to country. Partnerships involving several countries apply in the country where the lead partner is based.

The selection process from application to decision takes more than half a year. Applicants may download a Life Nature application file from the web-site, which also contains detailed information on the application procedure:

http://europa.eu.int/comm/life/nature/prepare.htm

or ask for one from the UK national authority, to whom applications must be returned.

European Wildlife Division
Department of the Environment, Transport and the Regions
Mr Richard CHAPMAN
Room 9/22, Tollgate House
Houlton Street , Bristol BS2 9DJ
Fax: +44 117 987 8182 / 987 8119
E-mail: european.wildlife.doe@gtnet.gov.uk

Assistance in drafting applications may be requested from:

ECOSYSTEMS
11 Rue Beckers, B -1040 Brussels
Tel: +32 2 646 6950
Fax: +32 2 646 84 66
E-mail: ecosystems.ltd@glo.be

In the European Commission:

DG XI.D.2 – Nature protection, coastal zones and tourism
Mr Bruno JULIEN, Head of Unit
174 Boulevard du Triomphe, B-1060 Brussels
Tel: +32 2 295 6133 / 296 3637
Fax: +32 2 296 9956
E-mail: bruno.julien@dg11.cec.be
Internet: http://europa.eu.int/comm/life/nature/index.htm

B4-3201

Life II

Part 2: Environmental protection

Budget 99 €67,000,000 (£46,900,000)

Eligibility Applicants may be all natural persons and legal entities in the EU.

Beneficial areas Environmental sustainability, in particular:
- maintaining the overall quality of life;
- maintaining continuing access to natural resources;
- avoiding lasting environmental damage;
- meeting the needs of the present without compromising the ability to meet future needs;
- integration of the environmental dimension in all major policy areas;
- replacing the command-and-control approach with shared responsibility between various actors.

Partners needed Partnerships are possible, including from applicant EU countries.

Types of grant The EU co-finances preparatory, demonstration, technical assistance, support or promotional measures designed to:
- promote sustainable development and integration of the environment in industrial activities;
- help local authorities to integrate environmental considerations in land use development and planning;
- strengthen the link and complementarity between environmental regulations and structural financial assistance, in particular from EU funds and financial instruments concerning the environment.

Grant maximum: up to 30% of the cost in the case of income-generating projects (e.g. clean technologies, recycling, etc.) or up to 50% of the cost of other actions, rarely exceeding €1 million. Exception: projects fundable from the Structural Funds, Cohesion Fund or other EU budget lines.

Examples
Projects supported in 1998 and 1997, most of them run by NGOs and NGO networks, can be found on the Life websites:

http://europa.eu.int/comm/life/envir/press98.htm
http://europa.eu.int/comm/life/envir/links2.htm

Information and applications Application deadlines: usually from end-November to end-December, but vary from country to country. Partnerships involving several countries apply in the country where the lead partner is based.

The selection process from application to decision takes more than half a year. Applicants may download an application file from the web-site, which also contains detailed information on the application procedure:

http://europa.eu.int/comm/life/envir/howto.htm

or order one from:

European Environment Division
Department of Environment, Transport and the Regions
Ms Verity SHERWOOD
Zone 5/G9 Ashdown House
123 Victoria Street, London SW1E 6DE
Fax: +44 171 890 6509

In the European Commission:

DG XI.B.2 – Management and Coordination of financial instruments in the environment
Mr Matti VAINIO, Acting Head of Unit
5 Avenue de Beaulieu, B-1060 Brussels
Tel: +32 2 296 6138
Fax: +32 2 296 9561
http://europa.eu.int/comm/life/envir/index.htm

B4-3300

Community cooperation on civil protection and environmental emergencies

Budget 99 €2,000,000 (£1,400,000)

Eligibility National, regional and local government organisations, national or private specialised training centres, the private sector.

Beneficial areas Civil protection and ecological emergencies including marine pollution caused by accidents.

Partners needed No.

Types of grant The Commission co-finances, on a case-by-case basis, self-tuition workshops; pilot projects; exchange of experts; annual simulation exercises; information, education, awareness raising among citizens; support projects. Proposals can be submitted with detailed technical programme and budget. Grants are given for one year and may be renewed on an annual basis.

Information and applications

European Commission
DG XI.C.4 – Civil protection
Mr Alessandro BARISICH, Head of Unit
174 Boulevard du Triomphe, B-1160 Brussels
Tel: +32 2 299 2248
Fax: + 32 2 299 0314
E-mail: alessandro.barisich@dg11.cec.be

CONSUMER POLICY

B5-100	Promotion of consumer interests	€13,850,000	£9,695,000
B5-103	Consumer health and safety	€10,000,000	£7,000,000

The budget lines for consumer interests are part of a 'General framework for Community activities in favour of consumers', which covers the 5-year period 1999–2004. There will therefore be no substantial changes until 2005, but every year there are priority themes or actions.

Consumer policy is the responsibility of DGXXIV of the European Commission. An overview can be found on the Internet:

http://europa.eu.int/comm/dg24/index.html

National and international consumers organisations are represented in Brussels by:

Consumers Organisation BEUC (Bureau Européen des Unions de Consommateurs)
36 Avenue de Tervuren, B-1040 Brussels
Tel: +32 2 743 1590
Fax: +32 2 735 7455
E-mail: consumers@beuc.org

B5-100

Promotion of consumer interests

Budget 99 €13,850,000 (£9,695,000)

Eligibility Consumer organisations.

Beneficial areas Consumer information, education, training; European umbrella organisations of consumers.

Partners needed Not necessarily.

Types of grant Funding for activities:
- raising consumer awareness of the most sensitive issues, by means of advice centres and the media;
- consumer education, for both children and adults;

- guaranteeing the interests of consumers in the single market, especially in financial transactions and services;
- organisations representing the interests of consumers at a European level;
- pilot projects promoting consumption models.

Grant maximum: generally not exceeding 50% of actual expenditure.

The EU funds European and international representation of consumers, as well as – to a limited extent – national organisations.

The European Commission co-finances (max. €200,000) European Consumer Infocentres, or Euroguichet, which form part of a European network and provide information and advice to the public, distribute the results of comparative tests, develop cross-border studies, provide assistance and advice on mediation, information concerning the procedures, first legal aid and orientation towards other authorities (address in the UK below).

Examples

In 1999 (call for proposals in September 1998) the focus was on training, in the areas of food and product safety, financial services, EU rights for consumers, new marketing techniques (electronic trading), comparative tests, standardisation of products and services, information society. European consumer organisations could present annual action plans eligible for funding. Out of 210 eligible projects, the Commission funded 53 projects (25%):

– 49 specific projects, to a total amount of €5,720,000;
– 4 projects (operating expenses of European consumer organisations), to a total of €1,420,000.

Projects in the UK:

– Consumers' Research & Testing Centre: training and resourcing teachers to teach consumer-related topics to 14-16 year olds;
– Consumers International: programme to increase the participation of consumer representatives in the setting of international food standards;
– Consumers Association: a training programme on business-sponsored materials and activities in schools;
– European Research Into Consumer Affairs (ERICA): training consumer organisations on children and the Internet;
– Consumers International: training to develop the establishment of specialised computer networks amongst African consumer organisations;
– Consumers International: training consumer representatives in consumer issues related to electronic commerce and data protection.

Information and applications Calls for proposals are published annually in the Official Journal of the EU, indicating the priority areas and the selection and award criteria. Ask the Commission for further information.

European Commission
DG XXIV.C.1 – Consumer Policy: Resources and coordination
Mr Gerard RIJSSENBEEK, Head of Unit

232 Rue Belliard, B-1040 Brussels
Tel: +32 2 295 3168 / 295 3703
Fax: +32 2 296 3279
E-mail: gerard.rijssenbeek@dg24.cec.be

DG XXIV.C.3, Development of consumer information, education and representation
Mr Jens NYMAND-CHRISTENSEN, Head of Unit
232 Rue Belliard, B-1040 Brussels
Tel: +32 2 299 5026 / 299 5027
E-mail: jens.nymand-christensen@dg24.cec.be
Internet: http://www.europa.eu.int/comm/dg24/general_info/budget01_en.html

European Consumer Infocentre in the UK:

Ms Nicola SIMPSON
National Association of Citizens Advice Bureaux
Myddelton House, 115-123 Pentonville Road
London N1 9LZ
Tel: +44 171 833 2181
Fax: +44 171 833 4371
E-mail: nicola.simpson@nacab.org.uk

B5-103

Consumer health and safety

Budget 99 €10,000,000 (£7,000,000)

Eligibility Experts.

Beneficial areas Consumer food and safety in the EU.

Partners needed Not applicable.

Types of grant Activities which clearly have an impact on consumer health and food safety.

This budget line is mainly used for scientific research and committees: preparation and elaboration of opinions of the scientific committees, expertise and inspection relating to controls in the food sector, technical expertise to assess risks relating to products. The Commission also supports the dissemination of information about dangerous products and potential risks, and projects of major importance for consumer health and safety.

Grant maximum: generally not exceeding 50% of total costs for projects not initiated by the Commission.

Information and applications

European Commission
DG XXIV.C.1 – Consumer Policy: Resources and coordination
Mr Gerard RIJSSENBEEK, Head of Unit
232 Rue Belliard, B-1040 Brussels
Tel: +32 2 295 3168 / 295 3703
Fax: +32 2 296 3279
E-mail: gerard.rijssenbeek@dg24.cec.be

DG XXIV.C.3 – Development of consumer information, education and representation
Mr Jens NYMAND-CHRISTENSEN, Head of Unit
232 Rue Belliard, B-1040 Brussels
Tel: +32 2 299 5026 / 299 5027
E-mail: jens.nymand-christensen@dg24.cec.be
Internet: http://europa.eu.int/comm/dg24/index.html

FREE MOVEMENT, SOCIAL ECONOMY, TOURISM

B5-300	Strategic programme on the internal market – Robert Schuman programme	€22,355,000	(£15,648,500)
B5-321	Measures in the social economy sector (cooperatives, mutuals, associations and foundations)	p.m.	
B5-325	Community measures to assist tourism	p.m.	

B5-300

Strategic programme on the internal market – Robert Schuman programme

Budget 99 €22,355,000 (£15,648,500)

Eligibility Institutions responsible in the member states – at local, regional, national or EU level – for initial or continuing vocational training of judges, prosecutors or lawyers such as bar associations, courts, ministries of justice, high Councils of the judiciary, universities, schools of law.

Beneficial areas Training and information initiatives in the area of EU law for judges and lawyers, to promote the use of EU law for the benefit of citizens, consumers and businesses.

Partners needed No.

Types of grant Apart from very exceptional ad hoc grants to third parties, the main beneficiary of this budget line is the Robert Schuman programme, €1,300,000 (£910,000) in 1999. The programme has 3 objectives covered by 3 types of financial support:

◆ training: courses, seminars and study days for legal practitioners;
◆ information: creation of practical information tools on paper or in electronic form on EU law for judges, prosecutors or lawyers;
◆ accompanying initiatives: any original initiative (not covered by the 2 previous categories) to raise awareness of EU law among judges and lawyers.

Eligible institutions submit practical, focused proposals for financial support for a 1- or 2-year period. They must undertake to keep the projects going for an equal period without EU funding.

Grant maximum and range: up to 80% of net costs, with a ceiling of €30,000 for 1-year projects and €60,000 for 2-year projects. Actual funding in 1997–1999 averaged €19,000–20,000; about 65 selected projects shared the €1,300,000 available for 1999.

Examples
– Lincoln's Inn, one of the great English Inns of Court, took part in the Robert Schuman Project with a 3-day seminar 'Fair trial: principles of European law'. The seminar was delivered by eminent figures to 60 participants, with a balance in participation from the different professions. This was one of the first UK projects and had a practical emphasis;
– UK projects selected in 1998 included Liberty (National Council for Civil Liberties), Middlesex University – London, SLS Legal Publications – University of Belfast, Southampton Institute, Law Society of Scotland, the University of Manchester and the University of Birmingham.

Information and applications Institutions interested in submitting proposals for funding under the Robert Schuman Project should reply to the call for proposals published every year in the Official Journal. Further information, such as the *Vademecum, The Robert Schuman Project, Pilot Phases 1997–1998, Analysis and first assessment*, and application forms are available from the Commission, and the web-site.

European Commission
DG XV.D.3, Internal market and financial services
Robert Schuman project
Mr Ludovic SODJAHIN
100 Avenue de Cortenberg, B-1040 Brussels
Tel: +32 2 299 0959
Fax: +32 2 299 3088
E-mail: ludovic.sodjahin@dg15.cec.be
Internet: http://europa.eu.int/comm/dg15/en/update/schuman/index.htm

B5-321

Measures in the social economy sector (cooperatives, mutuals, associations and foundations)

Budget 99 p.m.

Eligibility Cooperatives, mutual societies, associations and foundations (the CMAF sector).

Beneficial areas Evaluation of the effects of the internal market on the CMAF sector; improving their access to EU actions.

Partners needed Projects must have a European or transnational aspect.

Types of grant No grants in 1999, see note below. This budget heading would cover the costs of:
- research on the potential of the CMAF sector for job creation;
- promoting the image, raising the profile, strengthening the structure and networking of CMAF;
- increasing their job potential and capacity to respond to the needs of society and the market;
- setting up information centres for CMAF;
- training actions to develop a European management of CAMF;
- promoting the role of voluntary organisations and foundations in Europe, through, among other things, the preparation of a European year of voluntary organisations and active citizenship, with a special facility for the transnational work of associations.

Information and applications See note below.

European Commission
DG XXIII.C.3 – Social economy
Mr Per Ove ENGELBRECHT, Head of Unit
80 Rue d'Arlon, B-1040 Brussels
Tel: +32 2 299 2149/295 6797
Fax: +32 2 296 5857
E-mail: cmaf@dg23.cec.be
Internet: http://europa.eu.int/en/comm/dg23/index.htm

Note This is a budget line without a legal basis, except from being mentioned in the EU budget itself. The Court of Justice ruled that all funding must be based not only on the budget, but also on a decision for a programme adopted by the Council of Ministers. There will therefore be no funding until such a legal basis exists.

See also B5-501: Pilot projects on the third system, p 185.

B5-325

Community measures to assist tourism

Budget 99 p.m.

Eligibility Small and medium-sized enterprises (SMEs) in the tourism sector.

Beneficial areas Projects to implement an EU policy to assist tourism.

Partners needed Not applicable (see note below).

Types of grant There has been no new commitment under this budget heading since 1997 (see note below).

Themes are:
- cooperation with central and eastern European countries, the Maghreb, Cyprus and Malta on training, promotional strategies and marketing highlighting the tourism heritage of these countries, creation of SMEs in tourism.
- tourism and the environment: support for demonstration projects in the areas of visitor management and traffic management; development of a network on tourism and the environment to promote best practice, encourage partnership projects, publicise action taken by the EU, the tourism industry and other sustainable tourism groups and facilitate information and research.

The 1999 budget highlights the role of SMEs in the tourism sector which are active in green tourism.

Information and applications No applications were possible at the time of writing. Further information is available from the Commission.

European Commission
DG XXIII.D – Coordination of Community measures, and concerted actions, in relation to tourism
Mr Patrick HENNESSY, Director
80 Rue d'Arlon, B-1040 Brussels
Tel: +32 2 296 3355 / 295 1832
Fax: +32 2 296 1377
E-mail: patrick.hennessy@dg23.cec.be
Internet: http://europa.eu.int/en/comm/dg23/tourisme/tourisme.htm

Note The Commission proposed a First Multiannual Programme to assist European Tourism (Philoxenia 1997–2000) in April 1996, but the Council of Ministers has not been able to reach unanimous agreement on the programme. Therefore DG XXIII's Tourism Directorate is unable to provide any funding for individual projects. In the meantime, tourism initiatives can be supported by other programmes: the major funds for promoting regional, economic and social development in the EU (the Structural Funds, p 51); programmes on the environment, p 161; training, p 100; technological facility for small and medium-sized enterprises, p 189; stimulation of small and medium-sized enterprises, p 193; research and development, p 202; cultural heritage, p 108.

INFORMATION SOCIETY

B5-330	Info 2000	€6,100,000	£4,270,000
B5-331	Information Society	€6,000,000	£4,200,000
B5-336	Action against illegal and harmful content on the Internet	€5,500,000	£3,850,000

Many EU programmes provide funding for projects concerning the information society: they cover activities ranging from basic research to training and awareness raising and as many fields as education, training, healthcare, public administration, government, transport, environmental development, sustainability, consumers, tourism, arts, culture and entertainment, democracy, social services and participation, women, community development, small and medium-sized enterprises (SMEs), employment, languages.

Examples
– Forum: a Workshop about Public Debates on the Internet: the influence of modern communication media (information technology, or IT) on public debates with participants such as local or national policy makers, designers of web-sites, participants in public debates, moderators of public discussions, public relations and marketing specialists, and students in the field of information and communication technology. Experts and non-experts cooperate to producing concrete suggestions, supported by on-line visualisation;
– Tele-Abilities: workshops and dissemination campaign in easy teletraining and teleworking for recovery centres for physically disabled people. It aims at informing disabled people about existing telematics services and information technologies. This project is carried out by 4 Spanish and 1 UK partners;
– a project by NIACE (National Institute for Adult Continuing Education) in the UK produced a staff development pack for tutors, providing information technology education and training to groups of adults outside formal education or training programmes. The pack will show them how to provide an effective experience, to develop positive attitudes to and perceptions of information technology and to maximise the transferability of knowledge and skills.

Information and applications The Information Society Project Office (ISPO)of the Commission informs companies, organisations and individuals about opportunities, which are summarised in a brochure *Financial instruments for information society projects*. It is available from ISPO or from the ISPO web-site.

The web-site also provides full details about funding opportunities, current and past calls for proposals, examples of projects, a partner search facility, etc.

Contact:

Information Society Project Office (ISPO):
ISPO Help Desk
Tel: +32-2-296 8800/296 8900
Fax: +32-2-299 4170/299 4180
E-mail: ispo@ispo.cec.be
ISPO free phone in the UK: 0800 962 114
Internet: http://www.ispo.cec.be

Also see in this book:
- *Structural Funds: European Social Fund, Community Initiatives*, p 51
- education: Socrates, p 87
- training: Leonardo, p 102
- heritage: Raphael, p 110
- languages: B3-2004, p 115
- audiovisual: Media, p 120
- SMEs: B3-510, technological facilities for small and medium-sized enterprises and B3-512, stimulation of small and medium-sized enterprises, p 188
- telecommunications, p 198
- *Research and Technological Development*, p 202

B5-330

Info 2000

Budget 99 €6,100,000 (£4,270,000)

Eligibility
- Multimedia content owners, creators, developers (graphics, sound, music, images, texts);
- producers, agents and publishers of books, databases, newspapers, CD-ROMs, and so on;
- distributors (delivery channels such as optical and magnetic media, cable, satellite, telephone and mobile networks);
- end-users (small and large businesses, public administrations, professionals, researchers, the education and training sector, consumers and citizens associations).

Newcomers to the world of multimedia content are particularly welcome.

Beneficial areas Development of multimedia information content.

Partners needed No.

Types of grant The programme aims to stimulate the development and use of multimedia information content in order to contribute to economic growth, competitiveness and employment, and to individual professional, social and cultural development.

Multimedia content is defined as combinations of data, text, sound, graphics, animation, still and moving images stored in digital form and interactively accessible.

It supports projects – new products, new services, new distribution channels passing from 'scribe to screen' – which optimally exploit cultural, commercial, academic and industrial information by electronic publishing:

- stimulating demand and raising awareness;
- exploiting Europe's public sector information;
- catalysing the creation of high quality European multimedia content;
- promoting mechanisms for trading multimedia rights.

Grant maximum: normally not more than 50% of the costs, with progressively lower participation the nearer the project is to the market place. Special add-on incentives can be provided to encourage participation of SMEs and less-favoured regions.

Information and applications A call for proposals is normally published in the Official Journal each autumn.

European Commission
DG XIII.E – Information industry and market and language industry
Info 2000 Central Office
Mr Frans DE BRUÏNE, Director
Jean Monnet Building
Rue Alcide de Gasperi, L-2920 Luxembourg
Tel: +352 4011 62222
Fax: +352 4301 32847
E-mail: info2000@echo.lu

Overall coordination:

Mr Wolfgang HUBER
Tel: +352 4301 32879
Fax: +352 4301 34959
E-mail: wolfgang.huber@lux.dg13.cec.be
Internet: http://www.echo.lu/info2000/infohome.html

The Midas (Multimedia Information Demonstration and Support) network in the 17 countries of the European Economic Area (EU + Norway, Iceland and Liechtenstein) aims to stimulate awareness and use of multimedia information services and applications in Europe.

Internet: http://www.midas-net.org.uk

Two consortia are based in the UK:

Scottish Enterprise
Coordinator – John McCROSSAN
120 Bothwell Street, Glasgow G2 7JP
Tel: +44 141 248 2700
Fax: +44 141 221 3217
E-mail: john.mccrossan@scotent.co.uk

UK MM-SIG LTD
Coordinator – Neil SANDFORD
The Old Office Block, Elmtree Road
Teddington, Middlesex TW11 8ST
Tel: +44 181 977 7670
Fax: +44 181 943 3377

Info 2000 committee members in the UK:

Mr Paul AYSCOUGH
Department of Trade and Industry
CAIS-CII 4 – Z II Green
151 Buckingham Palace Road
London SW1W 9SS
Tel: + 44 171 215 1295
Fax: + 44 171 215 1370
E-mail: paul.ayscough@ciid.dti.gov.uk

Mrs Margaret HAINES, Chief Executive
Library and Information Commission
2 Sheraton Street, London W1V 4BH
Tel: + 44 171 411 0059
Fax: +44 171 411 0057
E-mail: libcom@lic.bl.uk

Dr Richard G. HOPKINS
Department of Trade and Industry
CAIS-CII 4 – Z II Green
151 Buckingham Palace Road
London SW1W 9SS
Tel: + 44 171 215 1219
Fax: + 44 171 215 1966
E-mail: dick.hopkins@ciid.dti.gov.uk

Mrs Susan MOORE
Department of Trade and Industry
CAIS-CII 4 – Z II Green
151 Buckingham Palace Road
London SW1W 9SS
Tel: + 44 171 215 1594

Fax: +44 171 215 1370
E-mail: susan.moore@ciid.dti.gov.uk

Note Info 2000 was adopted for 3 years (1996-1999): the Commission is currently (autumn 1999) discussing a proposal for a follow up programme. See also B3-2004, Promotion of linguistic diversity in the information society, p 115.

B5-331

Information Society

Budget 99 €6,000,000 (£4,200,000)

Eligibility Users, companies, voluntary organisations, national, regional or local administrations, social partners.

Beneficial areas Stimulating the information society in Europe.

Partners needed Transnational projects with partners from more than 2 member states have priority.

Types of grant Measures to raise awareness:
• dissemination of information and promotion of actions aimed at a better understanding of the opportunities, benefits and possible risks of the information society;
• demonstration of potential impacts of information society at regional level, the promotion of exchange of relevant information between cities and regions, and giving visibility to the general public of services which can meet their needs;

Measures to help establish the information society in Europe, for example:
• assessment of the opportunities and barriers which disadvantaged social groups and peripheral and less favoured regions may face in accessing and using information society products and services; the identification of appropriate measures to overcome these obstacles and to grasp the related benefits.
• contributions, on the basis of identified best programmes and practice, to Europe-wide inclusion of successful examples in information society policies, projects and services.

Measures to take into consideration and make use of the global dimension of the information society:
• inventory of initiatives taken word-wide, exchange of information with third countries (notably with developing countries), collaboration in the preparation of demonstration actions, bilaterally or with international organisations.

Information and applications

European Commission
DGIII / DGXIII, Information Society Activity Centre
Mr Joerg WENZEL
24 Avenue de Beaulieu, B-1160 Brussels
Tel: +32 2 296 3320/296 1843
Fax: +32 295 0688

To learn more about EU programmes relating to multimedia and telematics, contact:

Information Society Project Office (ISPO) help desk:
Tel: +32 2 296 8800/296 8900
Fax: +32 2 299 4170/299 4180
E-mail: ispo@ispo.cec.be
ISPO free phone in the UK: 0800 962 114
Internet: http://www.ispo.cec.be

B5-336

Action against illegal and harmful content on the Internet

Budget 99 €5,500,000 (£3,850,000)

Eligibility Self-regulatory bodies, the industry (access and service providers, content providers, network operators, software houses), user, consumer and citizens' rights groups, educational bodies and government bodies.

Beneficial areas
- encouraging the actors (industry, users) to develop and implement adequate systems of self regulation;
- initiating the development and application of technical solutions;
- alerting and informing parents and teachers, in particular through their relevant associations;
- fostering cooperation and exchange of experiences and best practice;
- promoting coordination across Europe and between actors concerned;
- ensuring compatibility between the approach taken in Europe and elsewhere.

Partners needed Yes: see below.

Types of grant The multi-annual Community action plan on promoting safer use of the Internet covers the 4-year period 1998–2001 with a total budget of

€25,000,000. The use of existing networks will permit cost saving, but additional financing is required to produce the relevant content.

Grant maximum: generally one-third of eligible costs.

Subjects and activities funded:

Action 1: **Creating a safe environment:** Encourage the actors (industry, users) to develop and implement adequate systems of self regulation by:

- a European network of hotlines or centres (20–25 participating organisations) which allow users to report content which they consider to be illegal and come across in the course of their use of the Internet, including links between this network and hotlines in third countries. They will have to demonstrate a forward-looking and innovative approach, in particular in their relationship to national law-enforcement authorities;

- encourage self-regulation and codes of conduct for the industry to contribute effectively to restricting the flow of illegal and harmful content through cooperation between them and the other parties concerned. The self-regulatory mechanism should provide a high level of protection and address questions of traceability.

Action 2: **Developing filtering and rating systems in order to make content easier to identify:** This can be done through a rating system which describes the content in accordance with a generally recognised scheme (for instance where items such as sex or violence are rated on a scale) and by filtering systems which empower the user to select the content he/she wishes to receive.

- demonstrating benefits of filtering and rating: validating rating systems, encouraging integration of rating into the content creation process and to demonstrate benefits of these technical solutions. Emphasis will be placed on usefulness and practicality in 'real-world' situations involving a large cross-section of typical users (such as business, institutional or educational users);

- facilitating international agreement on rating systems in order to ensure compatibility between operators and other concerned parties in the EU and their partners in other regions of the world.

Action 3: **Awareness actions:** To make parents, teachers and children aware of the potential of the Internet and its drawbacks and of the means available to protect children from undesirable content. Two stages:

- preparing the ground for awareness actions: the first phase identifies multiplier organisations and most appropriate channels, media and content to reach the target audience, prepare basic material, adapt it for linguistic and cultural specificity. The target audience are parents, teachers and the action will involve industry (Internet service providers, content providers) and multipliers, e.g. consumer associations, education organisations;

- encouraging implementation of full-scale awareness actions: initiatives which must contribute to make adults (parents and teachers) aware of the potential and the drawbacks of the Internet, and of the means to identify useful content and how to block harmful content.

Actions will be of two types:

- seminars, workshops, preparation and distribution of specific printed and multimedia material focused on teachers and educational institutions;
- special events, creation of web-sites, distribution of information material in schools, through access providers and through shops and other outlets selling computers, distribution of CD-ROMs in computer magazines, the media aimed at the general public (parents and children).

Support actions: such as assessment of legal implications, coordination with similar international initiatives (including an international conference), evaluation of the impact of EU measures, will be implemented after a call for tenders.

Information and applications Calls for proposals will be published regularly in the course of the programme.

European Commission
DG XIII.E.5 – Illegal and harmful content on the Internet
Mr Richard SWETENHAM, Head of Unit
Jean Monnet Building
Rue Alcide de Gaspieri, L-2920 Luxembourg
Tel: +352 4301 32400
Fax: +352 4301 38099
E-mail: iap@cec.be
Internet: http://www.echo.lu/iap
http://www2.echo.lu/legal/en/internet/internet.html

LABOUR MARKET INITIATIVES

B5-500	Projects for innovative approaches in the member states' labour markets	€12,000,000	£8,400,000
B5-501	Pilot projects on the third system	p.m.	
B5-502	Labour market	€8,550,000	£5,985,000

B5-500

Projects for innovative approaches in the member states' labour markets

Budget 99 €12,000,000 (£8,400,000)

Eligibility Check with the Commission.

Beneficial areas Support for the actions of member states in the field of employment and equal opportunities, developing a coordinated strategy for employment, promoting a skilled, trained and adaptable workforce.

Partners needed Yes.

Types of grant Support for innovative approaches, by pilot projects, evaluating experiences and disseminating results.

Example
In 1998, 9 projects were selected (sharing a total budget of €12,000,000). One of them was a 2-year demonstration project to enhance the transnational employability of young people at risk of exclusion. 425 young people aged 18–25 are carrying out transnational traineeships in companies. The project involves different types of partners, such as multinationals and small and medium-sized enterprises.

Information and applications No information was available at the time of writing. Contact for further information:

European Commission
DGV.A.4, Social Funds and Local Development
Mr David COYNE, Head of Unit
Mr Angelo BAGLIO, Desk Officer
27 Rue Joseph II, B-1040 Brussels
Tel: +32 2 295 5741 (Mr COYNE)

Tel: +32 2 295 7276 (Mr BAGLIO)
Fax: +32 2 299 9778
E-mail: angelo.baglio@bxl.dg5.cec.be

B5-501

Pilot projects on the third system

Budget 99 p.m.

Eligibility This action was launched in 1997 and there have been no new budget commitments since then. There might be a follow-up programme. Contact the Commission for further information and an update.

Beneficial areas Exploration and enhancement of the employment potential of the third system i.e. various non-profit organisations with an emphasis on social and neighbourhood services, the environment and the arts, and dissemination of the results throughout the EU.

Partners needed Yes.

Types of grant Innovative pilot projects at local level are supported.
Note: 'third system' refers to the economic and social fields represented by cooperatives, mutual companies, associations and foundations, along with all local job creation initiatives intended to respond, through the provision of goods and services, to needs for which neither the market nor the public sector currently appear able to make adequate provision.

This action was launched in 1997 and there have been no new budget commitments since then. There might be a follow-up programme. Contact the Commission for further information and an update.

Examples
Up to early 1999, 43 action research projects had been launched under this action, together with 9 research and communications projects.
– Empiric, Interarts Observatory of Urban and Regional Cultural Policies in Barcelona, Spain launched a 22-month project in December 1997: five cities in Europe (Palmela in Portugal, Tarragona in Spain, Olbernhau in Germany, Chorley in the UK, Marseilles in France) with cultural projects based on local initiatives collaborate in collecting, exchanging, evaluating and disseminating their experiences on employment and economic growth-oriented development in the Third Sector. The aim is to amplify employment possibilities in the regions and aid the economy by focusing on specific aspects of project design in which each project has an interest.
– Surrey Springboard, in partnership with Terre, Liege (Belgium) and the University of Portsmouth, UK, launched a project 'Promoting the Labour

Market Integration of Offenders with Particularly Significant Needs'. Surrey Springboard aims to demonstrate successful interventions for integration into the employment market. The experience of a number of UK and Belgian projects has shown that offenders experience particular difficulties in obtaining and retaining employment. Through action research, this project will further the currently limited knowledge in this specialist subject, focusing especially on offenders with particularly significant needs.

Information and applications

European Commission
DGV.A.4, Social Funds and Local Development
Mr Angelo BAGLIO, Desk Officer
27 Rue Joseph II, B-1040 Brussels
Tel: +32 2 295 7276
Fax: +32 2 299 9778
E-mail: angelo.baglio@bxl.dg5.cec.be
Internet: http://europa.eu.int/comm/dg05/empl&esf/3syst/index_en.htm

B5-502

Labour market

Budget 99 €8,550,000 (£5,985,000)

Eligibility Research institutes, organisations, universities, public services and authorities.

Beneficial areas Monitoring, research, studies, information about labour market trends and employment strategies and policies in the EU.

Partners needed No.

Types of grant Supported activities:
- establishment of a framework for regular cooperation between the member states and the Commission for multilateral surveillance of progress in reforming employment systems;
- monitoring of labour market trends, with statistics broken down according to gender, and review of member states' policies that have an impact on employment;
- experimental research projects to promote the exchange of experiences in the EU and the dissemination of good practice and skills in selected priority areas of employment policy;

- measures to ensure that the public as well as staff directly involved in job creation schemes, including self-help associations, are better informed about labour market trends and employment policies, including those at international level;
- exchanges and dissemination of information and best practice about employment policies;
- comparative analysis of and guidance to member states' employment policies.

Information and applications

European Commission
DGV.A.1, Employment policy
Mrs Ruth PASERMAN, Desk Officer
27 Rue Joseph II, B-1040 Brussels
Tel: +32 2 299 3638
Fax: +32 2 299 4571

SMALL AND MEDIUM-SIZED ENTERPRISES

B5-510	Technological facility for small and medium-sized enterprises	€118,000,000	£82,600,000
B5-511	European joint ventures	€32,000,000	£22,400,000
B5-512	Stimulation of small and medium-sized enterprises	€38,730,000	£27,111,000

The Commission defines small and medium-sized enterprises (SMEs) as those which have fewer than 250 employees; have either an annual turnover not exceeding €40 million or an annual balance sheet total not exceeding €27 million; and which respect the criteria of independence.

Enterprises of the social economy sector are eligible for funding and loans as small and medium-sized enterprises.

DG XXIII (enterprise policy, distributive trades, tourism, and cooperatives) compiled an *Information package on access to finance* for SMEs. In addition to the budget lines described here, it provides information on opportunities from the European Investment Fund (EIF) and the European Investment Bank (EIB).

European Commission
DG XXIII.B.3, Access to finance
Mr Rudy AERNOUDT
1 Rue de Genève, B-1140 Bruxelles
Tel: +32 2 295 9186
Fax: +32 2 295 2154
E-mail: rudy.aernoudt@dg23.cec.be

You may find it useful to contact INAISE, the International Association of Investors in the Social Economy, an umbrella organisation of banks investing in the social economy, which can tell you about members near you:

INAISE
40 Rue d'Arlon, B-1000 Brussels
Tel: +32 2 234 5797
Fax: +32 2 234 5798
E-mail: inaise@inaise.org
Internet: http://www.inaise.org

Note See also *Research and Technological Development*, and in particular B6-6311, Promotion of innovation and encouragement of participation of SMEs, p 214.

B5-510

Technological facility for small and medium-sized enterprises

Budget 99 €118,000,000 (£82,600,000)

Eligibility
- European Technological Facility (ETF) start-up: commercially-orientated funds, able to demonstrate the necessary capability and credibility to manage venture capital funds: at least €10,000,000 available for investments, 50% of the fund's capital from private sources.
- For the SME guarantee facility: primarily existing guarantee schemes operating in member states within the public and/or private sector including mutual guarantee schemes specialised in loan financing that the banking system would not provide without guarantee cover. For countries where no guarantee schemes exist, the EIF may choose financial intermediaries, including (exceptionally) the EIB, to guarantee directly portfolios of eligible loans.

Beneficial areas Venture capital and loan guarantees for SMEs (including the social economy, neighbourhood services) investing in new technologies.

Partners needed No.

Types of grant This budget line provides funding for:
- ETF start-up: This programme has an indicative budget of €170,000,000–190,000,000 for the 3 years 1998–2000. The Commission provides risk capital participation in young SMEs through investments in specialised venture capital funds. The funds supported undertake to invest in SMEs with growth potential, which have been recently set up, are in their early stages or are innovative. Priority will be given to SMEs with up to 100 employees. In principle the Commission takes a minority position of 10–25% of the total capital of the venture capital fund with a maximum of €10,000,000. The fund has to operate in the EU.
- SME guarantee facility: This programme has an indicative budget of €150,000,000-190,000,000 for the 4 years 1997-2000. The facility is managed by the EIF on behalf of the European Commission. The facility supports existing European guarantee schemes undertaking to provide loans to small enterprises (no more than 100 employees) in member states. The Commission supports guarantee schemes in covering the costs of guarantees for additional loans provided to small enterprises. The loan guarantee companies undertake to ensure that the risk covered by the facility will be additional to the risk that they would have underwritten under normal circumstances.

Information and applications

European Commission
DG XXIII.B.3 – Access to finance
Mr Rudy AERNOUDT
1 Rue de Genève, B-1140 Bruxelles
Tel: +32-2 295 9186
Fax: +32-2 295 2154
E-mail: rudy.aernoudt@dg23.cec.be

ETF Start up:

European Investment Fund
Mr Roger PETT
43 Avenue J.F. Kennedy
L-2968 Luxembourg
Tel: +352 426 6881
Fax: +352 426 688300
E-mail: info@eif.org

European Commission, DGII.A.1
Mr Giorgio CHIARION CASONI
Rue Alcide de Gasperi
Bâtiment Wagner (WAG A2/270)
L-2920 Luxembourg
Tel: +352 4301 36404
Fax: + 352 4301 36439
E-mail: giorgio.chiarion-casoni@sof.dg2.cec.be
Internet: http://www.cordis.lu/finance/src/schemes.htm

SME guarantee facility:

European Investment Fund
Mr Gerassimos THOMAS
43 Avenue J.F. Kennedy
L-2968 Luxembourg
Tel: +352 426 6881
Fax: +352 426 688300
E-mail: info@eif.org
Internet: http://eudor.eur-op.eu.int/

B5-511

European joint ventures

Budget 99 €32,000,000 (£22,400,000)

Eligibility
- small and medium-sized enterprises;
- for promotional actions: SME organisations of all types (i.e. national and regional associations of SMEs, chambers of commerce, Euro Info Centres, business and innovation centres).

Beneficial areas
- creation of transnational joint ventures for SMEs in the EU and support to enable them to benefit from the opportunities of the single market. See note below for joint ventures with partners outside the EU;
- promotion and information on business cooperation and the creation of transnational joint ventures.

Partners needed For the creation of joint ventures, there must be at least 2 SMEs from 2 different member states.

For promotional actions, partners are not necessary.

Types of grant This programme has a indicative budget of €105,000,000 for the 4-year period 1997–2000.

- Creation of European joint ventures: creating new economic activities, involving investment and employment creation within the EU, in any form of partnership between at least 2 SMEs or entrepreneurs, in the field of industry, services, trade or craft, from 2 different member states. No partner should own more than 75% of the shared capital of the joint venture.
  Eligible expenses: relating to the conception and setting-up of a joint venture; as part of the preparatory research, (market surveys, preparation of the legal framework, environmental impact assessment, technical standards, business plans, etc.) and for external and internal experts (for example travelling abroad). Grant maximum: €100,000 per project, covering up to 50% of the eligible expenses, or €50,000 plus, in a second phase, up to 10% of the total amount of the investment made.
  About 1,500 to 2,000 projects could be financed.
- Promotional action for the JEV programme. The Commission co-finances the development and distribution of promotional material, such as documentation material and/or the organisation of events to stimulate business cooperation and the creation of transnational joint ventures. SME organisations wishing to organise promotional actions have to introduce a proposal through one of the financial intermediaries.

Grant maximum: €10,000 for the development and distribution of promotional material and up to €20,000 for the organisation of events. The co-financing from the Commission will cover 50% of the expenses.

Information and applications A network of financial institutions specialised in investment finance (commercial banks, investment banks, venture capital funds), and selected by the European Commission, acts as intermediary between SMEs and the EU (see list on europa.eu.int/en/comm/dg23/guide-en/jev.pdf or ask the JEV Information Unit in Luxembourg for a copy).

European Commission
DG XXIII.C.2, Access to finance
Mr Rudy AERNOUDT, Desk Officer
1 Rue de Genève, B-1140 Brussels
Tel: +32 2 295 9186
Fax: +32 2 295 2154
E-mail: rudy.aernoudt@dg23.cec.be

European Commission, DG II.B.2
Mr Rainer RASS (contracts and payment)
Rue Alcide de Gasperi
Bâtiment Wagner (WAG A2/230)
L-2920 Luxembourg
Tel: +352 4301 36370
Fax: +352 4301 36439
E-mail: rainer.rass@sof.dg2.cec.be

JEV Information Unit
6 rue Jean Monet
L-2180 Luxembourg
Fax: +352 46 70 97
Internet: http://europa.eu.int/comm/dg23/guide_en/jev.htm

Note Two programmes support the setting up of joint ventures outside Europe:
- JOP (Joint Venture Phare Programme) supports SMEs from the EU intending to set up a joint venture in the central and eastern European countries (CEECs) and the New Independent States (NIS) and Mongolia;
- ECIP (European Community Investment Partners) supports SMEs from the EU intending to set up a joint venture in the ALAMEDSA countries (Asia, Latin America, Mediterranean countries, Republic of South Africa);
- the Commission finances preliminary information research, preliminary contacts and feasibility studies. In the case of JOP, grants related to success are available in CEECs following the implementation of joint venture projects. In the NIS and Mongolia, equity participation or guarantees are available. ECIP provides equity loans and equity participation up to 20% of the joint venture's capital.

Contacts:

JOP:

European Commission
DGII – Financial operations service
Section 2 – Financial engineering
Mr Rainer RASS, Deputy Head of Unit
Rue Alcide de Gasperi, Bâtiment Wagner
L-2920 Luxembourg
Tel: +352 4301 36370
Fax: +352 4301 36439
E-mail: rainer.rass@SOF.dg2.cec.be

ECIP:

European Commission
DGIB.0.3 –Trade, generalised tariff preferences and investments
MrTom ROE, Desk Officer
6 Boulevard Charlemagne
B-1040 Brussels
Tel: +32 2 299 0926
Fax: +32 2 299 1034
E-mail: andrew-thomas.roe@dg1b.cec.be

B5-512

Stimulation of small and medium-sized enterprises

Budget 99 €38,730,000 (£27,111,000)

Eligibility
+ for CREA (Capital-Risque pour les Entreprises en phase d'Amorçage): seed capital funds (created after 1 October 1997), with at least €4,000,000 available for investments in small enterprises and a maximum of 50% of the capital being of public-sector origin. Applicants must be from a member state of the European Economic Area (EEA). The services may be provided in the EEA and in the 11 applicant countries;
+ for business angel networks (business angels are former entrepreneurs, who – having sold their own companies – want to invest in new companies and assist them with their experienced advice): participants interested in doing feasibility studies on the creation of a business angels network or interested in creating a network itself must have proven experience in the area of financing young SMEs and in the general risk evaluation of young SMEs;

♦ for mutual guarantee schemes: applicants from member states of the EEA, who are experienced in SME financing and risk assessment. Services may be provided in the EEA and in the 11 applicant countries.

Beneficial areas
♦ CREA: creation of an EU-wide network for seed capital funds and promotion of the exchange of best practice and training to facilitate access for small enterprises to seed capital, in order to finance their creation or their transfer;
♦ setting up business angel networks in Europe;
♦ creation of mutual guarantee companies.

Partners needed No.

Types of grant This budget provides funding to implement the third multi-annual programme for SMEs, for which €127,000,000 are available (1997–2000). The aims are to:
♦ simplify and improve the administrative and regulatory business environment;
♦ improve the financial environment for enterprises (see Action 1 below);
♦ help SMEs to Europeanise and internationalise their strategies, in particular through better information services (in particular 'promote access by SMEs to the information society');
♦ enhance SME competitiveness and improve their access to research, innovation and training;
♦ promote entrepreneurship and support special target groups.

There are 3 different types of actions:

Action 1: CREA with a budget of €8,000,000 (£5,600,000) for 3 years (1998–2000).

The action facilitates the access of small enterprises to seed capital in order to finance their creation or their transfer. A predecessor of CREA was the Seed Capital action, where the Commission invested in 23 funds (see addresses in the UK below). Between 1989 and 1996, the 23 funds raised €52,000,000 in capital, of which €35,400,000 has been invested in 285 new enterprises, generating 2,876 direct jobs. CREA will pursue the following 2 activities:
♦ stimulate the supply of equity finance for the creation and transfer of innovative smaller businesses (fewer than 50 employees) with growth and job-creating potential by supporting seed capital funds or similar organisations;
♦ create an EU-wide network for seed capital funds and promote the exchange of best practice and training.
The Commission will support the seed capital funds by helping them to cover their operating costs in their start-up phase.
Grant maximum: up to 50% of the operating costs, to a maximum of €500,000 over 3 years.

Seed capital investments should stay in the investee company for a period of 5 years or more. If a fund should wish to withdraw from the investment sooner, the Commission should receive 10% of the capital gain for each early exit.

Action 2: Business angel networks are a forum where SMEs and business angels can make contact. They will give SMEs access to a new source of finance other than bank financing and formal risk capital.

Grant maximum: up to 50% of the costs of feasibility studies for the creation of business angels networks, as well as a maximum of 50% of the costs of pilot actions to set up a regional or national network. Feasibility studies of up to 1 year are financed, pilot actions of up to 3 years.

Seminars are also organised to disseminate the idea of business angel networks in Europe, especially dealing with the question of how to set up such networks.

Action 3: Mutual guarantee schemes. The Commission will finance feasibility studies on the creation of mutual guarantee companies and the establishment of mutual guarantee companies itself.

Grant maximum: 50% of the feasibility studies over a maximum peric 1 of 1 year and 50% of the running cost for the creation of mutual guarantee companies over a maximum period of 3 years.

Application deadline: 30 September 1999 at the latest.

Example

A call for proposals in 1998 (OJ C63, 20.8.98, with an open deadline until 30 June 2000) covers services for SMEs in areas such as: transnational partnership between structures and programmes for initial and continued training for cooperatives; access of independents to training; training and counselling for start-ups by young people. Eligible applicants are professional associations or other entities with appropriate knowledge of training, seminars, publications and counselling to SMEs. The Commission will fund up to 50% of total project costs.

Information and applications Calls for proposals are published in the Official Journal. Further information is available from the Commission and on the web-site.

European Commission
DG XXIII.C.2, Access to Finance
Mr Rudy AERNOUDT, Desk Officer
80 Rue d'Arlon, B-1040 Brussels
Tel: +32 2 295 9186
Fax: +32 2 295 2154
E-mail: rudy.aernoudt@dg23.cec.be
Internet: http://europa.eu.int/comm/dg23/guide_en/index2.htm

CREA:

Apply through the funds. Further information can be also be obtained through the European Commission or the European Venture Capital Association.

Internet: http://europa.eu.int/en/comm/dg23/guide_en/seedcap.htm

EVCA (The European Venture Capital Association)
Keibergpark, Minervastraat 6, Box 6
Zaventem, Belgium
Fax: +32 2 725 3036

Innovation Equity Limited
NIIP
Mr John STRINGER
Chamber of Commerce House
22 Great Victoria Street, Belfast BT2 7BJ
Tel: +44 1 232 241 619
Fax: +44 1 232 439 899

Korda Associates
Alex KORDA
The Outer Temple, 222 The Strand
London WC2R 1DE
Tel: +44 171 583 3377
Fax: +44 171 353 6320

Scottish Enterprise
Tayside
Mr John GARDNER
Enterprise House, 45 North Lindsay Street
Dundee DD1 1HT
Tel: +44 1 382 223 100
Fax: +44 1 382 201 319

TRANSPORT AND TELECOMMUNICATIONS

B5-700	Projects of common interest in the trans-European transport networks	€499,500,000	£349,650,000
B5-720	Trans-European telecommunications networks	€21,800,000	£15,260,000

B5-700

Projects of common interest in the trans-European transport network

Budget 99 €499,500,000 (£349,650,000)

Eligibility Organisations, companies, and so on in the member states.

Beneficial areas Interconnection and interoperability of national networks, access to these networks, taking into account the need to link island, landlocked and peripheral regions of the EU with its central regions.

Partners needed Not necessary, but projects must have a significant European dimension.

Types of grant The Commission provides funding for projects meeting objectives such as:
- promoting safety, consumer and environmental protection;
- expanding the Commission's knowledge and collating data in all transport sectors;
- promoting intermodal transport and logistics;
- preparing and defining appropriate policies for the revision of guidelines on trans-European networks;
- promoting improvements in local and regional passenger transport;
- promoting transport systems and legislation for people with restricted mobility;
- training users and policy makers in and outside Europe;
- promoting long distance cycle routes in Europe.

Projects can consist of:
- the collection and dissemination of information and good practice;
- measures aimed at avoiding accidents or mitigating their effects;
- improving the safety of infrastructures;
- the organisation by professional bodies (including consumer associations) and intergovernmental organisations of actions concerning the operation of the transport market, safety, working conditions and environmental protection;

- ◆ cooperation with international organisations working in the field of transport;
- ◆ training;
- ◆ examination and assessment of existing or proposed measures;
- ◆ information and publicity campaigns;
- ◆ pilot and demonstration projects;
- ◆ setting up networks.

Grant maximum: 10–50 % of total expenditure, depending on the specific merits of the project, in particular its value at EU level.

Information and applications Under the current call for proposals, proposals can be submitted at any time in 1999. The action programme in the field of transport continues thereafter and it is likely that there will be a similar call for proposals for 2000. Ask the Commission for further information.

European Commission
DGVII.1, Transport, Resources and Financial management.
Mr Dirk BECKERS, Head of Unit
Ms Silvia HAUPT, Desk Officer
33 Avenue de Beaulieu, B-1160 Brussels
Tel: +32 2 295 4261 / 296 8278 (Mr BECKERS)
Tel: +32 2 299 5929 (Ms HAUPT)
Fax: +32 2 296 8357
E-mail: subv@dg7.cec.be
Internet: http://europa.eu.int/en/comm/dg07/index.htm
http://europa.eu.int/en/comm/dg07/call_for_proposals.htm

B5-720

Trans-European telecommunications networks

Budget 99 €21,800,000 (£15,260,000)

Eligibility NGOs are eligible to apply as part of a consortium. The programme is open to both private and public organisations whose proposals fall within the list of eligible areas of activities.

Beneficial areas Development of trans-European networks in the telecommunications sector (TEN-Telecom).

Partners needed Yes: proposals should involve several member states, unless an activity in a single member state is of broader interest on the European level.

Types of grant TEN-Telecom focuses on 3 elements of the telecommunication networks:

- economically viable, demand-driven applications which match the socio-economic needs of the citizen and SMEs in the areas of healthcare (telemedecine), distance education and training, access to Europe's cultural heritage, services for SMEs, transport and mobility, environment and emergency management, city and regional information highways, and teleworking;
- the support of Internet-based generic services for SMEs;
- easy access to telecommunication networks, the development of broadband networks (mainly based on fixed, mobile and satellite technology) and the interoperability of all components of the global information infrastructure.

Proposals submitted to the annual calls must have successfully achieved their RTD phases, have a business case and a well defined financial commitment from public or private partners, and be ready to pursue short-term developments under real market condition.

TEN-Telecom aims to help by reducing the financial risk due to uncertainties about the short-term commercial viability of innovative telecommunication applications and services. TEN-Telecom will contribute to initial investment costs of a deployment through subsidies of the interest on loans, contributions towards fees for guarantees on loans or direct grants in justified cases. TEN-Telecom also funds studies into the commercial feasibility and validation of a proposal.

Contribution maximum: total contribution not more than 10% of the total investment cost; for feasibility studies and validation measures the financial contribution may be up to 50%.

Example

'Then': a technical-economical feasibility study of a global tele-healthcare network, based on an integrated communication satellite-terrestrial network. A tele-health centre as service provider and a network control centre are relayed to local centres in several countries. The tele-medicine application is the first social service to be operational, for possible extension to other application sectors such as tele-education.

Information and applications Calls for proposals are published in the Official Journal. The Commission also organises information days. The web-site includes a lot of up-to-date details.

European Commission
DGXIII.G.3, Transeuropean telecommunications networks
Mr Yvan CAPOUET, Head of Unit
Ten Telecom secretariat
29 Avenue de Beaulieu, B-1160 Brussels
Tel: +32 2 296 8995
Fax: +32 2 296 1740
E-mail: ten@dg13.cec.be
Internet: http://www2.echo.lu/tentelecom

JUSTICE AND HOME AFFAIRS

B5-800	Cooperation in the fields of justice and home affairs	€12,000,000	£8,400,000
B5-803	European refugee fund	€15,000,000	£10,000,000

B5-800

Cooperation in the fields of justice and home affairs

Budget 99 €12,000,000 (£8,400,000)

Eligibility Mostly government agencies, research institutes, also civil society organisations with thorough expertise.

Beneficial areas Legal practice (Grotius programme), trade in human beings and sexual exploitation of children (Stop), law enforcement (Oisin), asylum and immigration (Odysseus), combating crime (Falcone).

Partners needed At least 2 member states must be involved, preferably also from applicant countries.

Types of grant The Commission co-finances projects in the programmes mentioned above. Annual working programmes, with considerable variation in topics and activities, are published early in the calendar year in the Official Journal and can be obtained from the Commission. Stop and Odysseus in particular are relevant to the non-profit sector.

Information and applications The Commission publishes one joint call for proposals annually, with a deadline of 31 March for 1999. As representatives of the member states have the final say in the allocation of grants, assuring involvement or support from national authorities is recommended

European Commission, Secretariat General, Task Force for Justice and Home Affairs
Mr Adrian FORTESCUE, Deputy Director-General
9 Avenue des Nerviens, B-1040 Brussels
Tel: +32 2 295 5727 / 295 7531
Fax. +32 2 296 7481
E-mail: adrian.fortescue@sg.cec.be
Internet : http://europa.eu.int/comm/sg/tfjai/prog_en.htm

Note Another relevant programme is Daphne: Measures for combating violence against children, adolescents and women, B3-4109, p 142.

B5-803

European refugee fund

Budget 99 €15,000,000 (£10,000,000)

Eligibility Depends on potential involvement in fields of activities.

Beneficial areas Reception of refugees and displaced persons and voluntary repatriation of persons who found temporary protection in EU member states, including achieving an equitable balance of responsibility between member states.

Partners needed Ask the Commission.

Types of grant EU support may be given for activities regarding:
+ initial reception after a sudden influx;
+ improving the reception infrastructure of member states;
+ access to asylum procedures;
+ assuring a minimum standard of living conditions;
+ special assistance for vulnerable groups;
+ raising public awareness about the situation of refugees and EU policies;
+ voluntary repatriation and reintegration in the countries of origin (including counselling and vocational training).

Ask the Commission about implementation and the possibility of NGO involvement in the above fields.

Information and applications

European Commission
Secretariat General, Task Force for Justice and Home Affairs
Mr Adrian FORTESCUE, Deputy Director-General
9 Avenue des Nerviens, B-1040 Brussels
Tel : +32 2 299 5063 (for this budget line)
Fax. +32 2 296 7481
E-mail : adrian.fortescue@sg.cec.be
Internet : http://europa.eu.int/comm/sg/tfjai/prog_en.htm

RESEARCH AND TECHNOLOGICAL DEVELOPMENT

B6-6111	Quality of life and management of living resources	€553,000,000	£387,100,000
B6-6121	User-friendly information society	€857,000,000	£599,900,000
B6-6131	Competitive and sustainable growth	€646,000,000	£452,200,000
B6-6141	Preserving the ecosystem – Environment and sustainable development	€223,000,000	£156,100,000
B6-6142	Preserving the ecosystem – Energy	€223,000,000	£156,100,000
B6-6211	Confirming the international role of Community research	€78,000,000	£54,600,000
B6-6311	Promotion of innovation and encouragement of participation of SMEs	€78,000,000	£54,600,000
B6-6411	Improving the human research potential and the socio-economic knowledge base	€293,000,000	£205,100,000

The Fifth RTD Framework Programme

Research and technological development activities (RTD) are supported by the European Union (EU) through a broad multi-annual programme which is now in its fifth (revised and hopefully simplified) edition. The Fifth RTD Framework Programme (FP5) runs 1999–2002. For this 3-year period, FP5 has a total budget of €13,700,000,000.

FP5 differs considerably from its predecessors. It has been conceived to help solve problems and to respond to major socio-economic challenges facing Europe. To maximise its impact, it focuses on a limited number of research areas combining technological, industrial, economic, social and cultural aspects. Management procedures will be streamlined with an emphasis on simplifying procedures and systematically involving key players in research.

There are a number of specific programmes under this framework, which have common criteria (reflecting concern for increasing industrial competitiveness and the quality of life of European citizens) and harmonised management rules. FP5 should contribute to bringing together specialists from very different scientific fields, with industrial researchers, users, and political and economic decision makers. FP5 is based on 23 key actions implemented within each of the 4 thematic programmes (tackling specific areas of research) and the 3 horizontal programmes (activities involving all areas).

Thematic programmes: These are:
- Quality of life and management of living resources (B6-6111)
- User-friendly information society (B6-6121)

- Competitive and sustainable growth (B6-6131)
- Preserving the ecosystem: Environment and sustainable development (B6-6141); Energy (B6-6142)

Horizontal programmes: These are:
- Confirming the international role of Community research (B6-6211)
- Promotion of innovation and encouragement of participation of small and medium-sized enterprises (SMEs (B6-6311)
- Improving the human research potential and the socio-economic knowledge base (B6-6411)

Key actions: These cover the wide range of scientific and technological disciplines – both fundamental and applied – required to address a specific problem so as to overcome any barriers between disciplines or between the programmes and the organisations concerned.

These 23 key actions represent 70% of the budget. The remaining 30% are for basic research, i.e. research on basic knowledge or technologies in rapidly emerging sectors with a high potential for the future, and for research infrastructures.

General rules and information

Some selection criteria, application procedures and other characteristics are common to all the programmes described in this chapter. Each particular programme may have its own additional criteria.

Total Budget 1999–2003 €13,700,000,000 (£9,590,000,000)

Eligibility Legal entities established in the member states of the EU or the countries associated with the programme, e.g. individuals, industrial and commercial firms, universities, research organisations, including SMEs. The associated states include: the candidates for EU membership – Bulgaria, Cyprus, Czech Republic, Estonia, Hungary, Latvia, Lithuania, Malta, Poland, Romania, the Slovak Republic and Slovenia; EEA countries – Iceland, Liechtenstein, Norway; as well as Israel and Switzerland.

International cooperation in RTD will be pursued under FP5 through 2 complementary routes:
- a dedicated cooperation programme 'Confirming the international role of Community research' (see B6-6211), which will focus on specific RTD activities relevant to certain third countries or regions and not addressed by the other programmes of FP5;
- a dimension of international cooperation is integrated into each of the other specific programmes, which will allow the European research community to benefit from the knowledge and expertise of third countries and institutions, through their participation in projects of FP5.

Beneficial areas See the descriptions under the specific programmes.

Partners needed Yes: there must be at least 2 legal entities from different member states or from 1 member state and 1 associated state. However, certain actions may vary from this general rule, either by requiring more participants or by permitting a single one. A partner search facility is available on the FP5 web-site:

http://www.cordis.lu/fp5/src/eoi.htm

Types of grant Each of the specific programmes provides funding for:

The selection from the 23 key actions which are associated with it

RTD activities of a generic nature: In contrast to the mission-oriented and problem-solving key actions, which place the emphasis on the linkage between discovery and exploitation, RTD activities of a generic nature aim to build up the knowledge base in chosen areas of strategic importance, and to explore related ethical and socio-economic issues. Interaction between research laboratories and industry will be promoted. The networking of projects involving core centres and associated laboratories will be encouraged in order to create a critical mass, to promote interactions between basic and applied research and to ensure maximum transfer of knowledge to and from industry and undertakings.

Support for research infrastructures: The term 'research infrastructures' refers to facilities and establishments that provide essential services to the research community. It covers, for example, singular large-scale research installations, collections, special habitats, libraries, data-bases, integrated arrays of small research installations, as well as infrastructural centres of competence which provide a service for the wider research community based on an assembly of techniques and knowledge.

The budget of each specific programme covers:
- indirect actions;
- shared-cost actions (initiated by the Commission);
- grants for training;
- thematic networks;
- accompanying measures (evaluation, dissemination of results);
- coordination of RDT actions and other EU initiatives (including Phare, p 247; Tacis, p 254, European Investment Fund, Structural Funds, p 51 and European Investment Bank).

Information and applications Deadlines vary from one programme to another and, within each programme, from one action to another. A full overview of deadlines is available in the general documentation and the calls for proposals on these programmes, which are available from the Commission, the national contacts or the Internet.

The following types of calls for proposals are envisaged:

Periodic calls: These will be open for the submission of proposals for RTD projects and related activities, within a defined scope and with fixed deadlines, to be specified in the Official Journal and outlined in the indicative timetable for programme implementation.

Open calls: Calls for SME specific measures (exploratory awards and cooperative research), support for research infrastructure (thematic networks, concerted actions and RTD projects), training, international initiatives and accompanying measures, will be launched at the start of the programme and will remain open until the last year of FP5. Periodic evaluations will be carried out at least twice a year.

Dedicated calls: These will be published in the Official Journal normally once or twice a year and will be limited to a number of very specific topics and/or activities. The Commission may also publish a request for interested parties (Expression of Interest /Needs) to suggest ideas for activities that could be included.

In most cases, applications can be submitted by e-mail. For practical information, contact the Commission or the national contact points given under the description of each specific programme. The Cordis Internet server is a very detailed and up-to-date source of information on the large and complicated 5FP activities, including funding possibilities.

To obtain general information on 5FP:

European Commission
DG XII, RTD actions: Framework programme
Unit AP4, Communication
Mr Otto VON SCHWERIN, Head of Unit
8 Square de Meêus, B-1050 Brussels
Tel: +32 2 295 2559
Fax: +32 2 295 8865
E-mail: info@dg12.cec.be
Internet: http://www.cordis.lu/fp5/home.html

B6-6111

Quality of life and management of living resources

Budget 99 €553,000,000 (£387,100,000)

Eligibility See General rules and information, p 203

Beneficial areas Key actions:
- food, nutrition and health;
- control of infectious diseases;
- the 'cell factory';
- environment and health;

- sustainable agriculture, fisheries and forestry, and integrated development of rural areas including mountain areas;
- the ageing population and disabilities.

Partners needed See General rules and information, p 203

Types of grant See General rules and information, p 203

I Key actions
Food, nutrition and health:
- development of safe and flexible manufacturing processes and technologies;
- detection and elimination of infectious and toxic agents throughout the food chain;
- gaining a more profound understanding of the role of food in promoting and sustaining health.

Control of infectious diseases:
- vaccine development;
- strategies to identify and control infectious diseases;
- aspects of public health and care delivery systems.

The 'cell factory':
- developing innovative health-related processes and products;
- energy-efficient bioremediation and waste biotreatment processes; and new biological processes from cell factories.

Environment and health:
- diseases and allergies related to or influenced by the environment;
- risk assessment and risk management processes to reduce causes and harmful environmental health effects.

Sustainable agriculture, fisheries and forestry, and integrated development of rural areas including mountain areas:
- competitiveness and its direct implications for employment in rural and coastal areas, especially in light of the need to adapt to the evolution of the common agricultural and fisheries policies, of world trade and globalisation of the markets, to EU enlargement and to the limited availability of natural resources;
- reducing the vulnerability of the relevant sectors through the diversification of production;
- response to societal demands for sound environmental practices, sustainable use of renewable resources and for products complying with consumer health and environmental requirements.

The ageing population and disabilities:
- age-related illnesses and health problems to prevent, treat or delay onset; determinants of healthy ageing and the mechanisms leading to disability;
- demographic and epidemiological research on ageing and disability trends;
- delaying the onset of disability and improving the social and physical environment of older people;
- delivery and financing of health and social care services to older people.

II Research and technological development activities of a generic nature
The generic research activities are:
- chronic and degenerative diseases, cancer, diabetes, cardiovascular diseases and rare diseases;
- research into genomes and diseases of genetic origin;
- neurosciences;
- research on public health and health services (including drug-related problems);
- research relating to people with disabilities;
- biomedical ethics and bioethics in the context of respect for fundamental human values;
- socio-economic aspects of life sciences and technologies.

III Support for research infrastructures
- creating thematic networks in the various fields of research as a means of stimulating infrastructure operators to cooperate and pool resources among themselves, as well as with users of the infrastructure;
- R&D, demonstration and combined projects on developments in the following fields: biological information resources; biological collections; pre-clinical research facilities; clinical research facilities; facilities for aquaculture and fishery research.

It should be noted that this action will not provide support for the construction and operation of research infrastructures, or for the collection of data. The latter activities will be addressed through an open call.

Examples
- the European Vaccine Against AIDS project;
- a project aimed at identifying the bacteria responsible for chronic gastritis;
- a UK-led collaboration to establish compatible registries of Creutzfeld-Jakob Disease (CJD) cases in 5 European countries, allowing monitoring of the frequency of CJD according to standardised diagnostic criteria which were crucial in providing a solid base for establishing the existence of a new variant of CJD.

Information and applications See General rules and information, p 203

Contact:

Life Info-Desk
Fax: +32 2 299 1860
E-mail: life@dg12.cec.be
Internet: http://www.cordis.lu/life/home.html

National contact point:

Dr David COATES
Office of Science and Technology
26-28 Old Queen Street, London SW1H 9HP
Tel: +44 171 271 2012
Fax: +44 171 271 2016
E-mail: david.coates@osct.dti.gov.uk

B6-6121

User-friendly information society

Budget 99 €857,000,000 (£599,900,000)

Eligibility See General rules and information, p 203

Beneficial areas The objective is to realise the benefits of the information society for Europe both by accelerating its emergence and by ensuring that the needs of individuals and enterprises are met.

Partners needed See General rules and information, p 203

Types of grant See General rules and information, p 203. The programme's objectives focus both on the developments in technology of the information society and enable the close articulation between research and policy needed for a coherent and inclusive information society.

I Key Actions
- systems and services for the citizen;
- new methods of work and electronic commerce;
- multimedia content and tools;
- essential technologies and infrastructures.

II Research and technological development activities of a generic nature

III Support for research infrastructures

Examples:
The following examples are quoted from the UK permanent representation guide of 1997, which described the former equivalent RTD programmes: advanced communications technologies and services (Acts), information technologies (Esprit), telematics applications (applied research). There are no examples under the current programme, which has just started.
– Telematics and transport: the Romanse project in Southampton benefits from the FP4 Euroscope Project, aimed at demonstrating advanced transport telematics in the areas of traveller information, logistics, network management and evaluation. Euroscope will validate systems in user application sites across Europe, to achieve sustainable mobility for individuals;
– Telematics – Education and Training Technology: the Trends project which partners UK contributors with other European countries, including Greece, Italy, Portugal, France, Denmark and Spain. Its objective is to support education by developing teacher training through: multimedia telematics; implementing distance learning and validating it through over 2,000 teachers; and establishing a European teachers' training network;
– Telematics – Healthcare: UK organisations are very well represented in this programme, which covers 7 main areas of work: multimedia patient records;

assisting the work of healthcare professionals; departmental systems and advanced imaging; integration platforms and regional networks; tele-diagnostics, tele-consultation and emergency tele-medicine; information for citizens; and in the cross-sectoral supporting actions;

– Information technology – Esprit: I-See is an intelligent help system used to explain complex software to the user, which has been developed using Esprit funding. When the *Sea Empress* ran aground off Milford Haven in February 1996, a package known as Oil Spill Information System (Osis) was used by the Coastguards' Marine Pollution Control Unit to predict where the oil would come ashore. The latest version of Osis, developed by British Maritime Technology, incorporated I-See, making it easier to use.

Information and applications

IST Information Desk
European Commission, DGIII, Industry
105 Avenue des Nerviens, B-1040 Brussels
Fax: +32-2-299 4572
E-mail: ist@dg3.cec.be
Internet: http://www.cordis.lu/ist/home.html

National contact point:

Ms Margaret DENNIS
Department of Trade and Industry, CII 3c
151 Buckingham Palace Road, London SW1W 9SS
Tel: +44 171 215 1355
Fax: +44 171 931 7194
E-mail: margaret.dennis@ciid.dti.gov.uk
Internet: http://www.isi.gov.uk/isi/

B6-6131

Competitive and sustainable growth

Budget 99 €646,000,000 (£452,200,000)

Eligibility See General rules and information, p 203

Beneficial areas Research activities contributing to competitiveness and sustainability, particularly where these 2 objectives interact. Industry's role will not only be to identify areas for collaboration but also to bring together and integrate projects, especially cross-sectoral projects along the value chain, so that technology uptake and innovation are more effectively ensured across Europe.

Partners needed See General rules and information, p 203

Types of grant See General rules and information, p 203

I Key actions
Innovative products, processes and organisation
Sustainable mobility and intermodality: The 3 main components of a modern integrated transport system:
- a regulatory and accountable framework reflecting socio-economic objectives;
- an interoperable infrastructure which allows the operation of attractive, environmentally friendly and efficient transport means;
- modal and intermodal systems for managing operations and providing services.

Land transport and marine technologies
New perspectives in aeronautics

II Research and technological development activities of a generic nature
- new materials and their production and transformation (including steel);
- measurements and testing.

III Support for research infrastructures
This action will stimulate infrastructure operators to cooperate and pool resources among themselves, as well as with users of the infrastructure. In addition it will help to provide a relevant networked environment in the fields covered by the programme.

Examples
The following examples are quoted from the UK permanent representation guide of 1997, which described the former equivalent RTD programmes: Brite/Euram for industrial and materials technologies and Standards, measurements and testing.
– Brite/Euram: the development of a new type of membrane which helps to reduce pollution in the textile industry by purifying effluent and recovering chemicals used in dyeing; a car engine which includes a number of plastic components which reduce noise levels and gas emissions; several projects researching high-temperature super-conducting materials;
– Standards, measurements and testing: research aimed at devising a measurement method to identify the toxins contained in seafood and to determine whether it is fit for consumption.

Information and applications See General rules and information, p 203

E-mail: growth@dg12.cec.be
Internet: http://www. cordis.lu/growth/home.html

National contact point:

Mr Trevor FRASER
Department of Trade and Industry, EID 4d
151 Buckingham Palace Road, London SW1W 9SS
Tel: +44 171 215 1454
Fax: +44 171 215 1461
E-mail: trevor.fraser@eam.dti.gov.uk

B6-6141 and B6-6142

Preserving the ecosystem – Environment and sustainable development; Energy

Budget 99 €446,000,000 (£312,200,000)

Eligibility See General rules and information, p 203

Beneficial areas

Environment and sustainable development: Promoting environmental science and technology so as to improve our quality of life and boost growth, competitiveness and employment, while meeting the need for sustainable management of resources and protection of the environment.

Energy: Developing sustainable energy systems and services for Europe and contributing to a more sustainable development world-wide, leading to increased security and diversity of supply, the provision of high-quality, low-cost energy services, improved industrial competitiveness and reduced environmental impact.

Partners needed See General rules and information, p 203

Types of grant See General rules and information, p 203

Environment and sustainable development
I Key actions:
- sustainable management and quality of water;
- global change, climate and biodiversity;
- sustainable marine ecosystems;
- the city of tomorrow and cultural heritage.

II Research and technological development activities of a generic nature:
- fight against major natural and technological hazards;
- development of generic earth observation satellite technologies;
- study of socio-economic aspects of development of environmental change within the perspective of sustainable development (impact on society, the economy and employment).

III Support for research infrastructures:
- climate and global change research;
- marine research;
- natural hazards research.

Energy
I Key actions:
- cleaner, including renewable energy systems;
- economic and efficient energy for a competitive Europe.

II Research and technological development activities of a generic nature:
- ◆ study of socio-economic aspects of energy within the perspective of sustainable development (impact on society, the economy and employment).

Information and applications See General rules and information, p 203

Environment:
Fax: +32 2 296 3624
E-mail: eesd@dg12.cec.be
Internet: http://www.cordis.lu/fp5/src/t-4.htm

Energy:
European Commission, Energy Info Desk
75 Rue Montoyer, B-1040 Brussels
Fax: +32 2 296 6882
E-mail: helpline-energy@dg12.cec.be
Internet: http://www.cordis.lu/fp5/src/t-4.htm

National contact points:

Environment and sustainable development:
Dr Arwyn DAVIES
DETR
Great Minster House 4/24
76 Marsham Street
London SW1 4DR
Tel: +44 171 890 5271
Fax: +44 171 676 2356

Energy:
Mr David IRVING
Department of Trade and Industry, ENT 3
1 Victoria Street, London SW1H 0ET
Tel: +44 171 215 2812
Fax: +44 171 828 7969
E-mail: david.irving@hend.dti.gov.uk

B6-6211

Confirming the international role of Community research

Budget 99 €78,000,000 (£54,600,000)

Eligibility See General rules and information, p 203

Beneficial areas
- cooperation with third countries: pre-accession states, the independent states of the former Soviet Union (NIS) and other central and eastern European countries (CEECs) not in the pre-accession phase, Mediterranean partners, developing countries, emerging economy countries and industrialised countries;
- training of researchers;
- coordination: within FP5 and with other EU programmes; with Cost, Eureka, international organisations; and member states.

Partners needed See General rules and information, p 203

Types of grant See General rules and information, p 203

International RTD cooperation will be pursued in FP5 through the specific programme under this budget line, but also as an aspect of the other programmes, and in close coordination with them.

The specific actions provided for in this programme are:
- to pursue strategically defined activities aimed at the EU candidate countries, other CEECs, the Baltic states, the NIS and Mongolia, the Mediterranean partner countries and developing countries. In order to exploit fully the opportunities for cooperation and optimise the added-value at European level, this programme will also facilitate cooperation with certain industrialised and emerging economy countries;
- to increase the opportunities for training of researchers;
- to ensure coordination with other programmes of the framework programme, with other EU initiatives and policies, in particular external policies, as well as with policies and programmes of member states, international organisations and cooperation schemes such as Cost and Eureka.

Information and applications See General rules and information, p 203

E-mail: inco@dg12.cec.be
Internet: http://www.cordis.lu/fp5/src/t-5.htm

National contact point:

Dr Peter LEE
Office of Science and Technology
26-28 Old Queen Street, London SW1H 9HP
Tel: +44 171 271 2099
Fax: +44 171 271 2143
E-mail: peter.lee@osct.dti.gov.uk

B6-6311

Promotion of innovation and encouragement of participation of SMEs

Budget 99 €78,000,000 (£54,600,000)

Eligibility SMEs which
+ have fewer than 250 employees;
+ either an annual turnover not exceeding €40,000,000, or an annual balance-sheet total not exceeding €27,000,000, and
+ conform to the criteria of independence;

and in addition:
+ are not a research centre, research institute, contract research organisation or consultant;
+ are registered and operating in 1 of the member states or in a state associated to FP5.

This might include SMEs with little research capability of their own or high tech SMEs.

Beneficial areas Improving the economic and social impact of research activities by ensuring the better dissemination of results, by encouraging the participation of SMEs, and by encouraging the transfer and dissemination of technologies from various sources, taking into account the needs of customers and users.

Partners needed See General rules and information, p 203

To facilitate SMEs in this critical step of finding partners in other countries, several facilities are provided:
+ the national contact points, which can also assist in the drafting of proposals;
+ SMEs interested in submitting a European R&D proposal can submit an expression of interest (EOI) form to indicate that they are looking for additional partners;

- most of the SMEs selected to receive an exploratory award are also looking for additional partners. To further assist them in this first step, the Commission will load on the EOI database all the selected exploratory awards;
- the EOI database is publicly accessible and free of charge (further information from your national contact point).

Types of grant See General rules and information, p 203

To optimise the economic impact of EU RTD, the programme lubricates the effective use of EU RTD results. In areas such as intellectual property rights and innovation finance, the programme will provide help services to FP5 participants and carry out pilot activities. Particular emphasis will be given to help with the setting-up and development of innovative firms.

The programme serves 3 main functions:
- as a service provider, the programme offers information services and assistance to SMEs, other firms and relevant players and supports the thematic programmes in their approach to innovation and SMEs;
- as a clearing house, the programme collects innovation data and analyses trends, initiatives and policies at EU and member states level. It offers platforms for transnational experience exchange and contributes to EU policy initiatives;
- as a test bed, the programme launches pilot actions in the areas of innovation and SME participation and aims at the continuous improvement of EU instruments.

There are 2 types of support:

Innovation projects: Complementing the RTD and demonstration projects under the thematic programmes, innovation projects promote the transfer of technologies not stemming from the thematic programmes. They are combined research and demonstration projects dealing in parallel with tangible cases of transnational technology transfer (EU support: 35% of total costs) and methodological research to produce new knowledge on economic, social and organisational aspects of innovation (EU support: 50% of total costs).

SME specific measures: To facilitate the participation of SMEs in the EU RTD actions, the European Commission has set up SME specific measures. These consist of:
- getting information;
- preparing a project proposal with exploratory awards: grants allowing at least 2 SMEs from different countries with a common project idea to prepare a complete research proposal;
- finding partners (see above, under Partners needed);
- setting up a cooperative research (Craft) project (at least 3 partners): these enable transnational groups of SMEs with a common problem, but with limited or no in-house RTD capability, to sub-contract the research they need to a specialist (called an RTD performer). The Commission supports up to half the cost, and while the RTD performer is paid in full for its work, the results belong to the SMEs.

Information and applications Information concerning the SME specific measures can also be obtained from the SME helpdesk of the SME and innovation unit of the European Commission.

European Commission, DG XII, SME Help-desk
Tel: +32 2 295 7175
Fax: +32 2 295 7110
E-mail: sme@dg12.cec.be
Website: http://www.cordis.lu/sme/home.html

National contact point:

Mr David MOORE
Office of Science and Technology
26–28 Old Queen Street, London SW1H 9HP
Tel: 44 171 271 6518
Fax: 44 171 271 6523
E-mail: david.moore@osct.dti.gov.uk

Craft:

Mr Bob KEOWN
Beta Technology Ltd
Riverside House, Weedon Street
Sheffield S9 2FT
Tel: +44 114 242 2004
Fax: +44 114 256 0950
E-mail: bob@betatechnology.co.uk

B6-6411

Improving the human research potential and the socio-economic knowledge base

Budget 99 €293,000,000 (£205,100,000)

Eligibility See General rules and information, p 203

Beneficial areas
◆ improve and help to develop the knowledge potential of European researchers, engineers and technicians through greater support for the training and mobility of researchers and by enhancing access to infrastructures;

♦ mobilising and strengthening the socio-economic knowledge base to identify economic and social trends and requirements, both current and future, in order to contribute to the EU's competitiveness and the quality of life of its citizens.

Partners needed See General rules and information, p 203

Types of grant See General rules and information, p 203

I Improving human research potential
Supporting training and mobility of researchers: By research training networks and a coherent system of Marie Curie Fellowships. They will be open to all fields of scientific research that contribute to the EU objectives in research, technological development and demonstration, for projects chosen freely by the participants themselves:

♦ Research training networks: EU support for reinforcing the research teams of a network through the temporary appointment of young researchers coming from a country other that of the team concerned and contributing to the costs of coordinating the collaborative research project on which the network is based.

Each network will be required to define an appropriate training programme for its young researchers. This will benefit from the international nature of the network and, when relevant, the multidisciplinarity of its joint project, the complementarity of its teams and the network's connections with industry.

♦ Marie Curie fellowships: individual fellowships for young high-quality researchers with the necessary research experience, awarded for topics chosen by the researchers themselves.

The researchers participating are of 3 categories: postgraduates; young researchers with the necessary research experience; experienced researchers.

There are 5 different types of schemes:

♦ Marie Curie individual fellowships: advanced training through research. The research institutions will host young researchers with the necessary research experience;

♦ Marie Curie industry host fellowships: opportunities for young researchers to carry out research in industrial or commercial environments, including SMEs;

♦ Marie Curie development host fellowships: research institutions established in less-favoured regions with a need to develop new areas of competence will host young researchers;

♦ Marie Curie experienced researchers fellowships: the experienced researcher will come from an industrial or commercial enterprise and go to a university or research centre, or vice versa; or will come from or go to a research institution in a less-favoured region;

♦ stays at Marie Curie training sites: the scheme will provide young researchers pursuing their doctoral studies with the opportunity to undertake part of them at a Marie Curie training site.

Enhancing access to research infrastructures: This will be implemented primarily through the following actions:

- transnational access to major research infrastructures: EU support to selected infrastructure operators to provide free access to their facilities by transnational users;
- infrastructure cooperation networks: EU support to help coordinate joint activities that could lead to the more effective use and exploitation of present and future infrastructures relevant to the network. Participants in these networks will be operators of research infrastructures, research teams in universities, in research centres and in industry, representatives of users of the infrastructures, and equipment manufacturers.
- research infrastructure RTD projects: supporting cooperative research efforts that could have widespread significance at an EU level for enhancing access to and improving the service provided by infrastructures in a particular field. Such RTD projects will be particularly encouraged when they are in support of the work of the infrastructure cooperation networks of this programme or of the earlier training and mobility of researchers programme.

Promoting scientific and technological excellence:

- high-level scientific conferences: scientific conferences may be organised as Euro-conferences, courses, workshops or summer schools. They will, as a general rule, be small-scale events. Bigger events may be supported with the objective of facilitating the participation of young researchers. Non-traditional forms of scientific conferencing such as electronic conferences will be encouraged. Scientific conferences will be open to all fields of scientific research on topics freely chosen by the researchers themselves;
- distinctions for high-level research work: the Descartes Prize for outstanding scientific and technological achievements resulting from European collaborative research; an award to undergraduate students of higher education institutions in Europe who developed original scientific ideas or concepts in areas which are relevant to the advancement of European science; the EU Contest for Young Scientists, for scientific talents between 15 and 20 years old, to be organised in conjunction with the appropriate public awareness activities;
- raising public awareness: promoting European networking and the exchange of best practice between successful projects and initiatives at national or regional level; to arrange for regular encounters between scientists and science communicators; to promote the participation of women in science; to support the organisation of a European science and technology week as a showcase for the concerted and coordinated display of European efforts in science and research; to provide via electronic networks and other appropriate means information on topical scientific and technological subjects in a language that is understandable to the scientifically interested but non-specialist citizen.

II Improving the socio-economic knowledge base

RTD projects and thematic networks which can address one or more of the specified themes: social and economic challenges of changing family structures; changes in work and their effects on quality of life; challenges to European welfare systems; emerging concepts of work; the implications of societal changes for education and training; the relationship of the financial sector to the rest of the economy and society; the dynamics of knowledge in the economy; internationalisation, technology and employment in different geographical environments; the relationships between employment and economic growth; European integration and European identity; European construction and multilevel governance; governance and media.

III Support for the development of scientific and technology policies in Europe
Strategic analysis of specific political issues: This activity involves the provision of support for the analytical and collating work on a limited number of specific issues relating to scientific and technology policy. This work will be carried out by groups of experts from specialised national and international organisations and will include studies, seminars and conferences.

Common basis of science, technology and innovation indicators: Coordinating and funding the work needed in order to compile appropriate statistics and new indicators covering the EU and the main third countries.

Grant maximum: €1,500,000 for RTD projects of 1 to 3 years, and €20,000 per partner and per year for thematic networks. Proposals for RTD projects can also include an application for a bursary.

Information and applications Calls for proposals are published in the Official Journal twice a year (in 1999: March and November), with a deadline about 3 months after publication. A *Guide for Proposers* and the work programme are available from:

European Commission
DG XII-F-4, Socio Economic Knowledge base
Ms Marie-Grace VENTURA
Human Potential – Information Officer
Fax: +32 2 296 3270
E-mail: improving@dg12.cec.be
Internet: http://www.cordis.lu/improving

National contact point:

Mr Paul WRIGHT
Office of Science and Technology
26-28 Old Queen Street, London SW1H 9HP
Tel: +44 171 271 2113
Fax: +44 171 271 2016
E-mail: international.ost.ah@gtnet.gov.uk

THE EU IN THE WORLD:
EXTERNAL MEASURES

Introduction

Under the very general heading of External Measures, the European Union (EU) budget lists a great variety of budget lines, which exclusively or primarily deal with relations between the EU and other countries in a number of policy fields, as the titles above clearly indicate. These budget lines include traditional 'overseas development' relations with the ACP states, that is the former colonies in Africa, the Caribbean and the Pacific region, and have gradually been broadened to include other developing countries in Asia and Latin America. More recent extensions have covered relations with the Mediterranean area and with central and eastern Europe. The external measures section ends with a varied chapter on democracy and human rights. This whole B7 section has traditionally seen the close involvement of the non-profit sector, which has its own budget lines for EU support, and may receive EU funding for a variety of activities under other EU programmes. The youngest section of EU external relations, the Common Foreign and Security Policy (CFSP), has its own chapter in the budget, as it is a rather recent phenomenon with relatively limited EU policy involvement, budgetary provision and NGO relevance.

Further details of the reference numbers, titles and amounts of money available in each budget line are summarised in the introductions at the beginning of each sub-chapter, below.

Budget lines B7 are handled by DGs IA and IB, dealing with external relations, and DG VIII – Development. If more than one service is involved in a grant area, 'interservice groups' have been formed, for instance on human rights and on landmines. Details of contacts and procedures are given with each budget line below. For many programmes, it has become increasingly essential to liaise with the local EU delegations in recipient countries. DG units and Desk Officers will give guidance, and you may also find details on the web-sites below.

Once you decide to submit a request for funding, you will not only liaise with the responsible officials who prepare the decisions of the Commission. They will also give you details about the involvement of the Joint Service for the Management of Community Aid to Non-Member Countries (SCR) on the technical and procedural handling of your request.

General web-sites that are useful to consult are:

DG I: http://europa.eu.int/comm/dg01/projects.htm
DG IA: http://europa.eu.int/comm/dg1a/index.htm
DG IB: http://europa.eu.int/en/comm/dg1b/index.htm
DG VIII: http://europa.eu.int/comm/dg08/index_en.htm
ECHO (emergency aid): http://europa.eu.int/comm/echo/en/index.html
SCR: http://europa.eu.int/comm/scr/index_en.htm
EU delegations: http://europa.eu.int/comm/dg1a/site/contacts/delegations.htm (under construction at the time of writing)

A useful written source of information is DG VIII's *Digest of Community resources available for financing the activities of NGOs and other Governmental and/or decentralized bodies representing civil society in the fields of development cooperation and humanitarian aid*, which is published annually (but not in 1999). It can be ordered free of charge from DG VIII or downloaded from:

http://europa.eu.int/comm/dg08/publicat/ngo/digest_en.pdf

For NGOs, a useful contact in Brussels is the Liaison Committee of Development Non-Governmental Organisations to the European Union, which facilitates the contacts of European development NGOs and their umbrella networks with the European Commission. Their annual handbook gives extensive information on EU policies on development and human rights and further details on most budget lines in this section. Contact:

NGDO-EU Liaison Committee
10 Square Ambiorix, B- 1000 Brussels
Tel: + 32 2 743 8760
Fax: + 32 2 732 1934
E-mail: sec@clong.be
http://www.oneworld.org/liaison/

Note Many budget lines and programmes in the previous chapters, though primarily aiming at activities inside the EU, do allow the involvement of partners in non-EU countries. This is even encouraged in the case of applicant countries in central and eastern Europe, Cyprus and Malta.

ACP DEVELOPMENT

B7-1

European Development Fund: Cooperation with ACP (African, Caribbean and Pacific) states

Introduction

The European Development Fund (EDF) is the major instrument of the Lomé Convention on development cooperation between the EU and (mostly) the former colonies of the EU member states, the ACP countries. The EDF funds and policies are renewed every 5 years and €14.7 billion are available for the 1996–2000 period. These funds do not appear in the regular EU budget, as the member states contribute directly to the EDF from their national budgets. But on the implementation side the EDF is a real EU instrument, as most of it is jointly managed by the European Commission and the authorities of recipient countries. This makes it as relevant for NGOs as the 'regular' EU budget lines, which are partially or exclusively accessible to the non-profit sector. The amounts available vary from year to year and so does the division among different fields of activity: within regional programmes and national indicative programmes, project proposals are submitted and jointly decided on by the receiving countries and the local EU delegations.

General NGO opportunities

NGOs with an expertise in a relevant field (e.g. community development, primary health care, community or grassroots training) may be involved in the implementation of a project if its costs are less than €5,000,000, through a 'private contract'. Projects of over €5,000,000 are publicly tendered and NGOs are not eligible under that process. The EU delegation in each recipient country will be the primary contact for an NGO wishing to be involved in this general part of EDF implementation.

Decentralised cooperation

NGOs in ACP countries are explicitly mentioned as potential participants in projects, which aim at promoting cooperation between different local development players. Instead of a project-centred approach and cooperation with one implementing agency, decentralised cooperation encourages various players to work together in drafting and implementing development programmes, which includes cooperation between civil society and the state. In addition to concrete projects, explicit components of the philosophy of decentralised cooperation are 'strengthening the expertise and action capacities of grassroots organisations' and contributing to the 'emergence and strengthening of intermediate levels of responsibility'. More precise guidelines were being drafted by DG VIII at the time of writing this book, based on an 8-year trial period.

There are no specific amounts earmarked for decentralised cooperation and decisions are taken individually in each ACP state. Interested NGOs should contact the local EU delegation or the national authorising officer in a particular ACP country.

Micro-projects

Unlike decentralised cooperation, micro-projects are a facility under which ACP authorities and the EU may support a wide range of small scale projects of local or European NGOs outside the national indicative programmes. Eligible activities may vary widely, as long as they address the social and economic needs of the local community, in rural or urban areas. Projects must meet a real priority need, demonstrated and observed at local level and must be undertaken with the active participation of the local community.

Grant maximum: up to 75 % (to a maximum of €300,000) of the costs.

Information For the funding opportunities relevant to NGOs summarised above, information and advice can be obtained at central EU level from:

European Commission
DGVIII.A.4 – Civil society, NGOs and decentralised cooperation
Mr Sigurd ILLING, Head of Unit
Rue de Genève 12, Evere Green Building
B-1140 Brussels
Tel: +32 2 299 3269
Fax: +32 2 299 2847
E-mail: sigurd.illing@dg8.cec.be
Internet: http://europa.eu.int/comm/dg08/index_en.htm

The web-site will tell you which DG VIII officials deal with specific regions (http://europa.eu.int/comm/dg08/dg8org.htm) and which Desk Officers deal with a particular country (http://europa.eu.int/comm/dg08/desk.htm). They will then also be able to identify the relevant EU and national contacts in a particular recipient country.

The *DG VIII Digest* is a useful written source of information, and so is the NGO handbook of the Brussels-based Liaison Committee of NGDOs, which has staff with expertise in all development issues from an NGO perspective (see p 224)

Note Two EDF facilities are summarised in connection with other budget lines:
* Aid to refugees, returnees and displaced persons in ACP countries (B7-302 and B7-312)
* Emergency Aid, see ECHO (B7-21)

FOOD AND HUMANITARIAN AID

B7-20

Food aid and support operations

Budget 99 Three related budget lines are taken together here:

B7-200	Products mobilised under the Food Aid Convention	€151,000,000	(£105,700,000)
B7-201	Other aid (products, support actions, early warning systems and storage)	€250,000,000	(£175,000,000)
B7-202	Transport, distribution, flanking measures and monitoring implementation	€104,000,000	(£72,800,000)

Eligibility In addition to recipient countries, UN-related organisations and the Red Cross, European NGOs are eligible for EU funding of activities in this field, if they can show that they can successfully carry out food aid operations. They must have their headquarters in an EU member state, a recipient country or exceptionally, in the case of international NGOs, in a non-member country.

Beneficial areas Ensuring access to an adequate and appropriate diet and improving the availability and accessibility of foodstuffs to the public, consistent with local dietary habits, production and trading systems, particularly in food crises. The budget lines are applicable to developing countries, the Caucasus and central Asia.

Partners needed The Commission partly finances food security actions in cash, collaborating directly with NGOs in beneficiary countries and European NGOs. In other cases, funding is arranged and coordination and cooperation among various actors in this field is ensured through EuronAid in the Hague, a European network specialised in food aid and bringing together NGOs involved in food and emergency aid.

Types of grant Enhancing food security in recipient countries may involve broader activities than just food supply and include agricultural and food development and market restructuring. This may include early warning systems and data gathering, improvement of storage facilities and preparatory studies and training on these activities.

The aid should be integrated into the development policy and the food strategies of the country concerned, with special attention to vulnerable groups (particularly women) and pluri-annual programming.

The role of NGOs is becoming more important: they carried out 95 contracts worth €63,500,000 in 1998 against contracts worth €21,100,000 in 1997.

Grant maximum: operations under B7-200 are usually financed in full, including related costs like transport. Partial funding is possible for preparation, monitoring and supervision. Food security support operations are mainly co-financed and may receive funding of up to 75%. Projects under €300,000 will not be funded. At the time of writing, new operational directives for NGOs and local EU delegations in beneficiary countries were being prepared by DG VIII.

Information and applications In the division of responsibilities between EU units, the Food Aid Unit of DG VIII deals with projects relating to development geared towards food security and ECHO finances projects of a humanitarian/relief nature. Funding requests must be discussed with the EU delegation in the country concerned before they can be sent to DG VIII. More information and application forms from DG VIII, from EuronAid or from the EU-NGDO Liaison Committee in Brussels (see p 224).

European Commission
DG VIII.A.1 – Environment, rural development, food security
Mr Uwe WERBLOW, Head of Unit
Evere Building, 1 Rue de Genève
Tel: +32 2 299 3272 / 2736
Fax: +32 2 299 2908 / 3073
E-mail: uwe.werblow@dg8.cec.be
Internet: http://europa.eu.int/comm/dg08/psi/food-a-s.htm

EuronAid
PO Box 12, 2501 CA The Hague
The Netherlands
Tel: +31 70 330 5724
Fax: +31 70 364 1701

B7-21

Humanitarian aid

Budget 99 The European Community Humanitarian Office (ECHO) manages a series of budget lines on humanitarian aid which comprises assistance, relief and protection operations to help people in third countries, in particular the most vulnerable people in developing countries who are victims of natural disasters or man-made crises. The following budget lines are closely related and vary mainly in the beneficiary areas that they deal with:

B7-210   Aid, including emergency food aid to help the populations
of developing countries and others hit by disasters
or serious crises   €162,850,000   (£113,995,000)

B7-214	Humanitarian aid to the people of central and eastern		
	European countries	€98,000,000	(£68,600,000)
B7-215	Humanitarian aid to the people of the New Independent		
	States and Mongolia	€45,000,000	(£31,500,000)
B7-217	Operations to help refugees, displaced persons and returnees	€18,000,000	(£12,600,000)
B7-219	Operational support and disaster preparedness	€7,000,000	(£4,900,000)
B7-910	Emergency aid reserve	€346,000,000	(£242,200,000)
B7-1	European Development Fund, article 254 on		
	emergency aid 1996–2000	€346,000,000	(£242,200,000)
			for 5 years

Eligibility European NGOs are eligible for EU funding of activities in this field, in addition to international organisations and agencies, UN specialised agencies, specialised national agencies from the EU member states or the European Commission itself.

NGOs must show that they can successfully carry out food aid operations. They must have their main headquarters in a EU member state, a recipient country or exceptionally, in the case of international NGOs, in a third donor country.

Beneficial areas Assistance, relief, protection and emergency food aid to help people hit by natural disasters, man-made crises (wars, outbreaks of fighting etc.) or comparable emergencies for as long as is necessary to meet the humanitarian needs that such situations give rise to.

Partners needed No.

Types of grant Funding arrangements vary; the Commission often pays 100%, but always in the context of a framework partnership agreement with ECHO, which is based on ECHO's annual global plans.

In addition to the purchase and delivery of a wide range of goods and services, staff costs, shipment and so on, fundable activities include:

+ feasibility studies, monitoring, supervision, coordination and evaluation of humanitarian aid projects and plans;
+ strengthening EU coordination with member states, other donor countries, international organisations and NGOs;
+ public awareness and information campaigns;
+ mine clearance (including public awareness campaigns for local communities).

B7-214 has a special provision on the return of Bosnian refugees from European countries, in particular Germany.

B7-215 has a special provision on the situation in Chechnya.

B7-217 includes provisions on repatriation and on disaster prevention.

B7-219 specifically deals with disaster prevention, including scientific studies and the development of early warning systems.

Budget line B7-910 is a general reserve, supposedly available for quick responses to unpredictable events, but the required agreement between the European Parliament and the Council of Ministers on the release of these funds may well cause delays.

Information and applications NGOs interested in participation in emergency aid projects are advised to investigate thoroughly possibilities, criteria and procedures by contacting:

ECHO Information Service
Mr Giorgio Guarneri
Rue Belliard 232, B-1040 Brussels
Tel: + 32 2 299 3362
Fax: + 32 2 295 4544
http://europa.eu.int/comm/echo/en/index.html

A useful contact for information and advice for NGOs is a network of European NGOs, which has been set up to promote consultations and the exchange of information between NGOs and the EU on emergency aid issues. It is connected to and housed at the same address as the NGDO Liaison Committee (see p 224).

VOICE (Voluntary Organisations in Cooperation in Emergencies)
10 Square Ambiorix, B- 1000 Brussels
Tel: + 32 2 743 8775
Fax: + 32 2 732 1934
E-mail: voice@clong.be
http:://www.oneworld.org/voice

Note Asia and Latin America are covered by budget lines B7-302 and B7-312 respectively.

ASIA AND LATIN AMERICAN DEVELOPING COUNTRIES; SOUTH AFRICA

B7-300	Financial and technical cooperation with Asian developing countries	€312,500,000	£218,750,00
B7-302	Aid to uprooted people in Asian countries	€37,950,000	£26,565,000
B7-303	Rehabilitation and reconstruction operations in developing countries in Asia	€5,000,000	£3,500,000
B7-310	Financial and technical cooperation with Latin American developing countries	€202,500,000	£141,750,000
B7-312	Aid to uprooted people in Latin American countries	€21,350,000	£14,945,000
B7-313	Rehabilitation and reconstruction operations in developing countries in Latin America	€4,250,000	£2,975,000
B7-320	Cooperation with South Africa	€127,500,000	£89,250,000

B7-300

Financial and technical cooperation with Asian developing countries

Budget 99 €312,500,000 (£218,750,000)

Eligibility Check with the Commission.

Beneficial areas This budget line covers a broad range of activities, mainly in the field of macro-economic development and sectorial problems, but some aspects are relevant to NGOs.

Partners needed Check with the Commission.

Types of grant Activities covered include: strengthening of civil society, environment, education of women and children, promotion of consumer policy, drugs abuse control. NGOs dealing with street children, promotion and defending of the rights of vulnerable groups (women, children, ethnic minorities) are specifically mentioned. With regard to India and Pakistan, granting new allocations to NGOs has priority.

For details of possible support, check with the Commission.

Information and applications

European Commission
DG IB.C.4 – Programming and economic cooperation
Mr Erich MULLER, Head of Unit
Rue de la Loi 170, B-1040 Brussels
Tel: +32 2 299 0775
Fax: +32 2 29 5734
E-mail: erich.muller@dg1b.cec.be

B7-302

Aid to uprooted people in Asian countries

Budget 99 €37,950,000 (£26,565,000)

Eligibility The budget line is partially open to NGOs and international organisations.

Beneficial areas
- support to enable refugees, displaced people and other population groups who left their country because of conflicts, insecurity or other non-natural crisis situations, to meet their own needs;
- emergency, repatriation and relocation measures, including extension to the local population of the countries of reception and of origin, if economic circumstances so require;
- where necessary, support for preventative action.

Partners needed No, but coordination with other NGOs, agencies or local authorities is encouraged.

Types of grant These vary according to the type of project and local situation and may last from 2 to 3 years.

Information and applications

European Commission
DGIB.C.4 – Programming and economic cooperation
Mr Erich Muller, Head of Unit
170 Rue de la Loi, B-1040 Brussels
Tel: +32 2 299 0775
Fax: +32 2 296 7241
E-mail: erich.muller@dg1b.cec.be

B7-303

Rehabilitation and reconstruction operations in developing countries in Asia

Budget 99 €5,000,000 (£3,500,000)

Eligibility Includes non-governmental development organisations, civil society.

Beneficial areas Measures of limited duration (up to 24 months) to initiate the return to normal life of people in developing countries after critical situations (war, civil conflict, natural disasters): production, infrastructure (including mine clearance), institutional capacity.

Partners needed Yes: a local partner in the beneficiary country must be involved.

Types of grant Operations should cover programmes and projects implemented by NGOs and other civil society organisations and favour the participation of the beneficiary population at every level of decision making and implementation.

Activities typically relevant to NGOs and specifically mentioned are:
+ social reintegration, in particular of refugees, displaced persons and demobilised troops;
+ assisting with the needs of children, in particular children affected by war and child soldiers;
+ support for disabled people;
+ supporting women and women's organisations to reduce gender disparities.

Grant maximum: up to 75% of a rehabilitation operation, the remaining 25% being expected as a financial contribution of the initiating NGO.

Information and applications The local EU delegation in the beneficiary country is the main contact for NGOs in the identification and implementation of projects. Contact the Desk Officers dealing with a specific country, who can best be identified through the offices of the heads of the unit in which they work:

European Commission
DG IB.C – South Asia and South East Asia
Rue de la Loi 170, B-1040 Brussels
http://europa.eu.int/en/comm/dg1b/organi1b_gr_fr.htm

India, Nepal, Bhutan, Sri Lanka:
Mr Carlos CAMINO, Desk Officer
Tel: + 32 2 295 1053
Fax: + 32 2 299 1062/3

Pakistan, Afghanistan, Bangladesh, Maldives:
Ms Ruth ALBUQUERQUE, Desk Officer
Tel: + 32 2 295 3420
Fax: + 32 2 299 2463

South East Asia:
Ms Gwyn MORGAN, Desk Officer
Tel: + 32 2 299 2332
Fax: + 32 2 299 1061 / 1529

B7-310

Financial and technical cooperation with Latin American developing countries

Budget 99 €202,500,000 (£141,750,000)

Eligibility Check with the Commission.

Beneficial areas This budget line covers a broad range of activities, mainly in the field of macro-economic development and sectorial problems, but some aspects are relevant to NGOs.

Partners needed Check with the Commission.

Types of grant Activities covered include: strengthening of civil society, environment, cooperation between universities, education of women and children, promotion of consumer policy, drugs abuse control, promotion of the peace process in Guatemala. NGOs dealing with street children, the promotion and defence of the rights of vulnerable groups (women, children, ethnic minorities) are specifically mentioned.

For details of possible support, check with the Commission.

Information and applications

European Commission
DG IB.B.4 – Programming and economic cooperation
Mr Dieter OLDEKOP, Head of Unit
Rue de la Loi 170, B-1040 Brussels
Tel: +32 2 295 9845
Fax: +32 2 296 6630
E-mail: dieter.oldekop@dg1b.cec.be

B7-312

Aid to uprooted people in Latin American countries

Budget 99 €21,350,000 (£14,945,000)

Eligibility The budget line is partially open to NGOs and international organisations.

Beneficial areas Support to enable refugees, displaced people and other population groups who have left their countries because of conflicts, insecurity or other non-natural crisis situations, to meet their own needs.

Partners needed No, but coordination with other NGOs, agencies or local authorities is encouraged.

Types of grant These vary according to the type of project and local situation and may last from 2 to 3 years.

Fundable activities include emergency, repatriation and relocation measures, which may be extended to the local population of the countries of reception and of origin, if economic circumstances so require; where necessary, support for preventative action is possibile.

Information and applications

European Commission
DGIB.B.1 – Central America, Mexico, Cuba
Mr Manuel GOLDSTEIN, Head of Unit
Rue de la Loi 170, B-1040 Brussels
Tel: +32 2 299 0731
Fax: +32 2 299 1032
E-mail: manuel.goldstein@dg1b.cec.be

B7-313

Rehabilitation and reconstruction operations in developing countries in Latin America

Budget 99 €4,250,000 (£2,975,000)

Eligibility Includes non-governmental development organisations, civil society.

Beneficial areas Measures of limited duration (up to 24 months) to initiate the return to normal life of people in developing countries after critical situations (war, civil conflict, natural disasters): production, infrastructure (including mine clearance), institutional capacity.

Partners needed Yes: a local partner in the beneficiary country must be involved.

Types of grant Operations should cover programmes and projects implemented by NGOs and other civil society organisations and favour the participation of the beneficiary population at every level of decision making and implementation.

Activities typically relevant to NGOs and specifically mentioned are:
- social reintegration, in particular of refugees, displaced persons and demobilised troops;
- assisting with the needs of children, in particular children affected by war and child soldiers;
- support for disabled people;
- supporting women and women's organisations to reduce gender disparities.

Grant maximum: up to 75% of a rehabilitation operation, the remaining 25% being expected as a financial contribution from the initiating NGO.

Information and applications The local EU delegation in the beneficiary country is the main contact for NGOs in the identification and implementation of projects. Contact the Desk Officers dealing with a specific country, who can best be identified through the offices of the heads of the unit in which they work:

European Commission
DG IB.B – Latin America
170 Rue de la Loi, B-1040 Brussels
http://europa.eu.int/en/comm/dg1b/organi1b_gr_fr.htm

Central America, Mexico, Cuba:
Mr Manuel GOLDSTEIN, Desk Officer
Tel: +32 2 299 0731
Fax: +32 2 299 1032
E-mail: manuel.goldstein@dg1b.cec.be

Andean Pact:
Mr Cesare DE MONTIS, Desk Officer
Tel: + 32 2 299 0705
Fax: + 32 2 296 5261
E-mail: cesare.de.montis@dg1b.cec.be

Mercosur, Chile:
Mr Damian HERNANDEZ, Desk Officer
Tel: + 32 2 295 3666
Fax: + 32 2 296 1101 / 299 1103
E-mail: damian.hernandez@dg1b.cec.be

B7-320

Cooperation with South Africa

Budget 99 €127,500,000 (£89,250,000)

Eligibility South African NGOs, national, regional and local authorities, public bodies, public or private institutions and operators.

Beneficial areas The 1996–1999 European Programme for Reconstruction and Development in South Africa aims at promoting the South African government's policy of economic reform, private sector support, and delivery of social services and basic infrastructure to the very poor. The EU support is also intended to strengthen democracy and promote good government practice.

Partners needed Check with EU units listed below.

Types of grant The EU–South African Multi-annual Indicative Programme (MIP) 1997–1999 focuses on basic social services (education, health, water and sanitation), private sector development, democratisation and good governance, and regional integration. Specified in the 1999 EU budget:
- development programmes for local communities, implemented through the Kagiso trust, trade unions and churches;
- programmes to improve housing;
- programmes to improve education in rural areas and poor urban areas;
- programmes to improve vocational training;
- health programmes and projects in rural and poor urban areas;
- investments, including risk capital, joint ventures and employment projects;
- integration of consumer policy in development policy;
- transfer of technical knowledge on best practice on renewable energies.

Projects are jointly funded by the EU and the South African government.

Note EU-based NGOs are not normally eligible but have access, with their South African partners, to the general co-financing budget line B7-6000.

Information and applications

European Commission
DGVIII.E.3 – Southern Africa
Mr Jean-Claude BOIDIN, Head of Unit
Evere Green building
12 Rue de Genève, B-1140 Brussels
Tel: +32 2 295 7196
Fax: +32 2 296 9841
E-mail: Jean-Claude.Boidin@dg8.cec.be

EU delegation in South Africa
PO Box 945, 0027 Groenkloof – Pretoria
South Africa
Tel: +27 12 464 319
Fax: +27 12 469 923

MEDITERRANEAN COUNTRIES AND THE MIDDLE EAST

B7-410	Meda: Measures to accompany reforms of the economic and social structures in the Mediterranean non-member countries	€976,000,000	£683,200,000
B7-420	Community operations connected with the Israel-PLO peace agreement	€50,000,000	£35,000,000

B7-410

Meda

Measures to accompany reforms of the economic and social structures in the Mediterranean non-member countries

Budget 99 €976,000,000 (£683,200,000)

This large budget line deals with EU cooperation on a broad range of subjects and activities in Algeria, Cyprus, Egypt, Israel, Jordan, Lebanon, Malta, Morocco, the Palestinian Territories, Syria, Tunisia and Turkey, related to economic and social restructuring, including policies on environmental protection. Non-profit organisations have access to only a small part of the budget, through programmes that deal with issues that are typically of interest to the sector, summarised below.

Much of the description of Meda has to be provisional: after a crisis at the end of 1995, the Med programmes were temporarily suspended in order to re-examine and improve their management systems and mechanisms. An in-depth technical and financial evaluation of these programmes was undertaken and new management and control measures were put in place. In 1998 the programme was relaunched. At the time of writing, insufficient detail was available to allow a complete and systematic application of the subheadings (available budget, eligibility, beneficial areas, partners needed, types of grant) that are used in the descriptions of other budget lines and programmes in this book.

Meda activities were gradually resumed during 1999, with priority given to continuation and follow-up of existing approved projects. General information about the present state of affairs and the possibilities for submitting new proposals is best obtained from the appropriate service of the European Commission and from the Med secretariat (the Technical Assistance Office).

The Med-Campus, Med-Urbs and Med-Media programmes, the Meda Regional Indicative Programme, SMAP (environment), the Euro-Mediterranean Youth Action programme and the Morocco civil society programme are summarised below, with contact addresses. You can ask to go on the Med Secretariat mailing list to receive future publications as well as the new guidelines and application forms once they are available.

Note There are separate budget lines for the Israel/PLO peace agreement (B7-420) and the Meda democracy and human rights programme (B7-705). Activities in the Mediterranean region may also be eligible under general budget lines, e.g. NGO activities in developing countries (B7-6000), decentralised cooperation (B7-643) and most development-related budget lines on other specific subjects.

Applicant countries Cyprus and Malta also have access to the growing number of budget lines that have been opened for applicant countries since the late 1990s.

General information

European Commission
DG IB.A.4 – Programming and economic cooperation
Mr Patrick LAURENT, Head of Unit
170 Rue de la Loi, B-1040 Brussels
Tel.: +32 2 295 5255
Fax: +32 2 296 6653
E-mail: patrick.laurent@dg1b.cec.be
Internet: http://www.euromed.net

Decentralised cooperation: Med-Urbs, Med-Media, Med-Campus

Eligibility These programmes seek to encourage participation, initiatives and responsibilities by key groups in civil society – local authorities, universities, media bodies – and to promote between them contacts, understanding, cooperation and concrete expressions of interdependence. The actions undertaken must enable Euro-Mediterranean cooperation networks to be formed between municipalities (Med-Urbs), universities (Med-Campus) and media professionals (Med-Media). The programmes grant financial support for the creation of networks and for exchange of expertise and experience.

Partners needed Each project must include at least 4 partners from 4 different countries: 2 from the EU and 2 from the Mediterranean partner countries.

Types of grant Information can be obtained from the Med Secretariat. For all programmes, the total available amounts, range of amounts and conditions for individual grants were still to be established at the time of writing.

Information and applications New applications for the Med-Campus, Med-Media and Med-Urbs programmes are becoming eligible in the course of 1999. Information on calls for proposals, guidelines and application forms can be obtained from the contact people for each programme in the Med Secretariat.

MED Secretariat, Communication and Information
Ms Veronique DUBUS
63, Rue Montoyer, B-1000 Brussels
Tel: +32 2 237 0960
Fax: +32 2 237 0970
E-mail: v.dubus@med.ibf.be

Med-Urbs

Eligibility Municipalities and local authorities; civil society and its actors such as non-profit organisations, NGOs and grassroots organisations are encouraged to participate in cooperation with the local authorities and municipalities in the implementation of the programmes.

Beneficial areas The programme funds projects in 3 main areas:
◆ environment: environmental protection, water management, prevention of man-made environmental disasters, recycling of waste, and so on;
◆ urban management: town planning, local democracy, municipal management, local tax systems, and so on;
◆ social economic development: urban transport and infrastructure, culture, development of tourist industry, public health, participation of women in urban management, housing schemes, fight against social exclusion, and so on.

Further activities are identification and mobilisation of local human and economic resources, creation of twin towns.

Med Secretariat Med-Urbs Programme
Ms Assunta GLERIA, Manager
63 Rue Montoyer, B-1000 Brussels
Tel: +32 2 237 0960
Fax: +32 2 237 0970
E-mail: a.gleria@med.ibf.be

Med-Media

Eligibility Media professionals and journalists (press, radio or television) and media organisations from the public or private and non-governmental sector.

Beneficial areas Trans-Mediterranean cooperation between media professionals (press, radio or television) and media organisations from the public or private and non-governmental sector through the creation of media networks. The objective is to exchange information and skills, and to improve professional standards. Projects are limited to the field of practical training for journalists and media technicians (in radio, television or the press) in the Mediterranean countries.

Med Secretariat, Med-Media Programme Manager
Mrs Elyane LANKES
63 Rue Montoyer, B-1000 Brussels
Tel: +32 2 237 0960
Fax: +32 2 237 0970
E-mail: e.lankes@med.ibf.be

Med-Campus

Eligibility Higher education institutions such as universities, research institutes, business schools and training institutes. Public and private sector companies are also invited to participate in projects.

Beneficial areas Creation of genuine 'partnerships for knowledge', which will lead to increased efficiency, understanding and solidarity. The programme funds training activities to improve the technical and practical skills of teaching staff in higher education institutions in the Mediterranean. Subject areas may include environmental technologies and legislation, energy conservation, new technologies, management, language teaching and translation techniques, mass media and communication, consumer protection, financial markets and banking techniques. Other training activities include the contribution to the continuous training of high-level civil servants in public institutions and private sector management staff on subjects such as: management skills, environment, tourism, universities and higher education institutions, social and health services, local administration and small and medium enterprises.

Med Secretariat
Med-Campus Programme Manager
Ms Marie-Christine ASHBY
63 Rue Montoyer, B-1000 Brussels
Tel: +32 2 237 0960
Fax: +32 2 237 0970
E-mail: info@med.ibf.be

Meda Regional Indicative Programme

Beneficial areas Support for small-size operations for NGOs, associations and so on, under the Euro-Mediterranean Partnership:
• People-to-people activities within the framework of the Middle East Peace Process are meant to strengthen dialogue and to restore mutual trust among the civil societies of the parties to the peace process. This subject falls under the Meda democracy programme (see B7-705, p 288);
• Culture and information activities in the areas of fine-arts, photography, multimedia, music, drama and cultural festivals, history of civilisations, books and literature, publications, inter-religious dialogue.

Partners needed Priority is given to proposals that bring together the largest number of EU and Mediterranean partners.

Types of grants On the basis of satisfactory reporting, grants may be given a maximum of 3 times. Grants may not be combined with other types of Meda funding within the same period.

Grant maximum: not normally exceeding €200,000, with an (exceptional) maximum of €500,000. 100% is the norm for EU contributions, but co-financing is not excluded.

Information and applications Further documentation and application forms can be obtained from:

European Commission
DG IB.A.4 – Programming and economic cooperation
Mr Patrick LAURENT, Head of Unit
170 Rue de la Loi, B-1040 Brussels
Tel.: +32 2 295 5255
Fax: +32 2 296 6653
E-mail: patrick.laurent@dg1b.cec.be
Internet: http://www.euromed.net/social-cultural/small_size_projects/vademecum/

For further general information on information and culture from the technical assistance office:

MEDA Team 10
Mr Baher KAMAL
1-3 Rue Marie Thérèse 1-3, B-1040 Brussels
Tel: +32 2 209 0660/209 0658
Fax: +32 2 223 3747
E-mail: baher.kamal@medateams.belgonet.be
Internet: http://www.euromed.net/social-cultural/small_size_projects/vademecum/

Euro-Mediterranean Youth Action Programme

Budget €9,700,000 (£6,790,000) for 1999–2000

Eligibility National NGOs based in non-EU Mediterranean countries or in the EU, international and European organisations.

Beneficial areas Assisting young people to integrate into social and professional life and supporting the democratisation process of civil society in non-EU Mediterranean countries. Beneficiaries aged 15–25 years include in particular young women, youth association and club leaders, training professionals, youth workers, local and national leaders.

Partners needed Yes: for international exchanges.

Types of grants Youth exchange programmes follow the guidelines and rules of the Youth for Europe, Action D (see B3-1010, p 95) and the European Voluntary Services programmes (see B3-1011, p 98).

Maximum grant: up to 50% for EU and up to 100% for non-EU Mediterranean country participants and programmes, excluding permanent staff and equipment but including external trainers and experts. For voluntary service projects, 100% funding is possible when costs remain at reasonable levels.

Information and applications

European Commission
DG XX.C.2 – Youth Action
Mr Alexandros TSOLAKIS, Head of Unit
7 Rue Belliard, B-1040 Brussels
Tel: +32 2 295 9981
Fax: +32 2 295 4158
E-mail: alexandros.tsolakis@dg22.cec.be

For further information:

EU Youth Forum
120 Rue Joseph II, B-1000 Brussels
Tel: +32 2 230 6490
Fax: +32 2 230 2123
E-mail: youthforum@youthforum.org

Environment

The Short and Medium Term Priority Environment Action Programme (SMAP) is expected to become the common ground for the drafting and financing of environmental projects in the Mediterranean region, such as:
◆ integrated management of water resources;
◆ waste management;
◆ hot spots: polluted zones, endangered biodiversity;
◆ integrated management of coastal areas;
◆ the fights against desertification.

Relevant eligible activities for the non-profit sector include:
◆ public awareness raising campaigns;
◆ education and training activities;
◆ setting up of civil society partnerships;
◆ promotion of North-South and South-South networks;
◆ definition of sustainable development indicators and ecological monitoring.

Applications

European Commission
DG XI.A.4 – Development and Environment
Mr Christoph BAIL, Head of Unit
174 Boulevard du Triomphe, B-1160 Brussels
Tel: +32 2 295 4099
Fax: +32 2 296 3440
E-mail: christoph.bail@dg11.cec.be

Support for civil society in Morocco

As a pilot project for the Maghreb region, a support programme for civil society in Morocco was started in 1999. It is above all open to the NGOs in the beneficiary country. For further information, contact:

The EU Delegation in Morocco
2-bis Avenue de Meknès
BP 1302, Rabat, Morocco
Tel: +212 7 761 246/7
Fax: +212 7 761 156

B7-420

Community operations connected with the Israel–PLO peace agreement

Budget 99 €50,000,000 (£35,000,000)

Eligibility In general, this budget line is only used for aid for investments projects directly to the Palestinian Authority. Exceptionally, Palestinian or European NGOs may submit proposals to the Commission.

Beneficial areas Socio-economic development of the Palestinian population, in particular production, urban and rural development, education and training, health, water supply, environmental protection and the establishment of a Palestinian institutional apparatus.

Partners needed Yes: Palestinian organisation must be centrally involved.

Types of grant Regional cooperation between Israel and its neighbours, in the institutional and economic fields, water supply, environmental protection and energy. In all actions, the use of renewable energy sources must be encouraged. Activities to influence public opinion in favour of the peace process:

◆ common activities for Israeli and Palestinian youth;

◆ clear information in both languages;

◆ Israeli–Palestinian activities in the field of information and cooperation.

For NGO projects, co-financing arrangements will apply. Ask the donors for further information on conditions and procedures.

Information and applications

European Commission
DG IB.A.1 – Machrek and Israel
Mr Tomas DUPLA DEL MORAL, Head of Unit
170 Rue de la Loi, B-1040 Brussels
Tel: +32 2 299 2313
Fax: +32 2 299 0204
E-mail: tomas.dupla-del-moral@dg1b.cec.be

EU Delegation
PO Box 22207 Jerusalem
Tel: +972 2 228 1617
Fax: +972 2 228 1620

Palestinian organisations can submit proposals to the Palestinian Agency for Micro-project Development in Jerusalem. This agency was set up to promote and finance small, local community projects in the area of health care, education, training, rehabilitation and sport.

Palestinian Agency for Micro-project Development
PO Box 51035
Jerusalem, Wad El-Joz,
Khaled Obn Walied Street, via Israel
Tel: +972 2 282 408
Fax: +972 2 281 703

CENTRAL AND EASTERN EUROPE, NEW INDEPENDENT STATES AND MONGOLIA

B7-500	Aid for economic restructuring of the countries of central and eastern Europe (Phare, including Lien and Tempus)	€1,243,190,000	£870,233,000
B7-502	Transfrontier cooperation in the field of structural operations (part of Phare with Interreg)	€180,000,000	£126,000,000
B7-520	Assistance to economic reform and recovery in the New Independent States and Mongolia (Tacis)	€402,550,000	£281,785,000
B7-521	Transfrontier cooperation in the field of structural operations (part of Tacis with Interreg)	€20,000,000	£14,000,000
B7-522	Rehabilitation and reconstruction operations in the New Independent States and Mongolia	€10,000,000	£7,000,000
B7-541	Measures for the reconstruction of the republics formerly part of Yugoslavia	€200,000,000	£140,000,000
B7-543	Measures for the rehabilitation of the republics formerly part of Yugoslavia	€42,000,000	£29,400,000

B7-500

Phare

Aid for economic restructuring of the countries of central and eastern Europe

Budget 99 €1,243,190,000 (£870,233,000)

General introduction This large and varied budget line deals with the restructuring of the countries of central and eastern Europe: Albania, Bosnia-Herzegovina, Bulgaria, the Czech Republic, Estonia, Hungary, Latvia, Lithuania, Macedonia, Poland, Romania, the Slovak Republic and Slovenia. As most of them are EU-associated, applicant member states, general priority is given to activities in relation to their accession to the EU.

The 2 main priorities of Phare are institution building, for which nearly one-third of available funds are allocated, and infrastructure financing (around two-thirds). The official description in the 1999 budget also explicitly mentions:

- financing the assessment of gender impact of projects, targeted at institution building and investment support;

◆ development of industrial relations systems and social dialogue, to be promoted as part of the process of institution building, including information, training and dialogue and exchange with European social partners.

For general information and references to specialised agencies implementing aspects of the Phare programme, contact:

Phare – Tacis Information Office
19 Rue Montoyer, B-1000 Brussels
Tel: +32 2 545 9010
Fax: +32 2 545 9011
E-mail: phare.tacis@dg1a.cec.be
http://europa.eu.int/comm/dg1a/phare/index.htm

Overall responsibility for the Phare programmes lies with the European Commission:

DG IA.B1 – Horizontal Questions, Phare
Mr Alan SEATTER, Head of Unit
170 Rue de la Loi, B-1040 Brussels
Tel: +32 2 295 4998
Fax: +32 2 296 9501
E-mail: alan.seatter@dg1a.cec.be
http://europa.eu.int/comm/dg1a/phare/index.htm

For local Phare offices and EU delegations:

http://europa.eu.int/comm/dg1a/site/contacts/phare_tacis_info_centre.htm
http://europa.eu.int/comm/dg1a/site/contacts/delegations.htm

Phare and the non-profit sector Non-profit organisations in the EU and in recipient countries may to varying extents be involved in Phare-funded programmes and activities, which are introduced below from that angle. For general information on Phare funding possibilities, procedures, handling units and so on, contact the Brussels information office. As a first step, some systematic browsing of the Phare web-site is strongly recommended.

Programmes funded through Phare
NGO strengthening and networking: Partnership
Social projects, volunteers: Lien
Higher education: Tempus
Vocational education and training
Civil society programmes
Town twinning

Related programmes financed through other budget lines
Cross border cooperation: B7-502
Reconstruction and rehabilitation in former Yugoslavia: B7-541 and 543
Democracy and human rights: B7-700

Note In addition to Phare and other budget lines dedicated to central and eastern Europe, regular EU budget lines and programmes are increasingly opened to involvement by partners from applicant countries. Whether or not this is explicitly mentioned in the entries in this book, it is worth enquiring with the respective handling units in the European Commission.

Phare – Partnership and Lien beyond 1999

These dedicated programmes in support of civil society and NGOs in Phare countries have been implemented until 1999. At the time of writing, a follow-up programme was being drafted, provisionally and unofficially named Access, which is expected to keep the main aspects of the Lien and Partnership programmes, i.e. furthering links between non-profit organisations in the EU and in Phare countries, which may be (socio-)economically oriented NGOs (Partnership) or socially oriented NGOs involved in capacity building, targeting underprivileged sections of the population (Lien – Link inter-European non-governmental organisations). For general orientation, we summarise the characteristics of the 2 programmes as they were implemented in their first phase. A new call for project proposals will not be launched before the year 2000. For up-to-date information, consult the Phare website or contact the Phare-Tacis Information Office in Brussels (see above) or the specialised agencies in charge of each programme (see below).

Phare – Partnership up to 1999 The Phare partnership and institution building programme aimed at strengthening ties between non-profit making organisations in the EU and in the countries of central and eastern Europe and on reinforcing existing or emerging organisations in the beneficiary countries. Co-financing grants were provided for local development projects initiated by non-profit organisations for building sustainable partnerships to exchange skills, knowledge and experience. This included:
- local and regional development: improvement of community services, urban and regional planning, tourism development;
- human resources development and training: adult education, vocational training;
- socio-economic development: promotion of social dialogue, consumers' interests, job creation, strengthening of associations, cooperatives and other organisations with a socio-economic role.

Projects had to involve at least 2 eligible partners from 2 different countries, one being a central and eastern Europe country. Partners could be any type of non-profit making organisations: NGOs, trade unions, chambers of commerce, workers or consumers associations, etc.

The EU co-financed up to 75% of total costs for EU-Phare partnerships and up to 80% for Phare-Phare partnerships. Grants ranged between €15,000 and 200,000 and were given for macro-projects of up to 24 months that involved, in an international partnership, NGOs based in the EU or the Phare countries.

Micro-projects for NGOs in the Phare countries of up to 12 months could be co-financed up to 90% and grants ranged between €2,000 and 15,000. Priorities could differ locally and decisions were taken by the EU delegations in the Phare countries.

For further information, contact the Phare – Tacis Information Office in Brussels or:

Euroconsultants SA
13 Rue de la Presse, B-1000 Brussels
Tel: +32 2 223 7033
Fax: +32 2 223 7043
E-mail: euroconsult@arcadis.be

Lien up to 1999 Lien funded projects initiated by NGOs to stimulate citizens' initiative and to strengthen the capacity of NGOs based in recipient countries. It targeted projects in the social sector, in favour of disadvantaged groups of the population (women, the handicapped, the elderly, the sick, the unemployed) and exchanges of young volunteers (18-25 years old) to enable them to acquire experience in the sectors with which the programme was concerned.

At least 2 organisations from 2 different countries (one being eligible under Phare or Tacis programmes) needed to be involved from the start in the project.

The EU gave co-financing grants up to 80% of total costs; a minimum 10% had to be brought in cash by the partners, while the remaining 10% could be contributed in kind. In the case of micro-projects applicants did not need a partner from the EU, the criteria for eligibility were more simple and the Commission could cover up to 90% of total costs (€3,000–10,000 per project); applications needed to be made through the EU delegation in the country concerned.

For further information, contact the Phare – Tacis Information Office in Brussels or:

European Volunteer Centre
42/10 Rue de l'Industrie, B-1040 Brussels
Tel: +32 2 511 7501
Fax: +32 2 514 5989
http://sme.belgium.eu.net/cev/

Tempus

Tempus is a trans-European mobility programme to help with the modernisation of higher education in the associated countries:

- ◆ Joint European projects (JEPs) are 3-year projects and can receive up to €500,000. They focus on the introduction of new degree courses or restructuring of existing degree courses and their content; university management; creation of new institutions or faculties, or restructuring of existing institutions or facilities; development of universities' structural capacities to cooperate with enterprises and other local bodies (in particular to improve universities' delivery of continuing education).

Projects are proposed and implemented by a consortium of at least one higher education institution per partner state involved, one EU member state higher education institution and one university, enterprise or organisation from another EU member state.

◆ Individual mobility grants (IMGs) support teachers, trainers or administrative staff at higher education institutions and senior ministry officials or education planners for visits from EU member states to the central and eastern European partner states or vice versa.

Vocational education and training

The European Training Foundation manages 8 national vocational education and training reform programmes over the course of 3 years. All programmes have as their objective the reform and modernisation of the initial training systems or secondary vocational education and are designed to ensure a multiplier effect across the vocational education system as a whole. In each partner country a specific programme management unit (PMU) is in charge of the implementation of each programme at local level. The foundation is responsible for the overall supervision and coordination of the reform programme.

For further information contact:

European Training Foundation
Villa Gualino, 65 Viale Settimio Severo
I-10133 Torino, Italy
Tel: +39 11 630 2222
Fax: +39 11 630 2200
E-mail: info@etf.eu.int
http: //www.etf.it

Specifically on vocational education and training:

http://www.etf.it/etfweb.nsf/pages/phare#VET

Specifically on access to programmes of the European Social Fund (B2-14):

http://www.etf.it/etfweb.nsf/pages/pharesocial

Details of national Tempus offices in central and eastern European partner countries:

http://www.etf.it/etfweb.nsf/pages/Natempof

In the UK:

Tempus National Contact Point
The University Research and Development Building
Canterbury CT2 7PD
Tel: +44 1227 824 067
Fax: +44 1227 823 468

Overall responsibility for the Tempus programmes lies with the European Commission:

DG XXII.C.1 – Cooperation with third countries, Tempus, ETF
Mr Giuseppe MASSANGIOLI, Head of Unit
7 Rue Belliard, B-1040 Brussels
Tel: +32 2 295 0746
Fax: +32 2 295 5719

Town twinning

For further information on town twinning schemes contact:

European Commission
DG IA.B.5 – Enlargement process, pre-accession strategy and Europe agreements
Ms Carolyn Leffler-Roth, Desk Officer
170 Rue de la Loi, B-1040 Brussels
Tel: +32 2 296 7470
Fax: +32 2 296 7432

In the UK contact:

The EU Department (External)
Foreign and Commonwealth Office
Ms Vicky Lee-Gorton
Main Building, King Charles Street
London SW1A 2AH
Tel: +44 171 270 4267
Fax: +44 171 270 3514

For central and eastern European national contact points consult:

http://europa.eu.int/comm/dg1a/site/contacts/contacts_dg1a.htm

Civil society programmes

In addition to the possibilities for NGO support mentioned above, civil society programmes are financed from the funds available for each country which aim at strengthening NGOs and social movements in central and eastern European countries:
+ information and legal advice for NGOs;
+ education and training programmes;
+ small-scale NGO projects.

Conditions vary according to national preferences and priorities. Projects are initiated and primarily implemented by NGOs in the recipient countries. EU based NGOs may be involved in contributing expertise and financing. More information can be obtained through the local agencies for civil society programmes in each Phare country. For details, contact the Phare-Tacis information office in Brussels.

B7-502

Phare with Interreg

Transfrontier cooperation in the field of structural operations

Budget 99 €180,000,000 (£126,000,000)

Eligibility Non-profit organisations may participate on the same conditions as in Interreg programmes (see B2-1410, p61).

Beneficial areas Participation in Interreg activities (including tourism, human resources, culture, local democracy) in border regions between the EU and countries from central and eastern Europe as well as between central European applicant countries.

Partners needed See Interreg.

Types of grant See Interreg. Two-thirds of the funds are allocated to border regions between the EU and applicant states (pre-accession strategy framework) and one-third at most to other border regions. 10% of the funds are earmarked for small joint projects at local level, in particular by local authorities, EU regions, professional associations, trade unions and NGOs.

Information and applications

European Commission
DG IA.B.5 – Enlargement process, pre-accession strategy and Europe agreements
Ms Carolyn Leffler-Roth, Desk Officer
170 Rue de la Loi, 1040 Brussels
Tel. +32 2 296 7470
Fax: +32 2 296 7432
Internet: http://europa.eu.int/comm/dg1a/phare/programme_types/crossborder/crossborder.htm
http://europa.eu.int/comm/dg1a/phare/programme_types/crossborder/small_projects_funds/spf_eligible_organisations.htm

B7-520

Tacis

Assistance to economic reform and recovery in the New Independent States and Mongolia

Budget 99 €402,550,000 (£281,785,000)

Eligibility Non-profit organisations can participate in designated sections.

Beneficial areas A broad and varied programme of support for the transition to a market economy and to strengthen democracy in Armenia, Azerbaijan, Belarus, Georgia, Kazakhstan, Kyrghystan, Moldova, Russia, Tajikistan, Turkmenistan, Ukraine, Uzbekistan, Mongolia.

For details of Tacis programmes accessible to non-profit organisations, see sections below on Tempus and Lien

Information For general information about Tacis and revisions from 2000, contact:

Phare and Tacis Information Office
19 Rue Montoyer, B-1000 Brussels
Tel: +32 2 545 9010
Fax: +32 2 545 9011
E-mail: phare.tacis@dg1a.cec.be
http: //europa.eu.int/comm/dg1a/tacis/index.htm

For EU delegations and Tacis offices in the Tacis countries:

http://europa.eu.int/comm/dg1a/tacis/spp/address.htm

European Commission:

DG IA.C.1 – horizontal questions, Tacis
Mr John KJAER, Head of Unit
170 Rue de la Loi, B-1040 Brussels
Tel: +32 2 295 6413
Fax: +32 2 296 3379
http://europa.eu.int/en/comm/dg1a

Tacis and the non-profit sector Compared to Phare, the other large-scale assistance programme in Europe, NGO involvement is more limited and mainly consists of the Tacis version of the Small Projects Programme in which civil society and education and training are important components.

Related programmes financed through other budget lines
Emergency humanitarian aid: ECHO, B7-20
Transfrontier cooperation (Tacis with Interreg):B7-521

Rehabilitation and reconstruction: B7-522
Tacis – Democracy: B7-701

Tempus – Higher education and training As the Phare and Tacis versions of Tempus are very similar, refer to the Phare section, B7-500, for information. You may also consult the website of DG IA:

http://europa.eu.int/comm/dg1a/tacis/spp/tempus/htm

or that of the European Training Foundation:

http://www.etf.it/etfweb.nsf/pages/tempusp

Lien (Link inter-European non-governmental organisations) The Tacis version of the Lien programme focuses heavily on disadvantaged women and on social reintegration and sustainable social and health support for marginalised population groups.

The 1999 budget includes a special provision for a maximum amount of €10,000,000 to cover the implementation of an integrated programme in Azerbaijan aiming to support the civil society and social sector, in particular the displaced population, as well as to promote democracy and human rights.

Available funds vary from country to country and depend on national priorities. Grants of €10,000–200,000 cover up to 80% of project costs, with a contribution of at least 20% (10% in cash) from the applicant.

Due to the expiration of the legal basis for the Tacis programme and the revision of the Lien programme in 1999, priorities and conditions for 1999 and beyond were unclear at the time of writing. In 1999, a call for proposals may be published at the end of the year. For further information, contact:

IBF Department Consultant
Ms Sylvie Jacquet
63 Rue Montoyer, B-1000 Brussels
Tel.: +32 2 237 0956
Fax: +32 2 237 0955
E-mail: info@idp.ibf.be

Information about projects supported previously is available from:

Technical Assistance Unit CEV
42/10 Rue de l'Industrie, B-1040 Brussels
Tel: +32 2 511 7501
Fax: +32 2 514 5989

B7-521

Tacis with Interreg

Transfrontier cooperation in the field of structural operations

Budget 99 €20,000,000 (£14,000,000)

Eligibility NGOs may participate in partnership with local/regional authorities as applicants, as well as development agencies, chambers of commerce.

Beneficial areas Structural operations in border regions with the EU and with Phare countries, through joint programming and monitoring with Interreg (B2-1410). Environmental protection measures are specifically mentioned in the official budget description.

Partners needed
NIS-EU: one from each eligible bordering area;
NIS-Phare: one from each eligible bordering area and one from any EU area.

Types of grant NIS-EU and NIS-Phare: up to 80% of total costs, maximum of €200,000. The co-financing by project partners may be in cash or in kind. For a NIS–EU project there is no official minimum grant, in practice it amounts to €10,000. There is a special micro-project facility grant up to €10,000 for preparatory measures for a major project.

Information and applications For further details on fundable activities, procedures and deadlines, contact the Phare-Tacis information office in Brussels or:

Management Unit
Phare-Tacis CBC Project Facility Office
County of West Zealand, Alleen 15
DK-4180 Soro, Denmark
Tel: +45 57 872 315
Fax: +45 57 872 325

In Russia:

Valentina Chaplinskaya
Phare-Tacis CBC Project Facility Office
8 line 61, Vasiljev Island
199 004 St Petersburg
Russia
Tel: +7 812 218 6278
Fax: +7 812 327 0943

B7-522

Rehabilitation and reconstruction operations in the New Independent States and Mongolia

Budget 99 €10,000,000 (£7,000,000)

Eligibility Includes non-governmental development organisations, civil society.

Beneficial areas Measures of limited duration (up to 24 months) to initiate the return to a normal life of people in developing countries after critical situations (war, civil conflict, natural disasters): production, infrastructure (including mine clearance), institutional capacity.

Partners needed Yes: a local partner in the beneficiary country must be involved.

Types of grant Operations should cover programmes and projects implemented by NGOs and other civil society organisations and favour the participation of the beneficiary population at every level of decision making and implementation. Grant maximum: up to 75% of a rehabilitation operation may be financed, the remaining 25% being expected as a financial contribution from the initiating NGO.

Activities typically relevant to NGOs and mentioned specifically:
- social reintegration, in particular of refugees, displaced persons and demobilised troops;
- assisting with the needs of children, in particular children affected by war and child soldiers;
- support for disabled people;
- supporting women and women's organisations to reduce gender disparities.

Information and applications The local EU delegation in the beneficiary country is your main contact for NGOs in the identification and implementation of projects. You should contact Desk Officers dealing with a specific country, who can best be identified through the offices of their heads of unit:

European Commission
DG IA.C.1 – horizontal questions, Tacis
170 Rue de la Loi, B-1040 Brussels
http://europa.eu.int/en/comm/dg1a

Russia – DG IA.C.2.
Mr Jürgen KOEPPEN, Head of Unit
Tel: +32 2 295 3233
Fax: +32 2 296 4305

Ukraine, Moldavia, Byelorussia – DG IA.C.3
Mr Hughes MINGARELLI, Head of Unit
Tel: +32 2 296 2331
Fax: +32 2 296 3377

Caucasus, central Asia, including Mongolia – DG IA.C.4
Mr Cees WITTEBROOD, Head of Unit
Tel: +32 2 295 7312
Fax: +32 2 296 3912

B7-541

Measures for the reconstruction of the republics formerly part of Yugoslavia

Budget 99 €200,000,000 (£140,000,000)

Eligibility As implementing agencies of Commission projects.

Beneficial areas Reconstruction projects in the former Yugoslavian republics, including return and resettlement of refugees and displaced persons in Croatia, Bosnia-Herzegovina and Yugoslavia.

Types of grant Projects and activities are programmed by the Commission, which approaches agencies, which might be NGOs, to implement them on a case-by-case basis. The fields of activity funded include (NGO aspects only):
- the consolidation of democracy and civil society;
- the return of refugees;
- integration or reintegration of refugees, displaced persons and former soldiers into working life;
- the strengthening of NGOs, cultural institutions and educational establishments.

Information and applications For information about current and forthcoming activities and procedures contact:

European Commission
DG IA.D.1. Relations with other European countries
Mr Patrick RENAUD, Head of Unit
170 Rue de la Loi, B-1040 Brussels
Tel: +32 2 299 3806
Fax: +32 2 299 2198

Note For projects in Slovenia, contact DG IA.B.3(Phare) or the Phare-Tacis Information Office in Brussels (see B7-500).

B7-543

Measures for the rehabilitation of the republics formerly part of Yugoslavia

Budget 99 €42,000,000 (£29,400,000)

Eligibility As implementing agencies of Commission projects.

Beneficial areas A broad range of activities, comparable to the Phare programme, in the context of the democratisation and transition to a market economy of central and eastern European countries.

Partners needed Depends on the project.

Types of grant Projects and activities are programmed by the Commission, which approaches agencies, which might be NGOs, to implement them on a case-by-case basis. Within the wide range of activities, typical NGO fields of action include:

- cooperation with NGOs;
- education and training;
- health;
- cultural cooperation;
- environmental protection.

Information and applications For information about current and forthcoming activities and procedures, contact:

European Commission
DG IA.D.1. Relations with other European countries
Mr Patrick RENAUD, Head of Unit
170 Rue de la Loi, B-1040 Brussels
Tel: +32 2 299 3806
Fax: +32 2 299 2198

Note For projects in Slovenia, contact DG IA.B.3(Phare) or the Phare-Tacis Information Office in Brussels (see B7-500).

SUPPORT TO DEVELOPMENT NGOS, TRAINING, INFORMATION

B7-6000	Community contribution towards schemes concerning developing countries by NGOs	€200,000,000	£140,000,000
B7-610	Training and promotion of awareness on development issues	€4,500,000	£3,150,000
B7-611	Integrating gender issues in development cooperation	€3,300,000	£2,310,000
B7-612	Preparatory measures through NGOs against child discrimination	€5,000,000	£3,500,000

B7-6000

Community contribution towards schemes concerning developing countries by non-governmental organisations (NGOs)

Budget 99 €200,000,000 (£140,000,000)

Eligibility This budget line is reserved for EU based development NGOs. Organisations in developing countries or other non-member countries can only apply through EU based colleagues.

Beneficial areas About 90% of the funds is allocated to a wide range of social or economic development projects to help the poorest sections of the population in developing countries (which do not have to be EU associated countries); the remaining 10% is for programmes to promote public awareness in the EU and solidarity between people in Europe and in developing countries.

Partners needed Not obligatory, but possible as co-financers. The Commission encourages the creation of European NGO consortia for the financing and implementation of common programmes.

Types of grant Within the general aim of promoting the social or economic development of the poorest sections of the population, and awareness raising in the EU, special areas of attention include:
- a number of measures to promote the rights and welfare of children (including street children, forced labour, schooling);
- sustainable development measures regarding social, economic and environmental protection;

- education and training in developing countries on respecting the environment;
- clearance of landmines and revalidation of victims (main budget line: B7-661);
- consumer interests;
- education, health, reintegration, rural and social development and training in South Africa, Cambodia, Chile, Cuba, Vietnam, East Timor, Burma;
- NGO projects regarding Myanmar (Burma), the Kurdish, Tibetan and Western Saharan people.

Further details of the broad range of fundable areas is in the documentation available from DG VIII.

Substantial changes regarding the conditions of co-financing, including budgetary procedures, minimum and maximum amounts, were being prepared at the time of writing and expected to come into force as from January 2000, along the following lines:

Grant range and maximum: in general, not more than 50% of the total cost of a project (in exceptional cases 75%). NGOs must provide 15% of the direct costs from their own funds. Administrative funds are covered up to 6% of direct costs. Project duration may be up to 5 years, with annual EU contributions of up to €150,000 and varying from €40,000 to €500,000 for the full period. The maximum contribution may be up to €2,000,000 if a consortium is formed, which is highly recommended. Contributions to small projects may be considered within the framework of block grants to NGOs with successful experience of at least 3 years of co-financing.

The considerable backlog of applications from 1998 and 1999 will be processed according to previous regulations before new ones will be considered.

Information and applications Before applying, make sure that you read:
- DG VIII's *Digest of Community resources available for financing NGO activities in development cooperation and human rights* (see also p 223);
- DG VIII's *General conditions for co-financing* (1988 version for the considerable backlog of 1998 and 1999 applications submitted before the new conditions come into force).

The budget line is administered by the European Commission, DG VIII.A.4 (Civil society, NGOs and decentralised cooperation), which will also refer you for further information to regional administrators, depending on where the project is to take place (Asia, Pacific, Latin America or Africa), and to the Desk Officers in charge of individual countries.

These contacts can be made through and applications can be sent to:

European Commission
DG VIII.A.4 – Civil Society, NGOs and decentralised cooperation
Mr Sigurd ILLING, Head of Unit
Evere Green Building, 12 Rue de Genève
B-1140 Brussels
Tel: +32 2 299 3269

Fax: +32 2 299 2847
E-mail: sigurd.illing@dg8.cec.be
Internet: http://europa.eu.int/comm/dg08/index_en.htm

Further information is also available from the Liaison Committee of Development NGOs in Brussels (see p 224).

B7-610

Training and promotion of awareness on development issues

Budget 99 €4,500,000 (£3,150,000)

Eligibility Youth organisations which are not eligible for the co-financing programme (B7-6000).

Beneficial areas
- raising public awareness in Europe of development issues, especially among young people;
- (not for NGOs) audiovisual productions to improve public understanding of development issues and the need for North-South cooperation.

Partners needed No.

Types of grant At the time of writing, new guidelines were being developed for the first beneficial area (youth projects). The official description in the EU budget mentions training and awareness raising on the integration of sustainability and environmental concerns into mainstream aid.

Information and applications

European Commission
DG VIII.1 – Information and communication
Mr Dominique DAVID, Head of Unit
Astrid building
1 Rue de Genève, B-1140 Brussels
Tel: +32 2 299 9852
Fax: +32 2 299 2525
E-mail: dominique.david@dg8.cec.be

B7-611

Integrating gender issues in development cooperation

Budget 99 €3,300,000 (£2,310,000)

Eligibility Includes NGOs.

Beneficial areas Raising consciousness and promoting integration of gender issues in EU-funded development projects and programmes (follow-up from the 1995 World Conference on Women in Beijing)

Partners needed No.

Types of grant Flexible, from co-financing to full cost financing. Priority is given to:
- consultancy missions, by experts on women in development, for EU-financed programmes and projects;
- raising awareness and training of staff (within EU delegations and the European Commission);
- institutional reinforcement and awareness raising in relevant government departments.

Political lobby work of NGOs in ACP countries may be supported.

Information and applications The right to initiate action under this budget line rests with the European Commission. The programme is managed by Women in Development Europe (WIDE), a European network of development NGOs, women's organisations and individuals, organised in national platforms:

WIDE, Women in Development Europe
70–72 Rue du Commerce, B-1000 Brussels
Tel: +32 2 545 9070
Fax: +32 2 512 7342
E-mail: wide@gn.apc.org

Relevant units in the European Commission:

For developing countries in Asia, Latin America and the Mediterranean:

DG IB.D.2 – Relations with international organisations and integration of sectoral policies
Mr Hugo SCHALLY, Head of Unit
170 Rue de la Loi, B-1040 Brussels
Tel: +32 2 295 8569
Fax: + 32 2 299 0914
E-mail: hugo.schally@dg1b.cec.be

For developing countries in Africa, the Caribbean and the Pacific:

DG VIII.A.2 – Social, human and cultural development, gender issues
Mr Philippe DARMUZEY, Head of Unit
Evere Green Building, 12 Rue de Genève
B-1140 Brussels
Tel: +32 2 296 5592
Fax: +32 2 296 7141
E-mail: philippe.darmuzey@dg8.cec.be
Internet: http://europa.eu.int/comm/dg08/index_en.htm

Note NGO action to support women's organisations may be co-financed from budget line B7-6000.

B7-612

Preparatory measures through NGOs against child discrimination

Budget 99 €5,000,000 (£3,500,000)

Eligibility NGOs and European networks which address the problems of street children in developing countries and elsewhere.

Beneficial areas Combating violence against children and the exploitation of child labour, to support schooling and to provide food and protection for street children.

Partners needed Unclear at the time of writing.

Types of grant Co-financing contracts in general, including co-financing with NGOs which are members of the European Network on Street Children Worldwide. Further details not available at the time of writing.

Information and applications

European Commission, DG VIII.A.5
Mr Timothy CLARKE, Head of Unit
12 Rue de Genève, B-1140 Brussels
Tel: +32 2 296 1704
Fax: +32 2 299 2911

For Southern Mediterranean, Middle and Near East, Latin America, south and south east Asia:

European Commission, DG IB
Mr David TING
170 Rue de la Loi, B-1040 Brussels
Tel: +32 2 296 6070
Fax: +32 2 299 3703

ENVIRONMENT, HEALTH, DRUGS AND DEMOGRAPHY IN DEVELOPING COUNTRIES

B7-6200	Environment in the developing countries	€16,000,000	£11,200,000
B7-6201	Tropical forests	€45,000,000	£31,500,000
B7-6210	North-South cooperation schemes in the context of the campaign against drug abuse	€9,800,000	£6,860,000
B7-6211	Health programmes and the fight against AIDS/HIV in developing countries	€16,500,000	£11,550,000
B7-631	Aid for population and reproductive health policies and programmes in developing countries	€8,000,000	£5,600,000

B7-6200

Environment in the developing countries

Budget 99 €16,000,000 (£11,200,000)

Eligibility NGOs in the EU and beneficiary countries, universities and research centres, private consultancies (through tenders), authorities in beneficiary countries, international organisations.

Beneficial areas Promotion of sustainable development and securing the incorporation of the environmental dimension in the development process in ACP countries, Asia, Latin America and the Mediterranean.

Partners needed No, but one NGO may apply on behalf of two or more collaborating NGOs.

Types of grant For a broad range of activities such as trial and pilot projects, environmental impact studies, drawing up of guidelines and instruments, establishing green accounting systems, introducing environmental aspects in development cooperation projects. In 1998–1999 priority themes were:
+ national strategies for sustainable development;
+ transport, waste, water, air pollution in urban areas;
+ environmental protection of coastal areas, estuaries and wetland zones;
+ securing potable water resources through environmental measures;
+ sustainable agriculture and the fight against desertification.

Priority is given to local initiatives, low-cost innovative measures, building operational and institutional capacity with NGO support, involvement of the local (indigenous) population and regional cooperation.
Grant range and maximum: €100,000–1,000,000, up to 80%.

Information and applications Early applications are recommended, in October 1999 for projects in 2000.

Contact for ACP countries:

European Commission
DG VIII.A.6 – Environment and natural resources
Ms Maria SAVVAIDES, Head of Unit
Tel: +32 2 299 3952
Fax: +32 2 299 0961
E-mail: maria.savvaides@dg8.cec.be

For Asia and Latin America:

European Commission
DG IB.D.2 – Relations with international organisations and integration of sectoral policies
Mr Hugo SCHALLY, Head of Unit
170 Rue de la Loi, B-1040 Brussels
Tel: +32 2 295 8569
Fax: + 32 2 299 0914
E-mail: hugo.schally@dg1b.cec.be

B7-6201

Tropical forests

Budget 99 €45,000,000 (£31,500,000)

Eligibility NGOs may be eligible on a limited basis.

Beneficial areas Protection and conservation of tropical or subtropical forest ecosystems in regions between the 30° north and south parallels.

Partners needed No.

Types of grant This programme is mainly for funding large-scale projects in collaboration with the government of the recipient countries, but European and local NGOs might also have access to funding for small and medium-scale projects. In any case, projects must have a positive impact both on forest diversity and the indigenous people's quality of life.

The programme is for 4 years (1996–1999) with an annual average allocation of around €500,000,000. Projects below €200,000 are generally not financed. The initiative for a project can come from the European Commission itself, international, national, regional and local public bodies, and the private sector, including businesses, cooperatives and NGOs which include conservation of tropical forests as one of their stated aims and regular activities. 10% of these funds are allocated to small-scale local initiatives (Small Tropical Forestry Project Fund).

Information and applications Applications are examined on an ongoing basis, but as it takes 6 months for approval, you are advised to submit your application in the first quarter of the year.

For ACP countries:

European Commission
DG VIII.A.6 – Environment and natural resources
Ms Maria SAVVAIDES, Head of Unit
Tel: +32 2 299 3952
Fax: +32 2 299 0961
E-mail: maria.savvaides@dg8.cec.be

For Asia and Latin America:

European Commission
DG IB.D.2 – Relations with international organisations and integration of sectoral policies
Mr Hugo SCHALLY, Head of Unit
170 Rue de la Loi, B-1040 Brussels
Tel: +32 2 295 8569
Fax: + 32 2 299 0914
E-mail: hugo.schally@dg1b.cec.be

B7-6210

North-South cooperation schemes in the context of the campaign against drug abuse

Budget 99 €9,800,000 (£6,860,000)

Eligibility NGOs in EU member states and beneficiary countries; Mediterranean, Asian and Latin American developing countries; regional drug cooperation organisations; international organisations (especially the UN Drug Control Programme).

Beneficial areas Projects against drug abuse in developing countries, with priority for countries with official national anti-drugs policies (in particular Colombia, Peru, Bolivia and Ecuador).

Projects in Lomé countries are mostly financed from EDF funds (see B7-1, p 225).

Partners needed No.

Types of grant Projects may be on treatment and rehabilitation, information, education and awareness raising, or directing production away from illicit drugs. Grant maximum: 75% of costs in the EU and 85% in beneficiary countries.

Information and applications

Contact for general coordination:

European Commission
DG IB.D.2 – Relations with international organisations and integration of sectoral policies
Mr Hugo SCHALLY
170 Rue de la Loi, B-1040 Brussels
Tel: +32 2 295 8569
Fax: + 32 2 299 0914
E-mail: hugo.schally@dg1b.cec.be

For Asia:

DG IB.C.3 – South East Asia
Ms Laurence ARGIMON-PISTRE
170 Rue de la Loi, B-1040 Brussels
Tel: +32 2 296 2477
Fax: + 32 2 299 1529

For Latin America:

Mr Giovanni MASTROGIACOMO
DG IB.D.02
Tel: +32 2 296 9355
Fax: +32 2 296 5979

For ACP countries:

Mr Alkis DIAMANTOPOULOS
DG VIII.A.02
Tel: +32 2 295 7013
Fax: +32 2 296 7141

For Mediterranean countries:

Ms Laura BAEZA
DG IB.A.02
Tel: +32 2 296 1339
Fax: +32 2 299 1045

B7-6211

Health programmes and the fight against AIDS/HIV in developing countries

Budget 99 €16,500,000 (£11,550,000)

Eligibility NGOs in the EU and recipient countries.

Beneficial areas Combating AIDS/HIV in Asian, Latin American and Mediterranean developing countries.
   In ACP countries, funding is available from the EDF, B7-21, p 228.

Partners needed Cooperation is encouraged between European bodies, EU and local NGOs and ministries in the beneficiary countries.

Types of grant Full financing is possible. The range of fundable objectives and activities includes:
- reducing the transmission and spread of AIDS/HIV and other sexually or perinatally transmitted diseases;
- reinforcing health and social services;
- assessing the impact on the economy and on social groups, defining and implementing coping strategies;

- scientific, non-basic research of the epidemic and improving the quality of measures;
- combating tuberculosis;
- combating discrimination against and social and economic exclusion of AIDS/HIV-infected persons;
- pilot projects, improving access to anti-retroviral treatments, with priority for the prevention of mother-to-child HIV transmission and provision of care after birth.

Basic principles that need to be fulfilled include: integration with national health care and AIDS/HIV policies, adaptation to environments at risk, gender awareness, empowerment of individuals and communities, social training, adaptation to stages of the epidemic.

Information and applications Applications in ACP countries must be sent to the local EU delegation; those in Asian, Latin American and Mediterranean countries may go through the EU delegation or directly to the Commission in Brussels. In any case, you are advised to consult the EU delegation in the recipient country before applying.

European Commission
DG VIII.A.2 – Social, human and cultural development, gender issues
Mr Philippe DARMUZEY
Evere Green Building
12 Rue de Genève, B-1140 Brussels
Tel: +32 2 296 9321
Fax: +32 2 296 7141
E-mail: philippe.darmuzey@dg8.cec.be
Internet: http://europa.eu.int/comm/dg08/index_en.htm

B7-631

Aid for population and reproductive health policies and programmes in developing countries

Budget 99 €8,000,000 (£5,600,000)

Eligibility European and local NGOs in developing countries.

Beneficial areas Population, reproductive health and family planning: programmes in developing countries (design, implementation and evaluation), including follow-up of the 1994 Cairo action platform (ICPD) and the 1995 Beijing International Women's Conference; coordination of the work of EU NGOs in these fields.

Partners needed No.

Types of grant The broad range of subjects and activities include: free and informed choice on having children, reproductive health care (policies, improvement of services), information, education and awareness raising, information on family planning, development of grassroots structures, local NGOs, South-South cooperation.

For spending the limited funds available, priority is given to strategy development, operational research and pilot projects, complementary to direct aid projects. Other projects may be financed from budget line B7-6000.

Grant maximum: 100% financing is possible, although many projects are co-financed.

Information and applications Before making an application, consult the Commission services on the basis of a short project summary.

Coordination for Asian, Latin American and Mediterranean developing countries:

European Commission
DG IB.D.2 – Relations with international organisations and integration of sectoral policies
Mr Hugo SCHALLY, Head of Unit
170 Rue de la Loi, B-1040 Brussels
Tel: +32 2 295 8569
Fax: + 32 2 299 0914
E-mail: hugo.schally@dg1b.cec.be

For developing countries in Africa, the Caribbean and the Pacific:

DG VIII.A.2 – Social, human and cultural development, gender issues
Mr Philippe DARMUZEY, Head of Unit
Evere Green Building
12 Rue de Genève, B-1140 Brussels
Tel: +32 2 296 9321
Fax: +32 2 296 7141
E-mail: philippe.darmuzey@dg8.cec.be
Internet: http://europa.eu.int/comm/dg08/index_en.htm

SPECIFIC AID IN THE FIELD OF DEVELOPMENT

B7-641	Rehabilitation and reconstruction measures for the developing countries	€15,000,000	£10,500,000
B7-643	Decentralised cooperation for the developing countries	€4,000,000	£2,800,000

B7-641

Rehabilitation and reconstruction measures for the developing countries

Budget 99 €15,000,000 (£10,500,000)

Eligibility Includes non-governmental development organisations, civil society.

Beneficial areas Measures of limited duration (up to 24 months) to initiate the return to normal life of people in developing countries, in particular African, Caribbean and Pacific states, after critical situations (war, civil conflict, natural disasters): production, infrastructure (including mine clearance), institutional capacity.

Partners needed Yes: a local partner in the beneficiary country must be involved.

Types of grant Operations should cover programmes and projects implemented by NGOs and other civil society organisations and should favour the participation of the beneficiary population at every level of decision making and implementation. Grant maximum: up to 75% of a rehabilitation operation, the remaining 25% being expected as a financial contribution from the initiating NGO.

Activities mentioned specifically which are relevant to NGOs include:
- social reintegration, in particular of refugees, displaced persons and demobilised troops;
- assisting with the needs of children, in particular child soldiers and children affected by war;
- supporting women and women's organisations to reduce gender disparities.

Since 1999, a previously separate budget line for southern Africa has been integrated into this budget line.

Information and applications The local EU delegation in the beneficiary country is the main contact for NGOs in identifying and implementing projects. In Brussels, contact:

European Commission
DG VIII.04 – Priorities and programming
Mr Jean-Louis HOUDART, Head of Unit
12 Rue de Genève, B-1140 Brussels
Tel: + 32 2 299 2832
Fax: + 32 2 299 2874
Internet: http://europa.eu.int/comm/dg08/index_en.htm

B7-643

Decentralised cooperation for the developing countries

Budget 99 €4,000,000 (£2,800,000)

Eligibility Mainly NGOs from the EU and developing countries, local authorities, economic and social associations.

Beneficial areas Promotion of initiatives from civil society in developing countries through decentralised cooperation.

Partners needed Partnerships among Southern NGOs and between Southern and EU NGOs are encouraged.

Types of grant Activities promoted include:
- information and other activities to mobilise decentralised participants;
- strengthening the capacity of potential actors in decentralised cooperation to get access to existing financial sources or to strengthen their development capabilities;
- pilot programmes which may have an exemplary value;
- methodological and technical support and expertise.

Grant maximum: normally, co-financing is applied, to an unspecified percentage. Exceptionally, some projects may be fully financed.

Information and applications

European Commission
DG VIII.A.4 – Civil society, NGOs and decentralised cooperation
Mr Sigurd ILLING, Head of Unit
Evere Green Building, 12 Rue de Geneve
B-1140 Brussels
Tel: +32 2 299 3269
Fax: +32 2 299 2847
E-mail: sigurd.illing@dg8.cec.be
Internet: http://europa.eu.int/comm/dg08/index_en.htm

OTHER COOPERATION: TRANSATLANTIC RELATIONS, ANTI-PERSONNEL MINES AND SEX TOURISM

B7-6601	Cooperation agreements with third countries	€1,600,000	£1,120,000
B7-6602	New Transatlantic Agenda	€6,000,000	£4,200,000
B7-661	Community participation in action concerning anti-personnel mines	€4,000,000	£2,800,000
B7-663	Campaigns against sex tourism in third countries	€1,000,000	£700,000

B7-6601

Cooperation agreements with third countries

Budget 99 €1,600,000 (£1,120,000)

Eligibility Includes civil society groups.

Beneficial areas Bilateral relations with industrialised countries, in particular Taiwan, Korea and Canada (possibly to be extended from 2000).

Partners needed No.

Types of grant The budget line description mentions, among other activities, implementing social dialogue between economic and social groups, which may include political education.

More than half of the budget will be spent on tendered activities, the rest will be partly accessible for civil society organisations via calls for proposals or own-initiative applications.

Grant maximum: normally 50–80%, and exceptionally 100%.

Information and applications In the absence of clearly defined criteria for the subjects or activities covered by this budget line, you are advised to consult the Commission before applying and to check the web-site for calls for tenders, proposals and so on.

European Commission
DGI.1.0.01 – Personnel, budget, administration, external service
Mr Emiel WEIZENBACH
Rue de la Loi 170, B-1040 Brussels
Tel: +32 2 299 4953

Fax: +32 2 299 0599
E-mail: emiel.weizenbach@dg1.cec.be
Internet: http://europa.eu.int/comm/dg01/pubprono.htm

B7-6602

New Transatlantic Agenda

Budget 99 €6,000,000 (£4,200,000)

Eligibility Includes civil society organisations.

Beneficial areas Improving mutual understanding between key actors on each side of the Atlantic, through creation of an overarching framework for the 'people to people' and 'information and culture' exchanges in the Joint Action Plan of the Transatlantic Agenda.

Partners needed Yes: actions must involve EU and USA actors and organisations.

Types of grant Activities funded include joint pilot projects and preparatory actions on:
- education: research and exchange programmes, electronic resources and long-distance learning;
- people to people: social dialogue between labour, small and medium-sized enterprises and business;
- transatlantic houses, in particular in the Ukraine;
- civil society actions: coordination of initiatives, involving citizen-to-citizen links.

Information and applications

European Commission
DGI.B.1 – United States
Mr Eric HAYES, Head of Unit
170 Rue de la Loi, B-1040 Brussels
Tel: +32 2 299 1699
Fax: +32 2 299 0208
E-mail: eric.hayes@dg1.cec.be

B7-661

Community participation in action concerning anti-personnel mines

Budget 99 €4,000,000 (£2,800,000)

Eligibility Includes EU or local NGOs, mostly through DG VIII (see below under Information and applications).

Beneficial areas Mine clearance, prevention, awareness raising in developing countries.

Partners needed Check with the Commission services.

Types of grant Activities may include:
- mine clearance;
- medical care;
- reintegration of mine victims;
- education as a means of prevention;
- capacity building measures;
- support for NGOs which work on ratification of the Ottawa Treaty of December 1997 on the banning of anti-personnel mines.

Monitoring of operations in the field is done by EU delegations in recipient countries.

Grant maximum: funding through DG VIII can be up to 100%, limited to the running costs of the project.

Information and applications DG VIII accepts proposals initiated by NGOs, preferably in the first half of the calendar year. DG IA and IB normally publish calls for tenders to implement their own programmes, in which NGOs are not explicitly included.

Coordinator of the inter-service group on anti-personnel mines:

European Commission
DG IA.A1 – Security questions
Mr Geoffrey VAN ORDEN, Desk Officer
170 Rue de la Loi, B-1040 Brussels
Tel: +32 2 295 5551
Fax: + 32 2 295 0580

European Commission
DG VIII.04 – Priorities and programming
Mr Jean-Louis HOUDART, Head of Unit
12 Rue de Genève, B-1140 Brussels

Tel: + 32 2 299 2832
Fax: + 32 2 299 2874

For activities in Asia, Latin America, the Mediterranean, central and eastern Europe and the former Soviet Union, contact country Desk Officers in DG IA and IB.

Note Raising awareness in Europe is not covered by this budget line. Several other budget lines have provisions for various activities to do with landmines: B7-303, B7-313, B7-411, B7-522, B7-541, B7-543 and the EDF (all on rehabilitation), and B7-302, B7-312 and B7-21 (ECHO).

B7-663

Campaigns against sex tourism in third countries

Budget 99 €1,000,000 (£700,000)

Eligibility NGOs and professionals.

Beneficial areas Public awareness campaigns in Europe to oppose sex tourism affecting children.

Partners needed Yes: NGOs and professionals should develop joint projects.

Types of grant Check with Commission services.

Information and applications Applicants should respond to the commission's call for proposals. Further information is available from:

European Commission
DG XXIII.D.2 – Stimulation of competitiveness in tourism
Ms Joanna TACHMINTZIS, Head of Unit
80 Rue d'Arlon, B-1040 Brussels
Tel: +32 2 299 0428
Fax: +32 2 296 1377
Internet: http://europa.eu.int/en/comm/dg23/tourisme/tourisme.htm

DEMOCRACY AND HUMAN RIGHTS

B7-700	Support for democracy in the countries of central and eastern Europe, including the republics formerly part of Yugoslavia	€15,000,000	£10,500,000
B7-701	Support for democracy in the New Independent States and Mongolia	€10,000,000	£7,000,000
B7-7020	Human rights and democracy in the developing countries, in particular the ACP countries	€17,000,000	£11,900,000
B7-7021	Human rights and democracy in southern African countries	€4,000,000	£2,800,000
B7-7022	Special programme for democracy and good governance in Nigeria	€4,000,000	£2,800,000
B7-703	Democratization process in Latin America	€12,625,000	£8,837,500
B7-704	Grants to certain activities of human rights organisations	€15,000,000	£10,500,000
B7-705	Meda programme for democracy and human rights	€10,075,000	£7,052,500
B7-706	Support for the activities of international criminal tribunals and for the setting up of the International Criminal Court	€3,300,000	£2,310,000
B7-707	Human rights and democracy in Asian countries	€5,000,000	£3,500,000
B7-709	Support for, and supervision of, electoral processes	€2,000,000	£1,400,000

The European Union (EU) budget has a dedicated chapter for its European Initiative for Democracy and Human Rights, with a number of budget lines for specific regions or aspects of human rights. At the time of writing, a set of regulations was being drafted which will eventually serve as the basis for EU policies on human rights and the implementation of these budget lines.

The budget lines in chapter B7-70 deal exclusively with countries and regions outside the EU. With respect to the EU itself, a great variety of human rights are dealt with by budget lines in specific policy fields such as anti-discrimination, women's rights, social exclusion, and minority languages.

Generally, the main areas for which grants are given under chapter B7-70 are:
◆ promoting and defending the human rights and fundamental freedoms proclaimed in the Universal Declaration of Human Rights and the other international instruments concerning the development and consolidation of democracy and the rule of law;
◆ support to processes of democratisation;
◆ support for measures to promote respect for human rights and democratisation by preventing conflict and dealing with its consequences, in close collaboration with the relevant competent bodies.

Out of the 11 budget lines in this chapter, the 9 budget lines B7-700, 701, 7020, 7021, 7022, 704, 706, 707 and 709 are administrated within the common guidelines of the human rights units of DG IA (External relations – Europe and the New Independent States) and DG VIII (Development – External relations and development cooperation with Africa, the Caribbean and the Pacific).

The 2 regional budget lines B7-703 and 705 (on Latin America and countries in the Meda programme) are not covered by the common arrangements of DG 1A and DG VIII, but by the appropriate regional units in DG 1B (External relations – Southern Mediterranean, Middle East, Latin America, South East Asia and North-South cooperation). They each have their own priorities and procedures, which you will find under the description of individual budget lines. The general coordinator in DG IB is:

Mr David TING – Advisor to the Deputy Director General (general coordination)
170 Rue de la Loi, B-1040 Brussels
Tel: +32 2 296 6070
Fax: +32 2 299 3703

The rest of this introduction is taken from the *Guidelines for Applicants 1999* of DG IA and DG VIII, which deals with budget lines B7-700, 701, 7020, 7021, 7022, 704, 706, 707 and 709. The full text is available from the European Commission or can be downloaded from the web-site:

http://europa.eu.int/comm/dg1a/human_rights/intro/index.htm

The 1999 priorities for applications are:
* education and awareness-raising of civil society;
* protection and promotion of the rights of the child, including those of child soldiers, on the occasion of the 10th anniversary of the Convention on the Rights of the Child;
* innovative actions on conflict;
* promotion of inter-ethnic and inter-racial tolerance in preparation for the World Conference on Racism (2001) and in support for indigenous people;
* good governance: measures to promote transparency, accountability and the fight against corruption, notably those which would strengthen cooperation and dialogue between the EU and its partners.

Individual budget lines may have further specific priorities.

About half of the €75,300,000 available for these 9 budget lines in 1999 is spent on projects to a minimum of €50,000 and usually in excess of €500,000. The balance between larger and smaller projects may vary per budget line. Under B7-700 and 701 there are funding possibilities for micro-projects of €3,000–50,000, which are administered by the EU delegations in the recipient countries. Applications rejected because of a shortage of available funds may be put on the reserve list for the following year. The remaining half of the €75,300,000 is spent on activities that are generally not accessible to the non-profit sector, except possibly as allocations for urgent actions.

As a rule, the EU only co-finances projects and to various degrees. The levels of funding are sometimes negotiated on a case-by-case basis, with a maximum of 90%. Full financing is the exception. The remaining amount can be financed from the applicant's own resources (sometimes in kind) or other non-EU sources. Funding requests for separate parts of the same project may be submitted to several

Commission departments, but this must be clearly stated and double financing of the same expenditure is not allowed.

The deadline for applications is 2 months after publication of the call for proposals. The Commission expects to need a few months to process the anticipated large number of applications.

The administration of applications and implementation of the grants is shared between the DGs and the commission's Common Service on External Relations (SCR), as described in *The EU in the World: External Measures*, p 223.

Eligible applicants may be NGOs, regional or international organisations, national, regional and local authorities and official agencies, community-based organisations and public or private sector institutes and operators, acting either individually or in consortium with other eligible applicants. They must be public or private legal entities, properly constituted and registered under the law of their country of establishment. They must be non-profit-making, but media organisations may apply for a grant even if they are profit-making.

Activities that are not eligible include individual participation in conferences, individual scholarships for study and training, projects lasting over 36 months and projects supporting individual political parties.

For an overview of eligible costs and application procedures, see the *Guidelines for Applicants*.

For further information on budget lines B7-700, 701, 7020, 7021, 7022, 704, 706, 707 and 709, see each budget line description, the *Guidelines* or contact:

European Commission
DG 1A.A.2 – Human rights and democratisation
Ms Daniela NAPOLI, Head of Unit
170 Rue de la Loi, B-1040 Brussels
Tel: +32 2 295 5501
Fax: +32 2 295 7850
E-mail: daniela.napoli@dg1a.cec.be
Internet: http://europa.eu.int/comm/dg1a/human_rights/intro/index.htm

European Commission
DG VIII.A.5 – Democratisation, good governance, institution building
Mr Timothy CLARKE, Head of Unit
12 Rue de Genève, B-1140 Brussels
Tel: +32 2 296 1704
Fax: +32 2 299 2911
E-mail: timothy.clarke@dg8.cec.be
Internet: http://europa.eu.int/comm/dg08/index_en.htm

There is no EU-wide umbrella network in Brussels of human rights NGOs similar to the Liaison Committee of Development NGOs. Several international human rights organisations are represented in Brussels, such as Amnesty International and Human Rights Watch. They are very familiar with the human rights sections of the European Commission, but concentrate heavily on policy issues.

B7-700

Support for democracy in the countries of central and eastern Europe, including the republics formerly part of Yugoslavia

Budget 99 €15,000,000 (£10,500,000)

Eligibility NGOs and community-based organisations in the EU and in beneficiary countries, amongst others (see pp 278–280).

Beneficial areas Albania, Bosnia and Herzegovina, Bulgaria, Croatia, the Czech Republic, Estonia, Hungary, Latvia, Lithuania, Macedonia, Poland, Romania, the Slovak Republic, Slovenia and Yugoslavia.

Subjects and activities generally: see pp 278–280.

Specifically for this budget line: broadening democracy through strengthening advocacy and non-governmental bodies in applicant EU member states.

Partners needed Local partners obligatory for EU NGOs in micro-projects, consortia are possible for other grants.

Types of grant Specific subjects and activities funded include:
- the development of democracy, the rule of law and civil society;
- the peace process, appeasing tensions and developing democracy, including the promotion of free and independent media in the republics of former Yugoslavia;
- the media and freedom of the press;
- inter-ethnic dialogue;
- organisations involved in re-establishing democracy in civil society (including regional NGOs, trade unions and women's organisations);
- equal participation of women in decision-making processes;
- vulnerable groups.

Through the annual call for proposals (May-June in 1999, possibly earlier in following years), €3,500,000–4,000,000 may be distributed centrally by the Commission in Brussels on major projects (from €50,000, but mostly over €500,000). Commission delegations in beneficiary countries will administer €7,500,000 through micro-projects of €3,000–50,000. Closing dates vary from country to country.

Co-financing: on a case-by-case basis, generally up to 90%, only rarely 100%. For details, see pp 278–280.

Information and applications For further details and application forms, contact:

European Commission
DG 1A.A.2 Human rights and democratisation
Ms Daniela NAPOLI, Head of Unit

170 Rue de la Loi, B-1040 Brussels
Tel: +32 2 295 5501
Fax: +32 2 295 7850
E-mail: daniela.napoli@dg1a.cec.be
Internet: http://europa.eu.int/comm/dg1a/human_rights/intro/index.htm

B7-701

Support for democracy in the New Independent States and Mongolia

Budget 99 €10,000,000 (£7,000,000)

Eligibility NGOs and community-based organisations in the EU and in beneficiary countries, amongst others (see pp 278–280).

Beneficial areas Armenia, Azerbaijan, Belarus, Georgia, Kazakhstan, Kyrgystan, Moldova, Mongolia, the Russian Federation, Tajikistan, Turkmenistan, Ukraine and Uzbekistan.

Subjects and activities generally: see pp 278–280.

Specifically for this budget line: strengthening democracy, the rule of law, civil society.

Partners needed Local partners obligatory for EU NGOs in micro-projects, consortia are possible for other grants.

Types of grant Specific subjects and activities funded include:
*   democracy, the rule of law, internationally recognised human rights, protection of minorities, development of civil society;
*   infrastructure necessary for public and democratic life, with the widest participation of NGOs;
*   awareness-raising to strengthen civil society, civic education, the independent media.

Through the annual call for proposals (May-June in 1999, possibly earlier in following years), €3,500,000–4,000,000 may be distributed centrally by the Commission in Brussels on major projects (from €50,000, but mostly over €500,000). Commission delegations in beneficiary countries will administer €7,500,000 through micro-projects of €3,000–50,000. Closing dates vary from country to country.

Co-financing: on a case-by-case basis, generally up to 90%, only rarely 100%. For details, see pp 278–280.

Information and applications

European Commission
DG 1A.A.2 Human rights and democratisation
Ms Daniela NAPOLI, Head of Unit
170 Rue de la Loi, B-1040 Brussels
Tel: +32 2 295 5501
Fax: +32 2 295 7850
E-mail: daniela.napoli@dg1a.cec.be
Internet: http://europa.eu.int/comm/dg1a/human_rights/intro/index.htm

B7-7020

Human rights and democracy in the developing countries, in particular the ACP countries

Budget 99 €17,000,000 (£11,900,000)

Eligibility NGOs and community-based organisations in the EU and in beneficiary countries, amongst others (see pp 278–280).

Beneficial areas Developing countries, with priority for the ACP.
Subjects and activities generally: see pp 278–280.
Specifically for this budget line: activities linked to EU development cooperation.
Note: for southern Africa, see budget line B7-7021.

Partners needed Partnerships are preferred.

Types of grant Specific subjects and activities funded include:
♦ promotion of human rights and democracy, good governance, civil society, conflict prevention;
♦ technical advice on the rule of law, respect for human rights, institution-building, gender equality, electoral procedures, observation missions, training and media.

Co-financing: on a case-by-case basis, generally up to 90%, only rarely 100%.
Through the annual call for proposals (May-June in 1999, possibly earlier in following years), nearly €6,000,000 may be available for major projects (over €50,000). See also pp 278–280.

For smaller human rights projects, seek advice from the Commission.

Information and applications

European Commission
DG VIII.A.5 – Democratisation, good governance, institution building
Mr Timothy CLARKE, Head of Unit
12 Rue de Genève, B-1140 Brussels
Tel: +32 2 296 1704
Fax: +32 2 299 2911
E-mail: timothy.clarke@dg8.cec.be
Internet: http://europa.eu.int/comm/dg08/index_en.htm

B7-7021

Human rights and democracy in southern African countries

Budget 99 €4,000,000 (£2,800,000).

Eligibility NGOs and community-based organisations in the EU and in beneficiary countries, amongst others (see pp 278–280).

Beneficial areas Angola, Botswana, Congo, Lesotho, Malawi, Mauritius, Mozambique, Namibia, Seychelles, South Africa, Swaziland, Tanzania, Zambia, and Zimbabwe.

Subjects and activities generally: see pp 278–280.

Specifically for this budget line: good governance, development of civil society, gender equality, conflict prevention.

Partners needed Partnerships are preferred.

Types of grant Through the annual call for proposals (May-June in 1999, possibly earlier in following years), nearly €1,500,000 may be distributed centrally by the Commission in Brussels on major projects (over €50,000).
Co-financing: on a case-by-case basis, generally up to 90%, only rarely 100%.
See also pp 278–280.

For smaller human rights projects, seek advice from the commission.

Information and applications

European Commission
DG VIII.A.5 – Democratisation, good governance, institution building
Mr Timothy CLARKE, Head of Unit
12 Rue de Genève, B-1140 Brussels
Tel: +32 2 296 1704

Fax: +32 2 299 2911
E-mail: timothy.clarke@dg8.cec.be
Internet: http://europa.eu.int/comm/dg08/index_en.htm

B7-7022

Special programme for democracy and good governance in Nigeria

Budget 99 €4,000,000 (£2,800,000)

Eligibility Recognised Nigerian or European NGOs.

Beneficial areas Nigeria.

Partners needed Not specified.

Types of grant Specific subjects and activities funded include:
- development of democracy, peace and respect for human rights;
- respect for and implementation of internationally accepted norms;
- rule of law;
- strengthening of civil society, pro-democracy groups, women's organisations, trade unions, local organisations, religious and human rights organisations;
- conflict prevention in Nigeria and the sub-region;
- fulfilment by Nigeria of its international obligations to uphold human rights;
- protection of minority rights and vulnerable groups;
- humanitarian and legal aid to political prisoners and their families.

Co-financing: on a case-by-case basis, generally up to 90%, only rarely 100%. Through the annual call for proposals (May-June in 1999, possibly earlier in following years), nearly €1,500,000 may be distributed centrally by the Commission in Brussels on major projects (over €50,000).
  See also pp 278–280.
  For smaller human rights projects, seek advice from the commission.

Information and applications

European Commission
DG VIII.A.5 – Democratisation, good governance, institution building
Mr Timothy CLARKE, Head of Unit
12 Rue de Genève, B-1140 Brussels
Tel: +32 2 296 1704
Fax: +32 2 299 2911
E-mail: timothy.clarke@dg8.cec.be
Internet: http://europa.eu.int/comm/dg08/index_en.htm

B7-703

Democratization process in Latin America

Budget 99 €12,625,000 (£8,837,500)

Eligibility Latin American governmental institutions and NGOs have priority; European NGOs may exceptionally apply, but only at the invitation of the commission.

Beneficial areas Democratisation in the whole of Latin America, with priority in 1999 for setting up a multi-annual programme on democracy and human rights for the Andean Pact.

Partners needed Not specified.

Types of grant Specific subjects and activities funded include 4 strategic priority areas:
- exercise of public authority and reinforcing the rule of law: separation of powers, good governance, free elections, logistical support for democratic institutions (justice, human rights prosecutors, parliaments, armed forces, police);
- enhancing and empowering of civil society;
- support for vulnerable groups: children, women, indigenous peoples, refugees;
- reintegration into civil life of those who fought in Central America's civil wars.

Information and applications

European Commission, DG IB
Mr David TING – Advisor to the Deputy Director General
170 Rue de la Loi, B-1040 Brussels
Tel: +32 2 296 6070
Fax: +32 2 299 3703

Or contact:

DG IB.B.2 – Andean Pact
Mr Cesare DE MONTIS, Head of Unit
170 Rue de la Loi, B-1040 Brussels
Tel: +32 2 299 0705
Fax: +32 2 296 5261
Internet: http://europa.eu.int/en/comm/dg1b/index.htm

B7-704

Grants to certain activities of human rights organisations

Budget 99 €15,000,000 (£10,500,000)

Eligibility Only non-profit organisations.

Beneficial areas Globally, but excluding countries and regions for which there are specific budget lines.
Subjects and activities generally: see pp 278–280.
Specifically for this budget line: general promotion of human rights implementation.

Partners needed Not specified.

Types of grant Specific subjects and activities funded include:
- abolition of the death penalty;
- training on enforcement of human rights (judges, lawyers, civil servants, police and security forces, teachers);
- the rights of the child;
- women's human rights, including fighting the trafficking in women;
- rights of minorities such as gypsies;
- indigenous peoples' human rights world-wide;
- training with organisations specialised in the defence of human rights;
- human rights education and training;
- a European network on human rights and democratisation, dealing with EU human rights policies (collection, analysis, updating and dissemination of information).

On victims of torture:
- centres for the rehabilitation of torture victims;
- other practical help to the victims of human rights violations;
- specific attention to children who are the victims of human rights violation.

Priority is given to applicant organisations with scientific expertise in the medical rehabilitation of torture victims, extensive knowledge of and direct contact with existing rehabilitation services for torture victims world-wide, and experience in torture prevention, awareness-raising and advocacy.

Through the annual call for proposals (May-June in 1999, possibly earlier in following years), over €11,000,000 may be distributed centrally by the Commission in Brussels on major projects (over €50,000). Over half of that amount is allocated for projects to support victims of torture.
Co-financing: on a case-by-case basis, generally up to 90%, only rarely 100%.
For details, see pp 278–280.

Information and applications

European Commission
DG 1A.A.2 Human rights and democratisation
Ms Daniela NAPOLI, Head of Unit
170 Rue de la Loi, B-1040 Brussels
Tel: +32 2 295 5501
Fax: +32 2 295 7850
E-mail: daniela.napoli@dg1a.cec.be
Internet: http://europa.eu.int/comm/dg1a/human_rights/intro/index.htm

B7-705

Meda programme for democracy and human rights

Budget 99 €10,075,000 (£7,052,500)

Eligibility NGOs, associations, private, (semi-)public organisations, not political parties.

Beneficial areas Development of democracy, the constitutional state and civil society in countries covered by the Meda programme: Algeria, Egypt, Jordan, Lebanon, Morocco, the Palestinian Territories, Syria, Tunisia. Projects in Cyprus, Malta and Israel must involve other partner countries. Projects in Turkey may primarily fall under B7-704.

Partners needed Partnerships are possible.

Types of grant Specific subjects and activities funded include as main subject fields:
- political rights: electoral processes, awareness raising, training, polling institutes, institutional reform, training of civil servants, the prison system, administrative transparency, anti-corruption campaigns, inter-parliamentary relations;
- civil rights: freedom of expression, association and meeting, religion, movement (internal, international), media independence, right to privacy;
- social economic rights: joining trade unions, collective bargaining, working conditions, including trade union support and training;
- protection of target groups: women, children, minorities, refugees, displaced persons, torture victims, prisoners.

Co-financing: normally not exceeding 80%, full funding only exceptionally.

Information and applications Contact the Commission or EU delegations in Meda countries for details and documents.

European Commission, DG IB
Mr DavidTING – Advisor to the Deputy Director General
170 Rue de la Loi, B-1040 Brussels
Tel: +32 2 296 6070
Fax: +32 2 299 3703

DG IB.A.2 – Maghreb
Mr Robert van der MEULEN, Head of Unit
170 Rue de la Loi, B-1040 Brussels
Tel: +32 2 295 9335
Fax: +32 2 299 1045

DG IB.A.1 – Machrek and Israel
MrTomas DUPLA DEL MORAL, Head of Unit
170 Rue de la Loi, B-1040 Brussels
Tel: +32 2 299 2313
Fax: +32 2 299 0204
E-mail: tomas.dupla-del-moral@dg1b.cec.be
Internet: http://europa.eu.int/en/comm/dg1b/index.htm

Find EU delegations at:

http://europa.eu.int/comm/dg1a/site/contacts/delegations.htm

B7-706

Support for the activities of international criminal tribunals and for the setting up of the International Criminal Court

Budget 99 €3,300,000 (£2,310,000)

Eligibility NGOs and community-based organisations in the EU and in beneficiary countries, amongst others (for details, see pp 278–280).

Beneficial areas Global.

Partners needed Applicants must have a written statement of support for their proposal from the Registrar of the International Criminal Tribunal.

Types of grant Specific subjects and activities funded include:
- technical assistance to the existing criminal tribunals (Rwanda, former Yugoslavia);
- financial support for the preparatory work for the setting up and the functioning of a permanent International Criminal Court;

◆ training for the staff of the tribunals, including in the field of gender mainstreaming.

Through the annual call for proposals (May-June in 1999, possibly earlier in following years), around €1,000,000 may be distributed centrally by the Commission in Brussels on major projects (over €50,000).

Co-financing: on a case-to-case basis, generally up to 90%, only rarely 100%.

Information and applications

European Commission
DG 1A.A.2 Human rights and democratisation
Ms Daniela NAPOLI, Head of Unit
170 Rue de la Loi, B-1040 Brussels
Tel: +32 2 295 5501
Fax: +32 2 295 7850
E-mail: daniela.napoli@dg1a.cec.be
Internet: http://europa.eu.int/comm/dg1a/human_rights/intro/index.htm

B7-707

Human rights and democracy in Asian countries

Budget 99 €5,000,000 (£3,500,000)

Eligibility NGOs are included.

Beneficial areas In spite of the general title, this budget line mostly deals with China and highlights Hong Kong, Macao, Tibet, Xinjiang, Inner Mongolia and Tibet.

Partners needed Not specified.

Types of grant Specific subjects and activities funded include: promotion of human rights and democracy, exercise of public authority, development of civil society, conflict prevention, freedom of the media.

The budget line is managed by country Desk Officers in DG IB in line with the commission's national strategies. NGO eligibility and distribution of funds therefore varies from country to country.

Information and applications

European Commission, DG IB
Mr David TING – Advisor to the Deputy Director General (general coordination)
170 Rue de la Loi, B-1040 Brussels

Tel: +32 2 296 6070
Fax: +32 2 299 3703

Or contact Desk Officers dealing with a specific country, who can best be identified through the offices of the heads of the unit in which they work:

European Commission
DG IB.C – South Asia and South East Asia
170 Rue de la Loi, B-1040 Brussels
Internet: http://europa.eu.int/en/comm/dg1b/organi1b_gr_fr.htm

India, Nepal, Bhutan, Sri Lanka:

Mr Carlos CAMINO, Head of Unit
Tel: + 32 2 295 1053
Fax: + 32 2 299 1062/3

Pakistan, Afghanistan, Bangladesh, Maldives:

Ms Ruth ALBUQUERQUE, Head of Unit
Tel: + 32 2 295 3420
Fax: + 32 2 299 2463

South East Asia:

Ms Gwyn MORGAN, Head of Unit
Tel: + 32 2 299 2332
Fax: + 32 2 299 1061 / 1529

B7-709

Support for, and supervision of, electoral processes

Budget 99 €2,000,000 (£1,400,000)

Eligibility NGOs and community-based organisations in the EU and in beneficiary countries, amongst others (for details, see pp 278–280).
Specifically for this budget line: applicants must have experience in electoral observation in more than one country.

Beneficial areas Election monitoring projects outside the EU area.

Partners needed Not specified.

Types of grant Specific subjects and activities funded include:

- training of personnel taking part in electoral observer missions;
- creation of a pool of experts on electoral observation;
- media access during election campaigns.

The visibility of the EU in observation missions must be increased. This budget line will not be used if electoral assistance can be funded through other cooperation instruments.

Through the annual call for proposals (May-June in 1999, possibly earlier in following years), around €1,000,000 is distributed centrally by the Commission in Brussels on major projects (over €50,000).

Co-financing: on a case-by-case basis, generally up to 90%, only rarely 100%.

Information and applications

European Commission
DG 1A.A.2 Human rights and democratisation
Ms Daniela NAPOLI, Head of Unit
170 Rue de la Loi, B-1040 Brussels
Tel: +32 2 295 5501
Fax: +32 2 295 7850
E-mail: daniela.napoli@dg1a.cec.be
Internet: http://europa.eu.int/comm/dg1a/human_rights/intro/index.htm

ENVIRONMENT

B7-810 Life: Operations outside Community territory   €5,950,000   £4,165,000

B7-811 Contribution to international environmental activities, including

the Global Environment Fund   €6,935,000   £4,854,500

B7-810

Life

Operations outside Community territory

Budget 99 €5,950,000 (£4,165,000)

Eligibility Primarily national administrations, but also governmental and non-governmental organisations, technical assistance programmes and regional networks operating in the Mediterranean and Baltic regions for the protection of the environment; organisations and networks based in the eligible countries or territories.

Beneficial areas Application of general EU policy on nature conservation and other areas of environmental policy to countries bordering on the Mediterranean and the Baltic Sea: Albania, Algeria, Bosnia-Herzegovina, Croatia, Cyprus, Egypt, Israel, Jordan, Lebanon, Malta, Morocco, Syria, Tunisia, Turkey, West Bank and Gaza, and the Baltic shoreline of Russia (Kaliningrad and St Petersburg regions).

Partners needed Partnerships are encouraged and cooperation on a cross-border, transnational, or regional level is one of the selection criteria.

Types of grant Projects with total costs of €100,000–600,000 are favoured:
- technical assistance (up to 100%): through establishment and reinforcement of administrative bodies and structures – assisting the country concerned to manage better its environment and to promote strategies for sustainable development;
- nature protection (up to 50%): significant habitats of threatened species of flora and fauna;
- demonstration actions to promote sustainable development (up to 50%): new technical methods and/or innovative approaches, implementation of experiments and pilot projects which encourage sustainable development at national, sub-regional and/or regional level.

Other activities supported by the EU:
- strengthening of national environmental policies which increase environmental protection in the regions bordering the EU through institution and capacity building;

- strengthening and developing relations with international organisations (EIB, the World Bank, UNDP, IMO, MAP, etc.), regional networks and international NGOs operating in the eligible regions.

Proposals must have an immediate, practical application. They can include training seminars and/or a limited study phase, but they have to be targeted at the operational phase.

Not eligible: environmental studies, research, commercial or industrial projects, conferences or seminars, construction of infrastructures, purchase of equipment, purchase of land, and so on.

As the above applies to proposals submitted before February 1999, applicants should check with the Commission and other authorities involved about Life activities as from 2000.

Information and applications   Project proposals must be submitted in English or French through the national ministry of environment of the third countries concerned, or the European Commission.

European Commission
DG XI.A.4 – Development and the environment
Mr Christoph BAIL, Head of Unit
174 Boulevard du Triomphe, B-1160 Brussels
Tel: +32 2 295 4099
Fax: +32 2 299 4123
E-mail: christoph.bail@dg11.cec.be
Internet: http://europa.eu.int/comm/life/3countr/index.htm

Information packs and application forms can also be obtained from
- EU delegations or representations in the eligible third countries. Addresses of these delegations can be found on:
  http://europa.eu.int/comm/dg1a/site/contacts/delegations.htm
- the diplomatic missions to the EU of the eligible third countries.

B7-811

Contribution to international environmental activities, including the Global Environment Fund

Budget 99 €6,935,000 (£4,854,500)

Eligibility Includes NGOs 'to cover participation in work on existing and preparatory work on future agreements'.

Beneficial areas

- cooperation with international organisations on sustainable development and the environment;
- establishing Agenda 21 at local, regional or national level;
- implementation of the Rio 1997 conference (especially on tropical forests);
- EU participation in international environmental agreements and their implementation, in the fields of marine environment, protection of nature, the atmosphere and international waterways.

This includes the Euro-Mediterranean partnership and bringing laws in central and eastern Europe in line with EU legislation.

Partners needed Check with the commission.

Types of grant Check with the commission.

Information and applications

European Commission
DG XI.A.4 – Development and the environment
Mr Christoph BAIL, Head of Unit
174 Boulevard du Triomphe, B-1160 Brussels
Tel : +32 2 295 4099
Fax: +32 2 299 4123
E-mail: christoph.bail@dg11.cec.be

EDUCATION AND VOCATIONAL TRAINING

B7-830   Cooperation with third countries on education and vocational training   €2,500,00 £1,750,00

B7-830

Cooperation with third countries on education and vocational training

Budget 99 €2,500,000 (£1,750,000)

Eligibility Education and training institutions, businesses, NGOs, publishers, government departments, chambers of commerce, research institutes.

Beneficial areas EU cooperation on education and vocational training with the USA and Canada; dissemination of the results in EU cooperation with Latin American and Asian countries.

Partners needed Consortia must have 3 partners in at least 2 different EU member states and 3 in the USA or Canada.

Types of grant The EU will co-finance up to 50% of the cost of EU participants in projects on:
- development of organisational frameworks for transatlantic student mobility and exchanges of students, teachers, trainers and administrators;
- development of innovative curricula, teaching materials, methods and modules including those exploiting the new education technologies;
- short intensive programmes of a minimum of 3 weeks;
- teaching assignments as part of the curriculum in a partner institution;
- other innovative projects, including the use of new technologies and distance learning, to improve the quality and cost-effectiveness of transatlantic cooperation in education and training.

Grant average: depending on the number of partners, €100,000 is possible for a 3-year project.

Information and applications Documentation can be obtained from, and applications must be sent to:

European Commission
DG XXII.C.1 – Cooperation with non-member countries
Mr Giuseppe MASSANGIOLI, Head of Unit
7 Rue Belliard, B – 1040 Brussels
Tel: +32 2 295 0746
Fax: + 32 2 295 5719
E-mail: giuseppe.massangioli@dg22.cec.be
Internet: http://europa.eu.int/comm/dg22/call.html

UK ERASMUS Student Grants Council
The University
Research and Development Building
Canterbury, Kent CT2 7PD
Tel.: +44 1227 762712/764000 ext. 3673
Fax: +44 1227 762711
E-mail: erasmus@ukc.ac.uk

Central Bureau for Educational Visits and Exchanges
Ms Subha RAY
Ms Dawn LONG
The British Council
10, Spring Gardens, London SW1A 2BN
Tel.: +44 171 389 4426/4509
Fax: +44 171 389 4624/4517

THE EU FROM A TO Z

ACP   African, Caribbean and Pacific countries, mostly former colonies of EU member states, who negotiate with the EU on development cooperation on the basis of the Lomé Convention.

Amsterdam (Treaty of)   Signed 2 October 1997 in Amsterdam and came into force after ratification by the 15 member states in May 1999; updates the existing treaties that are the political and legal basis of the European Union:
* more powers for the European Parliament through application of the co-decision procedure (between Parliament and Council of Ministers);
* wider application of qualified majority voting in the Council of Ministers, instead of decision by unanimity;
* deepening of EU competence in various policy fields.

Applicant countries   Central and eastern European and Mediterranean countries which are expected successively to join the EU after 2000, first Estonia, Cyprus, the Czech Republic, Hungary, Poland and Slovenia, followed by Bulgaria, Latvia, Lithuania, Malta, Romania, the Slovak Republic and (possibly) Turkey.

Cabinet   Small group (5–6) of advisers to a European commissioner, who maintain contact with the services of the directorates general and other commissioners, and prepare the decisions of the Commission.

Commission of the European Communities – CEC   The European Commission has 3 major tasks:
* initiating EU policy;
* implementing decisions of the Council and Parliament and administering the EU budget;
* guarding the EU treaties against violation by the member states, which it can bring before the Court of Justice.

Its 20 members (commissioners) are appointed by the member states and confirmed in office by the European Parliament for 5 years.

The services of the Commission are organised into directorates general (DGs – equivalent to national ministries) with 14,000 officials, who work mostly in Brussels, otherwise in Luxembourg. Common services deal with matters that are not specifically assigned to one particular DG.

Committee of the Regions – CoR   Consultative body of the EU with representatives of regional and local authorities in the EU member states.

Common Agricultural Policy – CAP   Aims at increasing agricultural productivity through technical progress, ensuring a decent living standard for farmers, stabilisation of markets, guaranteeing supply and ensuring reasonable consumer prices.

CFSP   Common Foreign and Security Policy of the EU (second EU pillar).

Coreper   Permanent representatives (ambassadors) of all EU member states, who prepare the decisions of the Council of Ministers (abbreviation from the French: Comité des Représentants Permanents).

Council of Europe – CoE   Intergovernmental organisation of democratic European countries, founded after the Second World War, to safeguard the values of peace and democracy. Since the early 1990s, countries of central and eastern Europe and the former Soviet republics have joined the CoE. Not to be confused with the European Union or the EU Council of Ministers.

Council of Ministers   Meeting of the ministers of all EU member states, depending on the subject (e.g. agriculture council, environment council). Determines EU policy more or less together with the European Parliament in the co-decision or intergovernmental procedure (for instance the Common Foreign and Security Policy).

Court of Auditors   Examines the legality and regularity of EU income and expenses, controls proper financial administration by the EU institutions.

Court of Justice of the European Communities – ECJ   The Court of Justice guards the implementation of EU law and treaties, guarantees its uniform interpretation and application.

Directorate general – DG   The European Commission is primarily divided into the following directorates general (equivalent to national ministries). NB: the division below was valid for the 1994–1999 Commission. Revisions (restructuring, reduced number, renaming, numbering deleted) were expected at the time of writing but had not been finalised.
- DG I – External Relations: commercial policy and relations with North America, the Far East, Australia and New Zealand
- DG I.A – External Relations: Europe and the New Independent States, common foreign and security policy, and external missions
- DG I.B – External Relations: southern Mediterranean, Middle East, Latin America and south east Asia, North- South cooperation
- DG II – Economic and financial affairs
- DG III – Industry
- DG IV – Competition
- DG V – Employment, industrial relations and social affairs
- DG VI – Agriculture
- DG VII – Transport

- DG VIII – Development (external relations and development cooperation with Africa, the Caribbean and the Pacific, Lomé Convention)
- DG IX – Personnel and administration
- DG X – Information, communication, culture and audiovisual media
- DG XI – Environment, nuclear safety and civil protection
- DG XII – Science, research and development
- DG XIII – Information Society: telecommunications, markets, technologies – innovation and exploitation of research
- DG XIV – Fisheries
- DG XV – Internal market
- DG XVI – Regional policy and cohesion
- DG XVII – Energy
- DG XVIII – (formerly Credits and investments, merged with DG II)
- DG XIX – Budgets
- DG XX – Financial control
- DG XXI – Taxation and customs union
- DG XXII – Education, training and youth
- DG XXIII – Enterprise policy, distributive trades, tourism and social economy
- DG XXIV - Consumer policy and consumer health protection

ECHO European Community Humanitarian Office. Not to be confused with the EU database server European Commission Host Organisation.

Economic and Monetary Union – EMU Harmonises the economic and monetary policies of the EU, around the introduction of a common currency, the euro.

Economic and Social Committee – ECS Consultative body of the EU with employers, trade unions and various interest groups from the EU member states.

EDF European Development Fund, main EU financial instrument for development cooperation with the ACP countries.

Euratom See European Atomic Energy Community – EAEC.

Euro Common currency, with fixed exchange rate, of EU countries participating in the European Monetary Union (EMU), introduced in January 1999 by 11 of the 15 member states (exceptions: United Kingdom, Denmark, Greece and Sweden). Introduction of the euro into daily life, replacing existing national coins and bank notes, will take place 1 January 2002.

European Agricultural Orientation and Guarantee Fund – EAOGF Finances the EU Common Agricultural Policy, strengthens agricultural structures and develops rural areas.

European Atomic Energy Community – EAEC (Euratom) Third European Community (1958), promotes the use of nuclear energy for peaceful aims. Together with EEC and ECSC, it is the first pillar of the EU.

European Bank for Reconstruction and Development – EBRD   Gives loans for infrastructure projects in central and eastern Europe. The EU and its member states hold 51% of EBRD shares.

European Central Bank – ECB   In charge of EU monetary policy under the European Monetary Union, since the introduction of the euro.

European Coal and Steel Community –ECSC   The very first European Community (1950): common market of coal and steel products, integrating West Germany into western Europe after the Second World War. Together with EEC and Euratom, it makes up the first pillar of the EU.

European Commission – EC   See Commission of the European Communities. NB: confusingly, EC is used both for European (Economic) Community and European Commission.

European Community – EC   The European Community (or Communities) consist(s) of the 3 different communities (EEC, ECSC and Euratom) which together make up the first pillar of the European Union. NB: confusingly, EC is used both for European (Economic) Community and for European Commission.

European Conference on Security and Cooperation – ECSC   Intergovernmental organisation without executive power, a meeting and consultation body of European countries (east and west), Canada and the USA.

European Court of Human Rights   Part of the Council of Europe, with its seat in Strasbourg. Not to be confused with the ECJ.

European Court of Justice – ECJ   See Court of Justice of the European Communities.

European Economic Area – EEA   Economic cooperation structure, with common rules, between the EU and Iceland, Norway and Liechtenstein, which in this context participate in many European programmes.

European Economic Community – EEC   Second European Community (1958): promotes economic cooperation and expansion by creating a common market, as the basis for further political cooperation between EU member states. Together with ECSC and Euratom, it makes up the first pillar of the EU.

European Investment Bank – EIB   Major financial institution of the EU, which finances investments in the public and private sector in the EU, Mediterranean and ACP countries. Total of annual loans: €20 billion.

European Parliament – EP   Consists of 627 elected representatives of the EU member states, with the right of co-decision (with the Council of Ministers) on EU economic policy and several internal policy fields (e.g. energy, environment). In other fields it has the right to be consulted (common foreign and security policy). Approves the EU budget as a whole and in detail (exception: agriculture) and confirms the nomination of the European Commission

European Regional Development Fund – ERDF   One of the Structural Funds, supporting the development of economically backward regions of the EU and correcting regional gaps in development.

European Social Fund – ESF   One of the Structural Funds, supports national and transnational initiatives in the fields of employment and training.

European Union – EU   Economic and political union of 15 European countries, consisting of three pillars: European Communities (ECSC, EEC and Euratom), intergovernmental cooperation on the Common Foreign and Security Policy (CFSP) and on justice and home affairs (JHA).

Europol   European Police Office, EU cooperation on police affairs (in the third pillar).

JHA   EU cooperation on justice and home affairs (third EU pillar).

Meda   System of cooperation (economy, environment, research, media, civil society, etc.) between the EU and Mediterranean-Middle East countries.

Member states   The 15 member states of the European Union: Austria, Belgium, Denmark, Finland, France, Germany, Greece, Irish Republic, Italy, Luxembourg, Netherlands, Portugal, Spain, Sweden, United Kingdom.

Non-governmental organisation – NGO   Professional associations or non-profit interest groups at local, regional, national or international level.

Official Journal – OJ   Official journal of the European Communities: publishes all official EU legislation and many other EU documents, including calls for proposals.

Ombudsman   Receives and investigates complaints of EU citizens or conducts own investigations on improper administration by EU institutions or agencies.

Phare   Abbreviation of the programme formerly called Poland and Hungary, Action for the Reconstruction of the Economy, created in 1989 to give assistance to economic reconstruction of the central and eastern European countries, in relation to their future accession to the EU.

Pillar   With the treaties of Maastricht (1992) and Amsterdam (1999), the European Community(-ies) formed the first pillar of the European Union, together with cooperation on the Common Foreign and Security Policy (CFSP, the second pillar) and on justice and home affairs (JHA, the third pillar). The second and third pillars function as intergovernmental cooperation, in which unanimity or a qualified majority is needed in the Council of Ministers; the European Commission and Parliament have implementing and advisory roles only.

Permanent Representation/Representative – PR of an EU member state, equivalent to an embassy/ambassador.

Presidency Government of the EU member state which coordinates policies of the Council of Ministers, in a 6 monthly rotation system.

Tacis EU programme of technical assistance for the former republics of the Soviet Union and Mongolia (abbreviation of Technical Assistance to the Commonwealth of Independent States).

Troika The previous, current and next EU presidency, ensuring continuity from one presidency to another.

Western European Union – WEU Created after the Second World War as a branch of NATO; may develop into the defence component of the EU.

USEFUL CONTACTS AND ADDRESSES

EU addresses

European Commission

200 Rue de la Loi
B-1049 Brussels, Belgium
Tel: +32 2 299 1111

Jean Monnet Building
Rue Alcide de Gasperi
L-2920 Luxembourg
Tel: +352 4301 1
Fax: +352 436 124 or +352 4301 35049

Internet: http://europa.eu.int/comm/index_en.htm

Homepages of various DGs: http://europa.eu.int/comm/dgs_en.htm

EU officials (heads of unit and higher positions only): http://158.169.50.70/idea/ideaen.htm

Representations in EU member states: http://europa.eu.int/comm/offices.htm

Delegations outside the EU: http://europa.eu.int/comm/dg1a/site/contacts/delegations.htm
http://europa.eu.int/comm/sg/citguide/en/citgu35.htm

Information services: http://europa.eu.int/geninfo/icom-de.htm

European Parliament

Rue Wiertz
B-1047 Brussels, Belgium
Tel: +32 2 284 2111
Fax: +32 2 230 6933

Avenue de l'Europe
F-67000 Strasbourg, France
Tel: +33 388 174 001
Fax: +33 388 174 860

Plateau du Kirchberg
L-2929 Luxembourg
Tel: +352 4300 1
Fax: +352 4300 24842

Internet: http://www.europarl.eu.int/sg/tree/en/default.htm

Council of Ministers

175 Rue de la Loi
B-1048 Brussels, Belgium
Tel: +32 2 285 6111
Fax: +32 2 285 7397/81
Internet: http://ue.eu.int/en/summ.htm

Court of Justice of the European Communities

Boulevard Konrad Adenauer
L-2925 Luxembourg
Tel: +352 43031
Fax: +352 4303 2600 (press and information) +352 4303 2500 (switchboard)
Internet: http://curia.eu.int/en/index.htm

European Ombudsman

Palais de l'Europe
1 Avenue du Président Robert Schuman
P.O. Box 403
F-67001 Strasbourg Cedex, France
Tel: +33 388 174001, 172313, 179062
Internet: http://www.euro-ombudsman.eu.int

European Court of Auditors

12 Rue Alcide De Gasperi
L-1615 Luxembourg
Tel: +352 4398 45737
Fax: +352 4398 46430
E-mail: eurad@eca.eu.int
Internet: http://www.eca.eu.int

Economic and Social Committee of the European Communities

2 Rue Ravenstein
B-1000 Brussels, Belgium
Tel: +32 2 519 9011
Fax: +32 2 513 4893
E-mail: Jean-Pierre.Faure@ces.be
Internet: http://www.esc.eu.int

Committee of the Regions of the European Union

79 Rue Belliard
B-1040 Brussels, Belgium
Tel: +32 2 282 2211
Fax: + 32 2 282 2325
E-mail: info@cdr.be
Internet: http://www.cor.eu.int

ACP group of countries (general secretariat)

451 Avenue Georges-Henri
B-1200 Brussels, Belgium
Tel: +32 2 743 0600
Fax: +32 2 735 5573

European Investment Bank

100 Boulevard Konrad Adenauer
L-2950 Luxembourg
Tel: +352 43791
Fax: +352 437704

Information Office:
Tel: +352 4379 3122
Fax: +352 4379 3189
E-mail: m.bello@eib.org

227 Rue de la Loi
B-1040 Brussels, Belgium
Tel: +32 2 230 9890
Fax: +32 2 230 5827

368 Pall Mall
London SW1Y 5ES, UK
Tel: +44 171 343 1200
Fax: +44 171 930 9929

Internet: http://eib.eu.int/

European Central Bank

PO Box 16 03 19
D-60066 Frankfurt am Main
Kaiserstraße 29
D-60311 Frankfurt am Main
Germany
Tel: +49 69 1344 0
Fax: +49 69 1344 6000
Internet: http://www.ecb.int/

Office for Official Publications of the European Communities

2 Rue Mercier
L-2985 Luxembourg
Tel: +352 29291
Fax: +352 495719
Internet: http://eur-op.eu.int/indexen.htm

West European Union

4 Rue de la Régence
B-1000 Brussels, Belgium
Tel: +32 2 500 4456
Fax: +32 2 500 3519

European Bank for Reconstruction and Development

1 Exchange Square
London EC2A 2EH, UK
Tel: +44 171 338 6000
Fax: +44 171 338 6100

UK contacts

European Commission

Jean Monnet House
8 Storey's Gate
London SW1P 3AT
Tel: +44 171 973 1992
Fax: +44 171 973 1900/973 1910

9/15 Bedford Street (Windsor House)
Belfast BT2 7EG
Tel: +44 1232 240 708
Fax: +44 1232 248 241

4 Cathedral Road
Cardiff CF1 9SG
Tel: +44 1222 371 631
Fax: +44 1222 395 489

9 Alva Street
Edinburgh EH2 4PH
Tel: +44 131 225 2058
Fax: +44 131 226 4105

Internet: http://www.cec.org.uk

European Parliament

2 Queen Anne's Gate
London SW1H 9AA
Tel: +44 171 227 4300
Fax: +44 171227 4302
E-mail: eplondon@europarl.eu.int

9 Alva Street
Edinburgh EH2 4PH
Tel: +44 131 225 2058
Fax: +44 131 226 4105
E-mail: wscott@europarl.eu.int

Internet: http://www.europarl.eu.int/uk

Permanent Representation of the UK to the European Union

10 Avenue d'Auderghem
B-1040 Brussels
Tel: +32 2 287 8211
Fax: +32 2 287 8398

Internet: http://ukrep.fco.gov.uk

Euro Info Centres
Through
http://www.euro-info.org.uk/centres/centres.html
details can be accessed on Euro Info Centres in: Belfast, Birmingham, Bradford, Bristol, Chelmsford, East Anglia, Exeter, Glasgow, Hertfordshire, Hull, Inverness, Kent, Leicester, Liverpool, London, Manchester, Newcastle, Nottingham, Slough, Southampton, Stoke on Trent, Sussex, Telford and Wales.

European Briefing Unit
The European Briefing Unit provides EU training for the UK public and voluntary sectors. From international conferences to small training workshops, it offers a comprehensive training and development service, courses for European liaison officers in local authorities, education colleges and higher education institutions as well as training workshops on applying for European funding. It also delivers tailored training and development courses on clients' own premises. Other services include a subscription-based information service incorporating regular newsletters, updates on topical issues and monthly listings of conferences, seminars, courses and publications on European training issues.

European Briefing Unit
University of Bradford
Bradford BD7 IDP
Contact: Margareta Holmstedt, European Briefing Officer
Tel: +44 1274 235 821
Fax: +44 1274 236 820
E-mail: ebu@bradford.ac.uk

EU and related web-sites

Through

http://www.lib.berkeley.edu/GSSI/eu.html

a great number of EU and related web-sites can be accessed: EU institutions and agencies, offices in the EU member states and around the world, European documentation centres, UK members of the European Parliament, EU Information Initiatives, EU databases, business advice, education, employment and training sites, the euro, treaties and more.

Through

http://www.cec.org.uk/directry/index.htm

you will have access to: local sources of EU information, depository libraries, EU institutions and agencies in the UK, European related organisations in the UK, national sectorial organisations offering EU information and advice, UK MEPs, embassies, consulates and tourist offices of EU member states, sales agents for EU official publications, etc.

http://www.cec.org.uk/relays/relhome.htm

will lead you to EU information outlets throughout the UK:
Carrefours – rural advice and information centres
European Documentation Centres – for university students
European Information Centres – for the business community
European Reference Centres – for the academic community
European Resource Centres – for schools and colleges
Innovation Relay Centres – advice on technology and innovation
Public Information Relays – for the general public

EU depository libraries (EU legislation, Official Journal, etc.)

The British Library Document Supply Centre
Boston Spa, Wetherby
West Yorkshire LS23 7BQ
Tel: +44 1937 546 000
Fax: +44 1937 546 333
E-mail: Andrew Smith@bl.uk

Business andTechnology Library
William Brown Street
Liverpool L3 8EW
Tel: +44 151 225 5430/5434
Fax: +44 151 207 1342
E-mail: lvpublic@demon.co.uk

Westminster Reference Library
35 St Martins Street
London WC2H 7HP
Tel: +44 171 641 2034
Fax: +44 171 641 2040

Regional information
Regional information on the east of England, East Midlands, London, the north east, Northern Ireland, the north west, the west, Midlands, Scotland, the south east, the south west, Wales, Yorkshire and the Humber can be obtained from:

http://www.cec.org.uk/pubs/regions/index.htm

Regional brochures can be obtained from:

Publications Despatch Centre
European Commission
London SE99 6TT
Tel: +44 171 463 8177
Fax: + 44 181 694 0099
E-mail: eec@sr-comms.co.uk

Local contacts
You can access UK local government web-sites through:

http://www.tagish.co.uk/tagish/links/localgov.htm